What is the History of the Book?

What is History? series

John H. Arnold, *What is Medieval History?*

Peter Burke, *What is Cultural History?* 2nd edition

Peter Burke, *What is the History of Knowledge?*

John C. Burnham, *What is Medical History?*

Pamela Kyle Crossley, *What is Global History?*

Pero Gaglo Dagbovie, *What is African American History?*

Shane Ewen, *What is Urban History?*

Christiane Harzig and Dirk Hoerder, with Donna Gabaccia, *What is Migration History?*

J. Donald Hughes, *What is Environmental History?* 2nd edition

Andrew Leach, *What is Architectural History?*

Stephen Morillo with Michael F. Pavkovic, *What is Military History?* 3rd edition

Sonya O. Rose, *What is Gender History?*

Barbara H. Rosenwein and Riccardo Cristiani, *What is the History of Emotions?*

Brenda E. Stevenson, *What is Slavery?*

Jeffrey Weeks, *What is Sexual History?*

Richard Whatmore, *What is Intellectual History?*

What is the History of the Book?

James Raven

polity

Copyright © James Raven 2018

The right of James Raven to be identified as Author of this Work has been asserted in accordance with the UK Copyright, Designs and Patents Act 1988.

First published in 2018 by Polity Press
Reprinted 2019

Polity Press
65 Bridge Street
Cambridge CB2 1UR, UK

Polity Press
101 Station Landing
Suite 300,
Medford, MA 02155
USA

All rights reserved. Except for the quotation of short passages for the purpose of criticism and review, no part of this publication may be reproduced, stored in a retrieval system or transmitted, in any form or by any means, electronic, mechanical, photocopying, recording or otherwise, without the prior permission of the publisher.

ISBN-13: 978-0-7456-4161-4
ISBN-13: 978-0-7456-4162-1 (pb)

A catalogue record for this book is available from the British Library.

Library of Congress Cataloging-in-Publication Data

Names: Raven, James, 1959- author.
Title: What is the history of the book? / James Raven.
Description: Cambridge, UK ; Malden, MA : Polity Press, 2017. | Series: What is history? | Includes bibliographical references and index.
Identifiers: LCCN 2017018037 (print) | LCCN 2017047009 (ebook) | ISBN 9781509523207 (Mobi) | ISBN 9781509523214 (Epub) | ISBN 9780745641614 (hardback) | ISBN 9780745641621 (pbk.)
Subjects: LCSH: Books–History. | Printing–History | Bibliography–History. | Transmission of texts–History. | Book industries and trade–History. | Books and reading–History.
Classification: LCC Z4 (ebook) | LCC Z4 .R237 2017 (print) | DDC 200–dc23
LC record available at https://lccn.loc.gov/2017018037

Typeset in 10.5 on 12 pt Sabon
by Toppan Best-set Premedia Limited
Printed and bound in Great Britain by TJ International Ltd, Padstow

Illustration credits: 1: British Museum/Wikimedia Commons; 2: University of California Riverside/Flickr; 3: Wikimedia Commons; 4: University of Bologna/Wikimedia Commons; 5: Museum Georg Schäfer/Wikimedia Commons.

The publisher has used its best endeavours to ensure that the URLs for external websites referred to in this book are correct and active at the time of going to press. However, the publisher has no responsibility for the websites and can make no guarantee that a site will remain live or that the content is or will remain appropriate.

Every effort has been made to trace all copyright holders, but if any have been inadvertently overlooked the publisher will be pleased to include any necessary credits in any subsequent reprint or edition.

For further information on Polity, visit our website:
politybooks.com

Contents

Illustrations and Tables		vii
Preface		viii
Acknowledgements		x
1	*The Scope of Book History*	1
	Redefining the Book	9
	First Books First	16
2	*The Early History of Book History*	32
	Prehistories of the Book	32
	Towards Bibliography	40
3	*Description, Enumeration and Modelling*	47
	Retrospective Catalogues and Bibliometrics	58
	New Perspectives and Projects	68
	Circuits and Diagrams	77
4	*Who, What and How?*	83
	Economics	90
	Wider Horizons	94
	Control: Copyright, Censorship and Circulation	99
	Libraries	105
	Cautions and Precepts	110

5	Reading	115
	Identifying Readers	119
	Recovering Reading Practices	126
6	Consequences	136
Notes		145
Bibliography		154
Index		168

Illustrations and Tables

Illustrations

1. Cuneiform tablet found in Sippar, from around 600–500 BCE — 18
2. An unfolded Chinese bamboo concertina book: an eighteenth-century CE copy of *The Art of War* by Sunzi (Sun Tzu) 孙子 (c. 544–496 BCE) — 21
3. Codex Argenteus, a sixth-century manuscript, originally containing Bishop Ulfilas' fourth-century translation of the Bible into the Gothic language — 25
4. Codex Cospi, a pre-Columbian Mesoamerican pictorial manuscript believed to originate from the Puebla-Tlaxcala region — 28
5. *A Bibliophile Caring for his Extensive Collection* by Carl Spitzweg, 1850 — 106

Tables

1. Printing, paper and allied museums — 72
2. Centres for the history of the book — 73
3. International lecture series in bibliography, and the history of the book — 75
4. Earliest known printing by metal type cast in Europe and North America in selected towns and cities worldwide — 96

Preface

This book offers a fresh and suggestive exploration of the fast-developing field of book history. It investigates the scope of the 'history of the book' as understood by its practitioners worldwide and probes its theoretical and practical underpinnings. The following chapters chart the subject's distinctiveness, examining debates about its range, origins, methods and future direction. My aim is to test the boundaries of book history by exploring problematic examples of relevant historical investigation in bibliography, literature, communications and media studies. I am especially keen to suggest new directions by discussing periods and themes that are still underdeveloped and capable of further and different interpretation. Throughout, comparative examples, together with specific types of sources identified and explained, aim to illustrate the subject's development, strengths and weaknesses.

Given the enormous number of published contributions to this subject, the selection of cited individuals and examples is particularly invidious but also necessary in such a concise book. Notes are limited to the essential and specific. A bibliography offers broader references (including to authors mentioned in the text) as well as suggestions for further reading. These correspond where possible to the different sections of the book. References and recommendations, in line with the rubric of this series, are predominantly in English or translated into English. In deference to the global spirit of this volume,

I adopt BCE instead of BC. CE is used instead of AD but only where its omission might cause confusion.

I hope that students, teachers, researchers and general readers will benefit from an investigation that crosses disciplinary boundaries and intersects with literary, historical, communications, media, library and conservation studies. I have placed particular emphasis on book history's growing global ambition, contributing to debates about intellectual and popular culture, colonialism and the communication of ideas, the technologies, financing and economics of book production, and how study of reading practices opens up new horizons in social history and the history of knowledge. Robert Darnton, one of the pioneers of this enterprise, has written that the history of books can 'look less like a field than a tropical rain forest' in which an 'explorer can hardly make his way across'. Here goes.

Acknowledgements

Having used examples from around the world to explore different traditions in bibliography, palaeography, epigraphy and manuscript studies, I am hugely indebted to colleagues for their advice and criticism. The volume draws appreciatively upon the learning and expertise of dozens of fellow scholars and students, but, invidious as it is, I record particular thanks to Nicolas Barker, Isabelle Baudino, John Bender, Ann Blair, Cynthia Brokaw, Roger Chartier, Sophie Coulombeau, Robert Darnton, Margaret Ezell, Roger Gaskell, Alexandra Gillespie, Anthony Grafton, James N. Green, Germaine Greer, David D. Hall, George W. Houston, Leslie Howsam, Joseph McDermott, Jason McElligott, David McKitterick, Anne McLaren, Ian Maclean, David Pearson, Eleanor Robson, Leon Rocha, Daniel Roche, Graham Shaw, David Simpson, Clifford Siskin, Peter Stallybrass, Michael F. Suarez, Dominique Varry, Germaine Warkentin, William Warner, James Willoughby and Henry Woudhuysen. Many of these colleagues very generously offered extensive comment upon the text, identified errors and engaged in debate about particular controversies (and I owe a special debt to William Zachs for magnificently acerbic criticism and the suppression of the parenthetical). Earlier in my studies I was privileged to receive generous guidance from the greatly missed Giles Barber, Jeremy Black, Don McKenzie, Michael Treadwell and Michael Turner. Immense patience has been required from my editors at Polity and I am grateful for the support and encouragement of Andrea Drugan, Pascal Porcheron, Ellen MacDonald-Kramer and Ann Bone. Peter Burke first suggested that I write this volume and I continue to benefit enormously from his friendship and from the inspiration of his pioneering scholarship.

1
The Scope of Book History

What is now generally recognized as an interdisciplinary scholarly endeavour called 'the history of the book' began its modern life in the 1980s. Importantly, however, its intellectual roots reach back many centuries. As advanced today, book history or 'the history of the book' aspires to study the historical consequences of the production, dissemination and reception of texts, in all their material forms, across all societies and in all ages.

Separately, these are no new subjects of enquiry, even though scholars from different disciplines have increasingly used the designation of 'the history of the book' to advance more capacious questions about the past meaning and function of books, claiming fresh perspectives and promoting, in particular, an interdisciplinarity that extends and revises older methods and conclusions. In many ways, this last initiative has been the most productive aspect of the enterprise, bringing together in conversation and collaborative scholarship a great diversity of participants: cultural and social historians, literary scholars and critics, those concerned with the theory and practice of textual editing, bibliographers, codicologists, palaeographers, epigraphers, philologists, rare books' and special collections' librarians, book conservators, linguists and translators, historians of science,of ideas and of art, anthropologists, archaeologists and specialists in media, communications and graphic communication studies. By their different methods, these interpreters of books study texts as the products of collaborative human agency acting on material forms. Together with language, those material texts and the information their signs encode are the most powerful tools available to write a history of meanings.

It is important to appreciate the breadth of the history of the book. It is a history reaching back 5,000 years, not simply a history of the paper codex, or indeed of the printed book, but the history of how diverse peoples in different parts of the world, in different ways, for different reasons and with very different consequences have striven to store, circulate and retrieve knowledge and information. The balance between these objectives, together with other practical, local and ideological considerations, has affected the choice of materials and their shaping to record, transport, read and conserve since at least the thirty-third century BCE, the supposed age of the earliest surviving object claimed by some scholars to fulfil the definition of a book. Similarly, as this volume attempts to illustrate, activity in book history is worldwide, with new writing and research projects devoted to the history of the book in Africa, South America, China, India and South and Central Asia in addition to regions long associated with bibliographical and book historical studies. As will also be explored, a clear and developing incentive for histories of the book is to break free of national, imperial and otherwise political geographies – often the older and pragmatic organizing unit of study – and to pursue the linguistic, aesthetic, oceanic and postcolonial perspectives of what are manifestly *livres sans frontières*, books without borders. Sometimes, less obviously, these are also *livres sans lecteurs*, books without readers, where the historical human experience of books concerned an awareness or use of books that did not involve reading them.

These new agendas put the history of the book full square in the development of history itself, offering decisive contributions to developing interests in the history of class, ethnicity, gender and emotions, and revisions to the history of ideas, revolution, local and national politics, faith and belief, and diplomacy, among other fields. Contributory research, both of and within the material book, and in an astonishing range of extra-textual sources, informs fresh histories of censorship, copyright, the economics and geographies of publishing, the networks of distribution, the uses of libraries and the various source analyses offered in histories of reading and reception. The history of book production, circulation and influence intersects with and advances histories of revolution and ideas and of religious belief and practice, the social history of knowledge and histories of sociability and of intimate personal behaviour.

Drawing on a diverse heritage, by the early 1990s, numerous courses in book history, centres for the history of the book, and multivolume book history publishing projects advanced in Britain, France, many other European countries, the United States and Australasia. Most of the pioneers in the 1980s studied Europe and North America in the age of print. Robert Darnton in his seminal 1982 essay 'What is the History of Books?' proposed that 'it might even be called the social and cultural history of communication by print'.[1] Within a decade or more, medievalists and palaeographers, drawing on much earlier research, also led collaborative projects in publishing and broader book history, often nationally conceived.

The branding of this endeavour has been significant, and the history of the book has been both beneficiary and victim of institutional aggrandisement. The 'history of the book' appears to be a translation of the earlier coined *histoire du livre*, but many different traditions of bibliographical, literary and historical research informed the development of book history in different parts of the world. Intrinsic to the understanding of how meaning is conveyed by texts is the history of reading, itself subject to numerous methodologies, types of source and theoretical perspectives.

Printing dominates published book history, but print – word and image – is far from the only means of graphic communication used to convey messages. Texts might be impressed, imprinted, inscribed, written, drawn, stencilled, block- or letter-press printed, engraved, stereotyped, lithographed, or photographically or digitally reproduced. As an example – and one strikingly at odds with the emphasis of many late twentieth-century histories of the book – historians of the great majority of centuries of book production in regions that now comprise India, Pakistan, Nepal, Bangladesh and Sri Lanka are historians of the transmission of manuscript texts. Scribal productions were the only written texts until the mid-sixteenth century; they remained the preferred texts in South Asia until the early nineteenth century, almost three centuries after Catholic missionaries brought the first printing press with separately cast printing types to western India. Many more ancient texts in Sanskrit survive than those of equivalent age in Latin and Greek.

More broadly, although cultural historians and bibliographers of great distinction, including Roger Chartier, Robert Darnton and D. F. McKenzie, wrote pioneering studies in aspects of book history in the 1980s and 1990s, literary scholars subsequently exercised significant impact on its development. In the late twentieth century, objectives and techniques in literary criticism diverged. As new theoretical approaches advanced in literature departments across Europe and the Americas, some refugees from high theory allied their more historical interests to 'the history of the book'. More recently, however, a much broader range of approaches in literary scholarship and textual criticism has also contributed to historical study of authorship, publishing and reception.

In addition to extended work on the traditional corpus of canonical texts, or of what in effect remains a 'great tradition', canonicity itself attracted greater interest. A literary canon, and especially what has been both positively and negatively termed the 'Western canon', is the body of books, art and music accepted generally as the most influential in shaping culture. Histories of books assist with the identification and analysis of 'popular', 'minority' and specific 'genre' literature, together with research in women's, gender, queer and ethnic studies. Histories of books recover the non-canonical or what the critic Margaret Cohen has called, with teasing historical implications, 'the great unread'.[2] The replacement of many literature departments by departments of cultural studies, which embrace film and media studies, has further encouraged a new intersection with literary and gender theory and the literature of less familiar languages, as well as renewed interest in translation and untranslatability. The effect of much of this scholarship is to reintroduce historical, and especially social historical, perspectives into literary study. Among many outstanding examples, Michael Warner and then David Shields ingeniously reinterpreted early American literary, cultural and intellectual history, drawing upon very wide evidence of printed polemic, contest and conversation, where Shields also 'explores for the history of the book the arenas of manuscript publication'.[3] As a result of such studies, book history has enjoyed great and continuing popularity.

In recent years, another wave of book history has been more deliberately comparative, addressing non-European, extra-North American and postcolonial perspectives. New histories offer global comparisons in ways that are still in their infancy but also impossible without the secure underpinnings of accumulated, specialist, local and national bibliographical and archival research. To the fore are novel questions about transoceanic as well as transcontinental book production, circulation and reception, and of the localized creation and widely dispersed transmission of knowledge. The need to understand the economics of book production applies to book history in all ages and places: how a book was financed, why and how an individual or community met the costs of labour and acquisition, and what explains different levels of demand.

This volume identifies unknowns, uneven patterns of research and consequent future challenges. Western and non-Western comparisons in particular probe our understanding of the distinctions and overlaps, say, between commercial and non-commercial and institutional and private publishing, of the role of book and non-book printing by movable type, woodblocks, engraved plates or other processes, and of the relative efficiencies of different production, distribution and even reading practices. Study of Asian woodblock printing, for example, complicates more triumphalist histories of the European printing press by suggesting that the casting, composition, correction and painstaking redistribution of type is not always the most economically efficient method of printing.[4]

Taken together, the histories of books in different parts of the world contribute to a remarkable range of new scholarship from the history of news gathering and international journalism to the global history of particular works and of technological and knowledge transfer. Book history research informs, revises, problematizes and nuances broader narratives of practice, behaviour and representation, including diverse histories of subversion, revolution, reformation and conquest. Research on book production, circulation and reception has been conspicuous in recent explorations of the history of

6 *The Scope of Book History*

ritual, language, humour and emotions. An understanding of the transformative power of the book and especially of print and indigenous written texts has contributed largely to debates about the invention of traditions, the imagining of communities, colonial encounter, postcolonialism and subaltern studies.

Controversy and criticism have nevertheless accompanied book history, past and present, inviting debate about methodologies and assumptions. History is subject to both unconscious and deliberate emphasis upon certain prevalent values, and critical voices have accused influential studies in book history of anachronism and teleology. Those writing the history of book production and reception are warned against unthinking progressive narratives. Certain accounts, it is argued, brusquely assume an inevitable march to modernity and the subsumption of localized and critical differences within a globalizing totality. Others criticize the converse. In her final book, *Divine Art, Infernal Machine*, Elizabeth Eisenstein warned against current 'considerable ambivalence about Western technologies of all kinds. Triumphalism is out of fashion, along with ideas of progress and other "Whiggish" views of historical development.'[5] Concern with constraints to that development is not, however, abandoned in the discussion that follows here.

More bluntly still, for certain observers and even some participants, not all of this activity has actually been 'history', and for some, it is important that it is not. History concerns the recovery of past human experience. Some of the scholarship contributing to the 'history of the book' is liable to transgress the strict remit of historical study in the same way that many contributions to the 'history of art' or even the 'history of ideas' focus on aesthetic, material or philosophical questions rather than explicitly engaging with past behaviours and attitudes. In studies primarily involving critical theory and editorial scholarship, as well as antiquarian investigations of the minutiae of scribal and print productions, there were clearly some ways in which the history of the book was not, or very largely not, history at all. The depth of historical interest seemed relatively shallow in many bibliographical analyses of the construction of books and their exact printing, composition, paper and ink characteristics. Many codicological studies – the examination of manuscripts together with palaeography, the study of handwriting – used new technologies to reveal stylistic and literary developments but with limited historical contextualization.

At the same time, expansive writings in literary critical theory intersected with the interests of book historians especially in regard to authorship, readerships and the textual figuring of the author and reader, but this apparent interdisciplinarity has often been open to criticism and misunderstanding. To give one example, Gérard Genette popularized the idea of the 'paratext', typically including a book's title, cover, dedication, opening information, foreword, endpapers, colophon, footnotes, and many other materials not necessarily crafted by the author. Genette declared that 'we are dealing here with a synchronic and not a diachronic study – an attempt at a general picture, not a history of the paratext'.[6] He thought it 'appropriate to define objects before studying their evolution'. As Roger Chartier observes, in a study that actually questions this ahistoricist approach, 'this is a useful reminder if we want to avoid the false quarrels too often launched by historians against structuralist approaches that they took for bad history'.[7]

In the early days of modern book history, the main examples of the fusion of different approaches were the foundational *L'Apparition du livre* of Lucien Febvre and Henri-Jean Martin and later essays by Darnton, McKenzie and Chartier, among others. In different ways, their approach sought to bridge the early theoretical as well as bibliometric emphases of French and Continental contributions with the long tradition of collection-based bibliographical and empirical scholarship in the Anglo-American world. In the latter, British enumerative and retrospective national bibliography accompanied meticulous analytical bibliography – defined further in chapter 3 – and an emphasis on economic and material conditions. All contributors sought an understanding of the *historical* circumstances of textual production, circulation and reception. Examples range from the close reading of the work of monastic scribes to an understanding of the careers of stationers, printers and magazine and newspaper editors and proprietors. Investigations of the economics of publication and the workings of the literary marketplace vie with studies of patronage and censorship, the distinctions between commercial and private publications, and the multiplicity of readers and reading experiences.

Given the use of two terms in English, 'history of the book' and 'book history', it is worth pausing to consider differences between the two and parallels with other historical disciplines. The 'history of art' has been defined as a study of art analysing how stylistic, iconographic and technical 'patterns of causation' have shaped artistic development. In contrast, 'art history' has been defined as historical study, especially social and cultural, in which works of art provide tangible evidence for the understanding of individuals and societies. This division is by no means upheld by all art historians, but it usefully offers a parallel distinction in bibliographical studies between scholarship exploring the technical and even symbolic developments of books as material objects, and other histories which take books as evidence of broader types of human activity in the past. This difference of emphasis in writing the history of books certainly exists, but significantly does not seem to match any division in the actual usage of 'history of the book' and 'book history'. Indeed, for some writers and exponents, perhaps disappointingly so, the expressions seem interchangeable. For others, the somewhat limp 'book studies' offers a helpful escape from problematic boundaries of 'book history'.

If English speakers have been careless or inconsistent in terminology, then they share the weakness with German colleagues who use 'Geschichte des Buchwesens' interchangeably and apparently randomly with 'Buchgeschichte'. 'Buchwissenschaft' is reserved for 'book studies' in general. In many countries, and notably France and Italy, the distinction is not available and book historical study is singularly known as 'histoire du livre' and 'storia del libro'. In Spanish, 'historia del libro', that is, 'book', also in the singular, often adds reading, 'y de la lectura', as do French and Italian equivalents. The Portuguese 'história dos livros' is the 'history of books'. More appositely and in different languages, the terms 'book history' and 'history of the book' co-exist with other descriptors in bibliographical and graphic analysis and history, including publication and publishing history, printing and print history and, more capaciously, library history and reading history. Some of these distinctions, as we shall see, follow diagrammatic models and representations of the constituent parts of a book history or cycle of production and dissemination, but many also have a long tradition of their own as often represented by journals and centres devoted to their study. Self-evidently, such broad designations are often overlapping categories and often require contributors to draw on disciplines well outside their focus of study.

An even greater questioning of terminology applies to book history in China where in recent years interest in 'Western' book history has increased, together with fresh attempts at both comparative study and new types of research about China's own history of book production and its social consequences.[8] Some past scholars of Chinese book history such as Paul Pelliot, Thomas F. Carter and Zhang Xiumin variously used research about European printing. Conversely, Febvre and Martin evidence a certain understanding of the history of the Chinese book. New methods and research, however, benefit from the deep traditions of Chinese literary learning. The Chinese character binome 書籍 (in modern Mandarin Chinese pronounced *Shuji*) has been adopted as a translation of the 'book' of European and American histories, and carries sufficient inclusivity to describe, for example, unbound papers bearing written *or* printed characters.[9] More specifically, since at least the Song dynasty (960–1279), the word *banben* 版本 has been used to distinguish different, but usually printed, editions of an essentially unchanged text. Etymologically, the term is associated with a prized form of bibliographical learning, not least because of the privileged connections required to access and accumulate esoteric knowledge of rare books – and their resale value. More will follow on comparative bibliography, but the language used to describe books and their appreciation in East Asia highlights a perception of books that is only partially consonant with Western book history. Very obvious is a sense of difference in the balance between the material and the ideological and an emphasis on sacral and spiritual value in a modern intellectual world largely unmoved by religious and existential issues.

Redefining the Book

What therefore is a 'book' when its form has ranged from lengthy scrolls in the ancient world to concertina codices

10 *The Scope of Book History*

in Central America and palm leaf manuscripts in South Asia? In early South America and early Africa, in particular, our understanding of book forms has to combat a historical condescension that has disregarded and marginalized the intellectual, political and technological achievements of successive communities. 'Books', written and reproduced in many different ways and comprising many different literary forms, from prose to poetry to plays and dictionaries and listings, are characteristically taken by book historians to include, at the very least, pamphlets, periodicals and newspapers.

It is certainly not the case, despite such definitions on popular internet sites, that books are restricted to written, printed, illustrated or blank sheets made of ink, paper, parchment or other materials 'fastened together to hinge at one side'. But how adventurous can we be in attributing to material objects the characteristics which make them books, from clay to digital tablets? Given that animal skin parchment (such as vellum made from calf skin), silk and plant fibres (such as papyrus, hemp and early paper) are integral book components, we should also accept tree barks, leaves, untreated animal hides, mineral clays and terracottas. Some artefacts tantalize. Khipus (or quipus), the knotted string records of the Andean Incas, for example, apparently dating from about the tenth century CE, are more recent than the elaborate Mayan and Olmec recording systems and vessels, but offer a greater challenge to designations of the book and its various materialities, given that these also comprised portable, durable, replicable and legible (that is readable and communicable) means of recording and disseminating information. In considering the function and purpose of books, is the nature or absence of 'publication' determinate? And as forms of print and print in conjunction with script and illustration increased in complexity, how catholic does our definition of 'book' become? Do we include maps and sheets of music, fold-out panoramas, and gathered-together illustrations and prints? Newspapers, periodicals and gazettes, in all their worldwide and physical profusion, have long been established as fundamental to the study of the history of books, but are single-sheet printed productions to be included as 'books', even when many are simple jobbing pieces such as posters, tickets or commercial

The Scope of Book History 11

and legal agreements? Are the embroidered texts of samplers, often significant classroom exercises, or the roughly printed words on sacks or other containers admissible?

The answer for almost all of those pursuing book history is yes. And the reason for that is that whether the focus of enquiry is the minutiae of textual editing or the cultural or political context of ancient and unfamiliar material 'book' forms, the central concern is one of communication, of the creation and dissemination of meaning originating from a graphic and legible as well as a portable and replicable form. Whether made of clay, a skin or a natural fibre, or enabled by a digital screen, central processing unit, random access memory or a graphics card, books function as portable objects. Books might travel over very short or very long distances and serve, in varying degrees, as resilient transmitters of knowledge, information and entertainment. Such a definition, with its reliance on transportability, might exclude posters fixed on walls and inscriptions on immovable entities, and yet there is an undeniable connection between such texts and books, especially when a book might be created by multiples of small and otherwise non-book items. The contents and 'texts' of books remain reproducible and capable of being shared, stored and conserved even if later publishers and readers find their ——— obscure or even unfathomable.

——— ——— question our certainty about the defini- ——— ——— material form and conveyance, ma——— ——— elements. Is it the important o——— ——— is the more portability or of the po——— ——— Reading, self-evidently fundamen——— ——— tions epitomized by the history of books, o——— ——— its own right and one that entails numerous epistemo——— cal, methodological, interpretative and archival challenges. Genette followed Philippe Lejeune in describing the paratext as 'a fringe of the printed text which in reality controls one's whole reading of the text'.[10] In assessing reading influences, he further divided the paratext, and very much in terms of modern and Western books, between the 'peritext' or the title, epigraph, preface, author's foreword, preliminary remarks, notes and illustrations, all within the book itself, and the 'epitext' situated outside the book, including correspondence, diaries, journals and interviews.

The history of reading is notoriously problematic. The very act of reading eschews recording – few write down what they do. Some readers make marginal notes or doodles, some recall their reading to others or in a diary of reading, but evidence of reading practice, of the precise effect of the text upon its individual recipient, is essentially limited. The history of types of reading and literacies involves consideration of motivations, experiences, skills, aptitudes, places and consequences, yet the history of reading practices in the reception of texts can also diverge from the history of the engagement with books, where the material object might have been collected, displayed or otherwise used for symbolic, speculative, aesthetic, spiritual, emotional, sexual, pathological or other reasons. In certain circumstances and in very different places, ownership of books need not involve conventional reading.

A distinctive contribution of book history, therefore, is the re-evaluation of what makes a text, and one that engages usefully with the material interrogation of what defines a book. The meaning that the text conveys is crucially affected by the material form of the book, and, indeed, as D. F. McKenzie argued in exploring a 'sociology of texts', form actually *effects* meaning.[11] The common misreading of this, as 'affects', is nonetheless relevant to the appreciation of changes to textual forms and the conditions under which they are read and perceived. Readers of printed books know that other readers will be reading the 'same book' and yet this is a very different sameness from manuscript books and their reading. Changing valorizations of our own time also offer insights into how the relationship between book form and the signs conveyed by and within it has changed and is described differently in different ages. Current popular reference to a 'text', for example, is now given new meaning by the sending of a 'text' message, just as worldwide word processing and text messaging have brought about the rejuvenation but also the refiguration of the word 'font'. Font (or 'fount') is a word that only thirty years ago needed explanation to those introduced to typography – but now, exactly because of its casual usage, requires even more careful explanation by historians of the book.[12]

The Scope of Book History 13

Revisions to the material form of books are often radical, effecting new meaning. New editions are reset and reprinted and repackaged, and might be translated, given new critical apparatus or accompanying images, and be much travelled. All contribute to remaking a text among new communities, internationally, even globally and over many centuries and in very different cultural contexts. At each level, the intervention of manufacturers, publishers or editors might create multiple time-specific relationships between types of text, the work of the same or similar authors and other communities of books and readers, but it is also possible to chart this broader, cultural history of a single work over time and space. It is what Roger Chartier has conjectured as the 'biography of a book', to which analogy James Secord observed that books have no 'life' of their own independent from their use. 'Biography' or not, studies such Isabel Hofmeyr's appraisal of John Bunyan's *Pilgrim's Progress*, as it was translated and carried around the world and particularly across Africa, have advanced time and space histories of particular works. The history of the book has reinforced the contribution made by micro-histories to our understanding of the past by deepening research into particular texts and their reception, often in highly specific ways. Such history has also, however, expanded horizons by following the publication and circulation history of specific texts as ambitiously as possible, offering global histories of the long-term and far-reaching impact of authors' ideas.

As is frequently noted, the word 'text' derives from the Latin *texere*, to weave, a weaving that is intentional by its author, and also by later interventions, but which remains, however its form changes, open to different interpretations by its receiver. Casting bibliography as a 'sociology of texts', D. F. McKenzie encouraged such thought about texts as transactions in meanings. Textual editing and the creation of authorized editions, supposedly replicating most closely the author's original intentions, underpinned the development of much bibliographical study, but during the second half of the twentieth century many scholars radically transformed the nature of bibliographical textual study by investigating more expansively the collaborative and historical process of publishing and the unstable and mutable reception of a text by its readers. Ideas might be conveyed by physical forms that were extremely various, from a finger-length ticket to a poster higher than a house. The representation of the letters of the written might be placed and replaced and given particular meaning by the accompaniment of images and by the allocation of space. To the spatial construction of a page or other segment or component of a book is added a great diversity of paratextual features, including indexes to aid searching, footnotes and endnotes to provide referencing, jacket covers and advertisements. And whatever their size and form and how or not they are bound, all such texts might be 'unstable' in that their interpretation resides ultimately with the receiver, the reader who interprets according to the filter and control of material concerns and cultural circumstances.

For most practitioners of book history, the very mutability and cultural contingencies of the textual form are the challenge and delight of their study. The comparative is advancing all around us in the most recent history of the book, from analysis of the phonetics of the Mayans to examination of different Buddhist sutra forms ranging from Singhalese palm-leaf books to the block prints and thangkha scrolls of Tibet and Mongolia. Many feature a Buddhist deity on cotton or silk and are used for teaching and devotional purposes. New research in book history is adventurous and contentious and includes, among hundreds of specific projects, investigation of the relationship between block print techniques in Turkey and Russia, and the European printing of sacks and other commercial and very unconventional 'texts' by tillet blocks (large wooden blocks carved in relief for imprinting). It includes the chanting and rituals accompanying Japanese *hoso-e'* 細絵 woodblock prints intended to ward off plague and disaster and the later catfish-motif *namazu-e* 納馬祖 (ナマズエ) prints made after the 1855 Edo earthquake to protect against earth tremors.

In his hugely influential *Image, Music, Text* of 1977, Roland Barthes argued that while a literary 'work' might be 'held in the hand', a 'text' was 'held in language' and 'only exists in the movement of a language'. When we reread Barthes, however, we might now extend our examples beyond European and modern American material. We might think of Mesoamerican and Aztec peoples' fixed calendrical and mathematical calculations and collective memories of names and places on long paper codices and deerskin rolls as forms of textual creativity. Here also, text is linguistic structure, residing within but also liberated from the 'work' or the whole product. Around the world, and in societies very ancient as well as modern, hugely diverse linguistic structures host signs that convey meaning and allow interpretation.

Such definitional quandaries complicate many other types of history, but for the history of the book uncertainties about material and methodological scope have given a particular edginess to the study – and one much to its benefit, many would argue. Nevertheless, historians will continue to dispute the *historical* significance of those aspects of book history which appear to marginalize analysis of human actions and behaviours, just as scholars of literature will continue to question the *literary* significance of those aspects of book history which fail to demonstrate how the historical particularities of material forms affect textual meaning.

The history of the book therefore claims a distinctiveness from textual editorial studies and from traditional analytical, descriptive and even historical bibliography and yet these are also grounding disciplines and remain crucial scholarly components. Hands-on bibliographical analysis, for example, combining technical understanding with disciplinary rigour, is indispensable in understanding not simply the materialities but the contextual complexities of the objects of study. Nonetheless, the new developments, with all the dangers of false assumptions and shortcut scholarship that these carry, offer fresh and ambitious intellectual quests that make the history of the book a stimulating and provocative field of enterprise. How and why was it that certain communities, institutions and individuals supported professional scribes and printers and publishers, sometimes disproportionately to literacy levels in their societies? What political, religious and social roles were ascribed to books – and how did these relate to the use and appreciation of books not just as communicators but as the containers, transmitters, manipulators and censors of memory? Where, how and why did individuals, communities, institutions and nations invest in collections of books? What, indeed, distinguishes collectors from owners where owners are often but not always collectors but where collectors are always owners? The questions combine idealism and pragmatism, where books in all their variety were valued for their recording of knowledge, culture, spirituality and the approved rubrics and procedures of professional, social and political life, as well as the subversive and revolutionary opinions that sought to undermine it.

First Books First

The answers to questions about books in antiquity rest upon fragmentary evidence. The very posing of the questions, however, revises our thinking and assumptions. How, for example, in considering few but also very unfamiliar materials, might we gauge how controls or restrictions over book production – and communication – operated and how books might have been perceived differently? Who controlled production, what was the status of books, how did the relationship between the written and the oral change? In what ways, moreover, were people literate?

Men and women wrote, incised and imprinted signs and script on many objects long before the creation of tablet books, rolls of papyrus, parchment codices and bound sheets of paper. Form is dominated by the orthographic, that is, the invention of writing systems to offer graphic means of communication on diverse materials. Plant fibres, animal skins, cloths, other organic materials and mineral-based surfaces hosted ideograms and symbols used as either phonograms to represent sounds or logograms to denote words. Archaeological excavations in the Yellow River valley of northern China have uncovered thousands of fragments of tortoise shells 3,300 years old, whose flat bottoms and domed upper carapaces are inscribed with divinatory writing, recording royal inquiries about sacrifices, hunting and administrative matters. Other tortoise shells found in China, and believed to be more than 4,000 years older, bear markings which have been interpreted by some scholars as representing up to eleven separate symbols. Such identification is controversial and relevant more to the history of writing than of books, but the dating makes the ancient shells comparable to carved items recovered from the Palaeolithic era such as the notched bone plaques with notation systems and artefacts from the Grotte de Thaïs in southern

The Scope of Book History 17

France, plaques which might be up to 14,000 years old. The inscribed Chinese tortoise shells from the fourteenth to twelfth centuries BCE were used to consult the oracles in sacrificial divination practices, and in a further challenge for historians, have been termed 'pyro-osteomantic' books. The shells seem to have been conserved with their answers from the spirits in what Eleanor Robson has called 'a reference library of omens and their outcomes'.[13] The tortoise shells are of similar age to the oracle texts inscribed on ox shoulder-blades and the flat underpart of turtle shells. Examples of these bones held at Cambridge University Library are celebrated as among 'the oldest extant *documents* written in the Chinese language', and record divination questions from the court of the royal house of Shang 商, which ruled central China between the sixteenth and eleventh centuries BCE.

Graphemes or the smallest units of a writing system include premodern alphabetic letters, ideograms, digits, punctuation marks and other individual symbols, as well, in principle, as printing types and typographic ligatures. Epigraphical study of these inscriptions clarifies and classifies meanings according to chronological and cultural contexts, although epigraphy usually resists historical textual analysis. Indigenous writing has continued to develop among predominantly oral cultures in recent centuries, and notably in regions of North America, Africa and Central and South Asia, but four ancient and independent sites of writing are usually identified as the locales of writing systems without precursors: Egypt, Mesopotamia, China and pre-conquest Mesoamerica. There is much speculation about signs and writing inscribed in materials that have long since perished. The many fragmentary finds from the Middle East and China suggest rich and varied ancient literary traditions and, by implication, increase our awareness of how much loss plays in any understanding of ancient books. Inevitably, chance survival greatly affects our notions of the origin and forms of the earliest types of books, but the very mutability of the form also helpfully encourages consideration of the versatility of the book form – of the vessel used to record information, myths, stories and religious creed.

The world's first extensive books are often claimed to be the records made from pictograms and kept in the ancient Sumerian city of Uruk in about 3200 BCE. These flat clay tablets

18 The Scope of Book History

bearing the impressions of tokens and incised by schematic ideograms survive in their thousands. Such wedge-shaped cuneiform pressed into clay developed over many centuries from the clay tokens of Neolithic accounting systems recording wealth and trade and labour transactions. As different cuneiform languages increased, Uruk and other book-keepers also developed standardized exercises designed to school trainees in hundreds of word and number signs in a dozen different metrologies. Technically, it might be said that impression or punching in cuneiform is the simplest form of physical (im) printing (see figure 1).

Two thousand years before the dominance of Latin in Roman and medieval Europe, cuneiform became a common

1 Cuneiform tablet found in Sippar, from around 600–500 BCE

or 'vehicular' language that worked alongside vernacular languages and writing practices. Like Latin, cuneiform spread far afield, reaching Central Asia, North Africa and the coastal lands and islands of the eastern Mediterranean, including Cyprus. Bridging the universal and the regional, cuneiform multilingual dictionaries translated Sumerian and Akkadian terms into languages such as Hittite, Hurrian, Egyptian and Ugaritic and other Northwest Semitic languages, presaging the diffusion of Aramaic. As research into these ancient books continues, the suggestion of an early literature is also gaining acceptance. The cuneiform of the Euphrates valley denoted the sounds of the Sumerian and the very different Akkadian languages used in legal and institutional administration as well as in spoken and sung prayers and royal inscriptions. The clay tablets of instructions, codes, omens, medicines and mathematical training appear to have been intended as memory aids for the oral recall of knowledge and performative rituals and entertainments. It was this balance between oral and written forms of communication that fascinated Harold Innes in his pioneering communications and media studies publications of the 1950s in which he proposed a division between 'time-binding', durable media such as clay and stone tablets and the more ephemeral 'space-binding' media of modern radio, television, and mass circulation newspapers.[14]

The earliest known hieroglyphic inscriptions, dating from about the same time as Sumerian pictogram and cuneiform survivals, are carved on bone and ivory and painted on clay pottery. Recovered from a cemetery in the ancient Egyptian settlement of Abydos, these earliest known portable hieroglyphic inscriptions have raised many questions about how they were used and read, especially given their complexity which some scholars have linked to the preservation of an elite secrecy. These and dozens of other survivals suggest literate cultures but their functions are tantalizingly obscure. Some, suggesting calendrical, ceremonial or regnal tallies, prompt more questions than answers, even though the range of materials supporting writing increased during the second millennium BCE. In these centuries also, different groups simplified Egyptian hieroglyphs and spread new, more adaptable alphabets across languages. By the first centuries CE, the new alphabets replaced the higher-status cuneiform and hieroglyphic scripts.

The celebrated and as yet undeciphered Cretan Hieroglyphic and Linear A scripts appeared first on clay tablets in Crete from about 1600 BCE. Two centuries later, such scripts were used for Cretan administrative documents in Mycenean, the early form of Greek now known as Linear B. More than 5,500 such tablets have been recovered from Knossos, Pylos, Thebes and Mycenae, but many must already have been rivalled in their own day by the advance of simpler alphabetic scripts on other media. Ostraka or pieces of broken pottery on which ancient Greeks and Egyptians scratched or inked writing served as temporary exercise, recipe and account books from at least the New Kingdom onwards.

Thousands of miles away, at about the same period, signs made on pottery and found at Anyang in China anticipate a literacy associated with divination, administration and royal and official ceremonies. From the seventh century BCE, silk seems to have been used as writing material, with many bamboo and wooden strip books surviving from about two centuries later, most tied together like modern venetian blinds. Bamboo, flexible and light but also strong and durable, became the book material of choice throughout ancient China, save for northern regions where the climate cannot support bamboo and where, by the first centuries CE, book makers adopted willow, poplar, pine or tamarisk instead. Bamboo books, rolled like scrolls and tied with cords or folded like a concertina and bound by a wooden cover, were often sealed by clay over the knots of the cords. The cords tying together the bamboos strips feature in the Shang character sign *ce* for 'book'. In recent years, archaeologists have retrieved thousands of ancient bamboo and wood books from hundreds of tombs of officials and scholars in all regions of China. Hosting a great diversity of texts, many of the books survive in superb condition (figure 2).

As exciting as the bamboo book discoveries was the recovery in 1973 of a dozen silk book rolls during an excavation of a second-century BCE tomb near the northern city of Changsha. Silk's lightness, strength, water resistance, portability and durability ensured its use for literary and common writing during the Han period. The Changsha rolls included copies of the fourth-century BCE *De Jing* by the Daoist Laozi, a celebrated divinatory manual entitled *The Book of Zhuangzi* and the *Intrigues of the Warring States*, a history dating back

2 An unfolded Chinese bamboo concertina book: an eighteenth-century CE copy of *The Art of War* by Sunzi (Sun Tzu) 孙子 (c.544–496 BCE)

to 475 BCE, all of which extended the known, later editions of these texts by several thousands of characters. Against its advantages, silk remained expensive and writers found it difficult to erase characters from its surface. As a result, paper made from hemp fibres began to replace both the awkward bamboo and expensive silk, and during the course of the next six centuries became the staple of book production.

The earliest surviving fragments of paper, probably used for wrapping rather than writing, are those recovered from a tomb in the Han dynasty capital Chang'an (modern Xi'an) and sealed a few years either side of 100 BCE. An official history written six centuries later, however, somewhat specifically records modern paper as invented by Cai Lun in 105 CE.[15] Cai Lun, a senior official of the dynasty, is said to have introduced Emperor He to a paper-making method apparently inspired by wasps' nest-building and involving the pounding of inner bark from mulberry trees with waste hemp fibre. The oldest surviving paper book is a copy of the Buddhist *Piyujing*

Sutra copied in 256 CE, but at least a century earlier we know that Chinese paper makers dipped screens of woven ramie into vats of pulp to make thin sheets then glued into rolls. In later centuries, rattan, straw, jute and flax were added to strengthen and decorate paper sheets.

Late in the first millennium CE, block-printing techniques enabled variants of Chinese script to circulate in Japan, Korea and Vietnam. The westward spread of Chinese paper technologies also gradually reduced indigenous bark paper production in the Indian subcontinent. Birch-bark and palm-leaf books, almost all Buddhist sutras or Hindu scriptures, appeared in South Asia from about the second century BCE. Recopying was essential because the materials decayed rapidly in the humid climate or because they proved as attractive to rodents and insects as they did to readers. This advance continued to northern Pakistan and then Afghanistan from the sixth century. Hemp-based paper had certainly replaced birch and palm by the thirteenth-century arrival of the Mughals. Much-travelled books, many originating from Baghdad, heralded a new era in written communication and textual culture. Clay tablets continued over many centuries, and with a certain revival in the Persian Empire *c*.500 BCE, but the material had reached its technological limits. The size of a clay tablet restricted how much could be written on it. Bulky and dense, clay was easily fractured and hardly ideal for travel over long distances.

The earliest surviving visual depictions and archaeological specimens of waxed wooden writing boards originate from the royal cities of Assyria from the eighth century BCE, precursors of the waxed *tabula cevata* of the Greco-Roman period. Inside, writers used a bronze or iron stylus on a recessed surface filled with coloured wax. The flat end of the stylus smoothed the wax, enabling reuse. Wooden leaf tablets of birch or alder were also common, stitched together or folded and fastened together by a thong or clasp. A wall painting uncovered at Pompeii depicts a young woman holding a tablet with four leaves, and examples of the thin wooden slips have been uncovered in remote regions of the Roman world such as at Vindolanda in north Britain prior to the building of Hadrian's Wall (*c*.85–130 CE). A debtor note, the earliest datable document of Roman Britain, from 57 CE, was found recently among some 400 writing boards in a London excavation. Later, Romans substituted parchment for the wooden leaves of the *tabula* to form the notebook or *membranae*, a suggestive prototype of the modern folded and gathered book.

Papyrus books also endured over more than three millennia. The oldest extant papyrus is a blank roll from a tomb at Memphis near modern-day Cairo, from *c*.2950 BCE. But the earliest surviving inscribed papyri are from a few centuries later, with languages and graphics suiting different intentions. The Egyptians used hieroglyphic script for the ostentatious display of names, numbers and objects on high-status items and monuments. Such script contrasted with the workaday papyri used for administration – and which is increasingly the subject of specialist research. In 2013, for example, at the harbour site of Wadi el-Jarf on the Red Sea, excavators found several hundreds of papyri fragments, many accounts of food deliveries for the labourers, dating to *c*.2550 BCE, and re-employed as a filler between stone blocks.

Papyrus carried many languages to many peoples over many centuries and certainly into the first millennium CE. The earliest surviving papyri in Greek date from the fourth century BCE and scribes continued to use papyrus for either hieroglyphic and late cursive or demotic Egyptian in addition to international Aramaic. Among revelatory finds were eighteen papyri recording in Hebrew and Aramaic slave sales from the mid-fourth century BCE, uncovered in 1962 in a cave in Wadi Daliyeh, in the modern West Bank. Similar recoveries confirm radical changes in the use of papyrus by scribes and consumers over the centuries. Traditionally, papyrus was rolled in lengths that varied between about 1.5 and an unwieldy 6 metres, but stretches measuring more than 30 metres have also been found. From the first century CE, however, many makers and users made concertina-folded papyrus notebooks which were more compact, transportable and searchable.

By the fifth century CE, the use and the quality of papyrus declined, although its manufacture continued after the Muslim invasion of Egypt in 639 CE, and enjoyed popularity among Arabs until at least the tenth century. Nonetheless, parchment and local paper making advanced rapidly, with the latest known Egyptian papyrus document in Arabic written in the 1080s. Papyrus had always been prone to decay in humid lands, and the making of parchment and of paper was also less geographically confined. Although papyrus rolls were durable, unrolling them caused abrasion. Even though writing only on one side reduced the problem of wear, it was inefficient and made the roll even more cumbersome to store. As a result, the makers of books, some still making papyrus notebooks, experimented from the mid-first century CE with folding parchment sheets into what were usually quires or gatherings of eight leaves, which were then tacketed and sewn together to form codices.

By about 300 CE such parchment codices had become the dominant form of the book throughout the Mediterranean world, with bibles the most prominent productions. Early Christian readers, it is suggested, preferred the page-turning of codices to compare gospel accounts rather than the more cumbersome unrolling of scrolls. Unlike earlier untanned leather parchment, the leather of the late first millennium, as with medieval parchment, was dehaired by being soaked in lime and then scraped, stretched and dried, rubbed smooth with pumice and cut into sheets. The parchment of some luxurious late antique bibles was dyed purple, scribes then using gold or silver ink, as in the sixth-century Codex Argenteus (figure 3), now preserved at Uppsala with 188 of the original 336 folios surviving. The same process beautified Greek books of similar age. Written in a majuscule script that is clear and aesthetically pleasing, the texts were written in narrow columns that echoed late antique conventions of word separation.

The preservation of papyrus books in drier climes exemplifies the relationship between ancient book survival and climate. The physician and philosopher Galen reviewed the hazards in a letter itself newly rediscovered in a uniquely surviving fifteenth-century manuscript now in Greece. Galen blamed the natural environs of Rome for the archival tragedy that 'the papyri are completely useless and cannot even be unrolled because they have become glued together by decomposition since the region is both marshy and low-lying, and stifling in summer'.[16] Parchment made from animal skins, soon the staple component of the codex, required greater effort and expense in its manufacture, but offered greater resilience against humidity – and even against fire. The Dead Sea Scrolls dating from between the last three centuries BCE and the first century CE comprise some rolls of papyrus, but over 85 per cent of

3 Codex Argenteus, a sixth-century manuscript, originally containing Bishop Ulfilas' fourth-century translation of the Bible into the Gothic language

the nearly 1,000 rolls are made of the skins of goats, calves, ibex and gazelle.

In northern India, paper scrolls, primarily used for official documents, horoscopes and almanacs, were made of the inner bark of birch trees as well as beaten cotton cloth and were rolled for storage, To date, the earliest examples discovered are thirteen first-century CE birch-bark scrolls from the Buddhist kingdom of Gandhara, spanning modern Afghanistan and Pakistan. Elsewhere, Indian scribes wrote with a reed pen and ink on the boiled, dried and polished leaves of the talipot palm, a species of palm native to eastern and southern India and Sri Lanka. A vigorous trade in palm leaves developed, largely from the south. Often cited is a seventh-century description of commercial cultivation of talipot in a travelogue by the Chinese Buddhist pilgrim Xuanzang 玄奘. By about 1500, however, palmyra began to replace talipot in manuscript publication. Scribes incised the more resistant palmyra leaves with an iron stylus. The reader wiped the leaves with a cloth soaked in oil and lampblack, leaving the ink in the incised characters. Cords strung through holes in the leaves bound talipot and palmyra-leaf books, creating a distinctively narrow and horizontal book format.

Many recovered graphic artefacts from the ancient Middle East, Mediterranean and India, also from disparate parts of China, await fuller contextual analysis, but just as tantalizing for historians of ancient books are the ongoing excavations and decipherments of the symbolic writing systems of the early Americas. Many finds are unsettling to modern concepts of the book and complicate the understanding of the relationship between writing and spoken language, where books containing Aztec and Mixtec pictographs still appear to be unconnected to linguistic systems. Of the various Mesoamerican writing clusters, Mayan, dating back two millennia, is the best understood. Less well deciphered are Isthmian of the first centuries CE, and Olmec and Zapotec of the first millennium BCE.

Writings in the central Americas boast a history of some 3,000 years, although a discovery such as the massive 22 kg Olmec Cascajal Block from Veracruz, found in 1999 and dating from c.900 BCE, is too immovable to be termed a book. Its as yet undeciphered text of 62 characters and stylized pictograms, however, suggests an ancient literacy and the existence of lost, more portable – and more perishable – Mesoamerican texts, as well as rubbings made from the stone inscriptions. Similarly, later languages and hieroglyphic scripts, carved on thousands of Zapotec, Mixtec, Aztec and Mayan buildings and monuments, suggest the existence of scribes and artists, some apparently named in carved 'name tags'. Scribes are even depicted on pottery from what is known as the Classic Maya period (*c*.250–900 CE). Other portrayals include conch-shell inkpots and headdresses adorned by quill pens. The 1993 excavation of a scribal workshop at Aguateca in Guatemala, and other discoveries since, suggest a network of producers. In association with glyphic texts, archaeologists recovered abandoned pigment grinders and shell inkpots. The name of an elite owner inscribed on one inkpot offers crucial evidence of the high and possibly royal status of Mayan scribes. Nevertheless, there are still many unknowns and, not least, the link between the older monumentalism and the production of more portable and legible books.

It is both extraordinary and disappointing that so few Mesoamerican books have survived to modern times, and all – twenty at most – date from the fourteenth to sixteenth centuries CE. Dating is itself often approximate. One extant Mixtec manuscript, called the Codex Cospi, dates from between 1350 and 1520 CE and consists of concertina-folded deerskin in twenty pages (figure 4). The Mayan book now known as the Madrid Codex is constructed from a single nearly 7-metre strip of fig-tree bark and contains calendrical, astronomical and divinatory material taken from several sources by as many as eight or nine different scribes. Recent research confirms that this codex, like so many other similar survivals, conveys a long genealogical history and suggests that such books were copied and extended over many generations. The Mesoamerican book represented a sophisticated conveyance tool for collective memory, whose creation and access is still debatable. Removed from their original functional sites, these books are also notable examples of interrupted appreciation, subject to different periods of neglect, misunderstanding and accelerated interest. The pitifully few surviving books of pre-Hispanic Mesoamerica all now reside in European collections, where they were largely ignored until their rediscovery in the nineteenth century.

Assuredly, such artefacts and ancient books should not be regarded as 'primitive', but understood in ways that inform and fortify our understanding of the role of graphic forms of communication. Study of centuries-old and what seem to us exotic and mysterious book forms adds to our decoding of geographically and chronologically far-reaching endeavours.

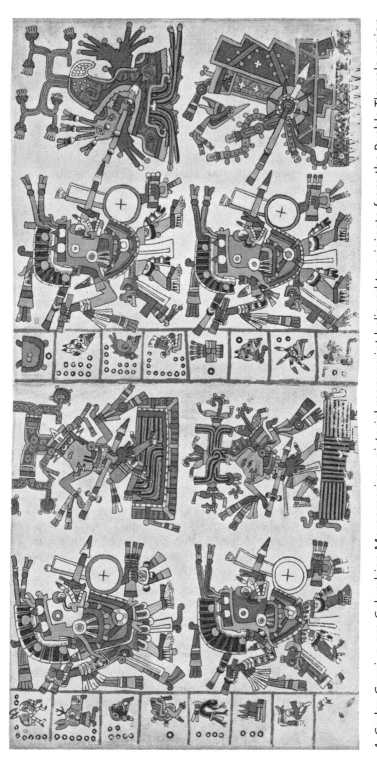

4 Codex Cospi, a pre-Columbian Mesoamerican pictorial manuscript believed to originate from the Puebla-Tlaxcala region and preserved in the library of the University of Bologna

The survivals question many assumptions we make about the efficiencies, effectiveness and specific historical contexts of books produced during the last few centuries, and especially of their many moves from their original sites to where they were acquired, read or preserved. Take, for example, ongoing research into the animal skins of the Lakota people of the North American plains. Known as winter counts, these community annals, drawn on buffalo, deer and cow hides, feature the oldest events at the centre, spiralling out anticlockwise to the most recent. Like Mesoamerican books, most winter counts are now divorced from their original communities and contain references to events many centuries old. Up to a hundred winter counts survive in national and local museums, with greatly varying chronologies and subjects.

Similar removal from original sites affects the book-form interpretation of beads and knotted strings from different parts of the Americas. Wampum beads, shells worn in strings on belts, acted as more than units of monetary exchange among many indigenous peoples of North America. Wampum, it is claimed by members of Native American communities, served to record and communicate stories, historical events and treaties and act as ceremonial gifts. Germaine Warkentin, in pioneering research in early book history, has used her investigations of wampum to interrogate what 'writing' and 'reading' actually means and meant. She suggests that the most significant problem is distinguishing between cultures that exhibit 'bookishness' and those that do not. What is meant by 'bookishness' here is very broadly conceived, with tensions and overlaps between the picture-based (semasiographic) and the language-based (phonographic), which encompasses the logographic, syllabic and alphabetic systems of aboriginal signification.[17] Nonetheless, research on wampum moves the history of the book to much broader and deeper cultural experiences and behaviours and readdresses questions about what books are, their genesis, proliferation and function, and who does what with them, and when and how and with what effect – to anticipate later chapters in this book.

Thousands of miles to the south of wampum collectors, South American Incan officials made the complex knotted string records called khipus in Quechua and with antecedents that stretch back as far as the seventh or eighth centuries CE.

About 600 khipu examples survive today from the period *c.*1400–1530 CE, some from archaeological excavations – notably of tombs. Khipus, like many pieces of Greek and Egyptian ostraka, also resurface in illicit sales of antiquities. Khipu cords were spun from cotton or llama hair and dyed, although the significance of colour is now not fully understood. About 80 per cent of the surviving khipus record (primarily at least) counts and quantifications, but the remainder are thought to bear narrative records. The interpretation of khipus remains basic and unsatisfying, even though we have tantalizing evidence of their use from colonial testimony, and matches between surviving sections of different khipus invite new interpretative attempts. In early conquest years, khipus, portable, reconfigurable and adaptable to a variety of different uses, formed admissible evidence in Hispanic courts of law, before khipus fell out of official use in the mid-sixteenth century. Accounts survive of witnesses and the accused reading their khipus – often by feel rather than sight, as fingers ran over the knots. Some khipus were huge. One of the largest known khipus, with 762 pendant cords, appears to have been organized calendrically, with 730 of those cords grouped into 24 clusters of about 30 pendants each.

In examining such books of antiquity, we must be aware that the word 'ancient' conceals a vast stretch of time and one that is subject to critical rediscovery and reinterpretation, often by removing colonial legacies. Many of the revelatory reports have their basis in a wave of nineteenth-century excavations, but more recent archaeological and electronic retrieval techniques have introduced more radical findings from the reading of buried and scorched texts from Roman Herculaneum to the decoding of Middle Eastern cuneiform and Mesoamerican glyphs by digital recording, manipulation and comparison. These various concerns are evident in one prominent survival, the mid-fourth century Codex Sinaiticus whose 400 surviving parchment sheets comprise one of the earliest and most complete of all Greek bibles. Rediscovered in St Catherine's Monastery in the Sinai in 1844, the codex contributed to reawakening interest in very old books in the nineteenth century. Now much travelled and divorced from the site of its original community, the codex is also divided between libraries in London, Leipzig and St Petersburg.

Some previously unknown parts were also discovered at the monastery in 1975, underscoring how we can lose, forget or not recognize such materials. A digital edition created by international collaboration now offers amendments to the text and the comparative imaging of pages and parchment textures under both standard and raked lighting.

The loss of the opening books of the Old Testament in the Codex Sinaiticus reminds us again of the prominence of loss. In ways similar to the rediscovery of classical learning in the Renaissance, the resurfacing of such texts after centuries of neglect or concealment attests to gaps in apparently accumulated knowledge. Exigencies of recovery, as well as debates over ownership and access, mark textual and communications history. The chance of rediscovery in some cultures seems remote. In southern Asia, birch-bark and palm-leaf books decomposed in the heat and humidity of the Indian subcontinent. Some worn-out texts were periodically recopied before their ritual destruction, but very few early Indian manuscripts have survived, or survive in only partial states, including those thirteen surviving first-century CE scrolls, believed to be only a portion of the Gandharan Buddhist canon. The meagre survival rates frustrate our knowledge about the scope of ancient book culture and the relationship between textual circulation and oral transmission. Rather than a continuum or linear development, the history of books encompasses a fitful account of burial and rediscovery, obscurity and enlightenment – or apparent enlightenment. It invites a *longue durée* of a social history of intellectual achievement that is uneven, unexpected and always capable of revision and reappraisal.

2
The Early History of Book History

Prehistories of the Book

Historical appreciation of book production and reception began early. In the first century CE, Pliny the Elder, having seen documents written on papyrus 200 years earlier, observed that upon papyrus 'the immortality of human beings depends'.[1] Papyrus had by then been a common writing material for 3,000 years.

Words matter to those writing the history of graphic communication. The word *paper* (*papier* in French and German) itself derives from the Latin, *papyrus* and the Greek πάπυρος (*papuros*). From the Greek βύβλος (*bublos*), a word said to derive from the name of the Phoenician city of Byblos, *biblos* came to mean the roll made from papyrus, and then a codex book and the Bible, but other bibliographical terms also descend from the ancients. The *charta*, relates Pliny, comprised a papyrus roll of no more than twenty sheets or about 4.5 metres. By 537–8 Cassiodorus was reporting that 'antiquity gave the name of *liber* to the books of the ancients; for even today we call the bark of green wood *liber*'.[2]

Further language study is illuminating. 'Biblos', 'volumen' and 'liber' could all mean book in the sense of the division of a work, where a work was too long to fit into one papyrus roll. The Books of the Bible are its divisions. The standard way of reading was to unroll or, in the Latin, *explicare*, 'to unfold'. Because of its resemblance to a block of wood, the tablet came to be called a *codex* (from the Latin *caudex* 'a tree trunk'), a term certainly used by the poet Martial (40–104 CE). There is a similar association in the Latin *liber*, which originally meant 'bark'. Such comments tempt us to construct a bibliographical chronology. In 84–6 CE, for example, when rolls dominated, Martial noted that a parchment codex was convenient for travel and storage space. Some scrolls unfolded vertically (resembling the 'scrolling down' textual reading of the modern computer screen), but the more general horizontal scroll, with divided-up text, looked more like the codex. Many note that the earliest full description of a scroll is by Catullus (b. *c.*84 BCE) when he rebuked a fellow poet for writing not upon an erased flat sheet but on rolled and polished *carta regia* with ivory handles wrapped in red parchment and tied with red thongs.[3]

Some 200 years later, the legal scholar Ulpian noted that codices were now acceptable and he anticipated much later reflective, even romantic observations such as those by Cassiodorus (537 CE) who, looking back, mused that papyrus remained unequalled for preserving great thought:

> For previously, the sayings of the wise and the ideas of our ancestors were in danger. For how could you quickly record words which the resistant hardness of bark made it almost impossible to set down?...The tempting beauty of paper...opens a field for the elegant with its white surface; its help is always plentiful; and it is so pliant that it can be rolled together, although it is unfolded to a great length. Its joints are seamless, its parts united; it is the snowy pith of a green plant, a writing surface which takes black ink for its ornament; on it, with letters exalted...there discourse is stored in safety, to be heard for ever with consistency.[4]

The roll was stored upright in a *capsa*, or book box, horizontally on a shelf, or in a pigeonhole. Most works required more than one roll kept together, and owners and early librarians placed valuable rolls in a chest or wrapped them in a protective sleeve of parchment tied with thongs. Such physical limitations – the length of the roll and the number of rolls that could be stored together – often defined the divisions of literature, but also brought criticism of such filing systems. Title tags were often mislaid and citation from papyrus rolls proved difficult and often inaccurate.

Such discussion of material forms and of how codices were coming to be preferred to rolls accompanied an awareness of the risks threatening the preservation of books. In his rediscovered letter, Galen describes how a fire that ravaged the city of Rome in 192 CE affected books and their owners: 'when Philides the grammarian's books were destroyed in the fire, he wasted away and died as a result of discouragement and distress. What is more, for quite some time, people went around in black garments – thin and pale like mourners.'[5] This European perspective, however, obscures even older descriptions and appreciation of the production and function of books. Until this point, in answering 'What is the History of the Book?', sustained discussion of printing has been deliberately withheld, not only to underscore the length and depth of book history before print, but in order to emphasize the rich and comparatively neglected history of books in Asia. As noted, greater study is required of the history of silk and bamboo books, but the invention of printing in East Asia also predated the invention of printing by movable type in Europe by 800 years. Printing supposedly began in China in 636 CE and definitely by 868. It is reasonable to expect therefore an earlier history of the book to have been developed, however different in its perspective or inspiration.

As many scholars in Europe and North America remind us – and most recently, Cynthia Brokaw, Peter Kornicki and Joseph McDermott – a great variety of global book culture technologies originated in China and East Asia. Like Assyrian cuneiform centuries before, Aramaic and Sanskrit, which developed from the much older Brahmi in South Asia, classical Chinese operated as the *lingua franca* of East Asia for two or more millennia. Just as Sanskrit carried practical learning and the edicts of authority, in both Korea and Japan classical Chinese was promoted as the language of government and the male elite, with particular reverence for Chinese classical books as virtuous sources in ethics and politics.[6] Gender remained critical. In Korea before about 1800 literate men wrote in Chinese, whereas women depended on Korean.

Extracts from Chinese literature were also widely adopted as an exemplar of approved writing, so that from early medieval years the various cities and settlements of East Asia supported a relatively unified language and similar forms of textual production. Scribal and manuscript production and distribution did not simply predate printing but continued alongside its deployment and expansion. From the seventh century, however, Chinese and then Korean and Japanese artisans devised a number of different techniques based on different printing technologies: the carving of artisanal characters, xylography or woodblock printing and movable type made from earthenware, wood and metal. This style of printing proved appropriate for the multiple characters of Asian written languages in the same way that movable type supported simpler alphabets.

Xylography, more than metal moveable type, remained the predominant technology of print until the early twentieth century. Even in Korea, where metal movable type was developed by government officials, xylography was the more commonly used technology. In medieval China this form of woodblock printing sustained a great expansion in publishing. By the early modern period the major form of book manufacture was printing and one that was to hugely influence the book histories of Korea and Japan. The first printing in Japan comprised a style of woodblock impression (木版画, *mokuhanga*) intimately connected to belief, emotion and prayer.

Although under-researched, it appears that the complexity of early and medieval Asian book production and reception did not inspire attempts to write histories of book production and effects. Even more than in Europe, it seems that from what is known at present we should not over-estimate the development of book studies in ancient Asia. In the era of the first Chinese print revolution, few wrote about their own bibliographical history. This is also true of Korea, where by the early thirteenth century, artisans at the Korean court were experimenting with metal movable type. Nonetheless, we do have hints, in ways reminiscent of Renaissance and post-Reformation Europe, that the new technology was prized and very much associated with progressive ideals. The early rulers of the Korean Joseon dynasty (1392–1910), for example, were quick to recognize the value of printing in administration and governance. As a 1403 edict of King Taejong of Joseon 이방원 explained, 'if the country is to be governed well, it is essential that books be read widely…It is my desire to cast copper type so that we can print as many books as possible and have them made available widely.' Reflections on literacy also increased. Chinese scholars were, from an early period, interested in cataloguing books, and, in the first century CE, Liu Xin 劉歆 developed the first cataloguing system. Later, many Chinese scholars worked on collating editions and developing principles of textual criticism, particularly in the eleventh and twelfth centuries when printed books became more common. Even so, Chinese and Japanese interest in what we think of as bibliographical history seems not to have prospered until the late nineteenth and early twentieth centuries.

The chronicles and literature of medieval Europe included diverse references to the production and use of books, including depictions of books read, held and stored in drawn and painted images and above all in the iconography of religious paintings and murals. Such depictions, many of which are contained within books themselves, offer valuable evidence about book manufacture, circulation and reading. Modern historians and literary scholars locating the premodern representation of the book and its significance have been much exercised by illustrations such as that of Ezra, perhaps representing Cassiodorus himself before his book cupboard at Vivarium, in the seventh-century Codex Amiatinus, the earliest surviving manuscript of the nearly complete Bible in the Latin Vulgate. Much later, 'Lady Hagiography' stands in front of opened books and book furniture in a mid fifteenth-century copy of an English translation of *Le Pèlerinage de l'homme* (Pilgrimage of the Life of Man) by Guillaume de Guileville. This and many other drawings have fuelled productive debate about the material and cultural history of books. The creation and consumption of such images in their own time, however, also contributed, in ways yet to be fully recognized perhaps, to an interest in the nature and even the history of the 'book'.

Despite the commentaries about new technologies and their possibilities, we can overstate early modern interest in books and in printing in Europe. Printing with movable type began in Europe in the 1450s and its introduction by Johannes Gutenberg created a historical watershed that underpinned intellectual, scientific, religious and political revolution – at least as most clearly calibrated by later historians. But as Thomas Hobbes argued in an opening early section to *Leviathan* in 1651, 'the Invention of printing, though ingenious, compared with the invention of Letters [which he facetiously attributes to Cadmus], is no great matter'. Uncertainty and mystery about the invention of printing fuelled the early modern myths and rival claims discussed later, but these have also endured to the modern day with new and sometimes outlandish theories about the creation of type in the fifteenth century and also the more politically sensitive claims about where printing first developed. Recent discoveries about printing along the Silk Road have reinforced ideas about the transference of technology, and especially the argument of Thomas F. Carter in 1925 about very early European appreciation of Chinese printing technology. Such arguments, together with the provocative and ultimately unconvincing propositions of Timothy H. Barrett, have encouraged a certainty among Chinese and Korean scholars that their countries' block printing and movable type had helped fashion European culture and the modern world. To date, the only textual evidence of any European awareness of East Asian printing before Gutenberg resides in eight post-1253 reports by travellers, all silent on production processes, but noting Mongol and Chinese printing of paper money.[7] The first recorded European awareness of Chinese printed books dates from 1513, when the King of Portugal donated a Chinese imprint to the Pope.

For all their disagreements, those researching this early history of the book have recovered a patchwork of significant comments and activities, and other historians might yet pay more attention. It is also the case that a century before Hobbes, a few well-placed individuals followed their passions, and, because of their bibliographical devotion, to them we owe the survival of ancient manuscripts and literature. For England, René Wellek long ago acknowledged the literary and bibliographical achievements of John Bale when accompanying John Leland's tour of the emptying monasteries of the 1540s. Bale's 1548 *Illustrium majoris Britanniae scriptorium summarium* and 1549 'A Regystre of the Names of Englysh Wryters' were catalogues that fashioned virtual libraries. In bibliography, Bale found salvation, and with Leland became celebrated among an increasing number of enthusiastic book collectors – in an appreciation that went beyond simple book ownership. Bale condemned the monkish avarice that 'hath made an ende both of our lybraryes and bokes' and attacked the destroyers of monasteries for regarding books simply as 'commodytees'. Bale reflected, even then, about how the market value of books might reduce their cultural worth.[8] In Hobbes's century also, much changed in the consideration of books. Many writers offer clues to an awareness of the history of books and a sense of both foreboding and opportunity. A particular debate concerns continuing reactions to 'information overload', as well as perceptions of overproduction and slipshod publication designed to satisfy an increasingly commercial market. Stern voices offered vivid warnings against an escalating obsession with the collection of books. Following from medieval witnesses like Vincent of Beauvais (c.1190–c.1264) and Richard de Bury, whose early fourteenth-century *Philobiblon* urged clerical pursuit of learning and love of books, Ann Blair has argued that the 'multitude of books' continued to awe and perplex and that many authors reflected on what it was to be a scholar. Much cited is the early preface to Conrad Gesner's *Bibliotheca universalis* of 1545, an immense book-cataloguing attempt with more than 10,000 titles listed in its first edition. Gesner warned of the 'confusing and harmful abundance of books' that kings and the learned must remedy.

Debate continues over the ways in which fears of a superfluity of books led to books being used and read in different ways, to the development of new aids to study and note-taking, and even to the physical cutting of texts. Concern about obsessive book collecting also reflected anxiety about the lack of use of books as much as their growing quantity. But all this also attests to a type of book history then circulating. Very soon after the increase in production and sales of books in the second half of the seventeenth century, pronouncements about an avalanche of publication featured in European news-sheets, journals and letters. Gottfried Leibniz, himself a distinguished librarian, typified mid-seventeenth-century concern, proposing that in order to contain the 'horrible mass of books', bad books should be banned before they were printed and that Louis XIV should prescribe a set of canonical texts as recommended by appointed specialists.[9]

Such expostulations did not invoke the word 'bibliomania' until the beginning of the eighteenth century. The earliest use in England – actually of the 'bibliomanie' – apparently dates from 1719 when Myles Davies reported in his news-sheet *Athenae britannicae* that a Mr Menschen, then editing writings by the Library Keeper to the King of Denmark, 'declared against those who are troubl'd with Bibliomanie, of having too many Books: that is, who will neither read them themselves nor let any Bode else'. The activity also highlights the distinction between the bibliomania of new publication – the torrent of new books – and the enhanced market in antiquarian books. The activities of book collectors proceeded against a rash of warnings across Europe against indiscriminate purchase and reading. The motivation for collection was many-faceted. The pursuit of books was one in which intellectual enquiry, specific interest, an urge to improvement, practical problem-solving and entertainment subtly combined with prestige, status, family pride and the concern to preserve and bequeath a collection, whether to kin or to a favoured institution or community.

David McMullen's work on the intellectual and institutional history of medieval China reveals that some Chinese were already complaining of too many books during the Tang dynasty (618–907 CE), but the concern seems to have matured in the last century of the early modern Ming period (1368–1644) in ways that have resonance thousands of miles to the west. Peter Burke has drawn parallels between the early production of popular encyclopaedias in China and Europe in response to demands for readers' digests to cope with the surge in printing in the sixteenth century.[10] As the preface of one of the popular Ming encyclopaedias, written in 1599, asked, 'The number of books is now boundless as the ocean – how can we read them all?', then explaining that what followed offered the answer by condensing all the information one needed in one work of forty-three chapters.[11] Joseph McDermott's research in early modern China echoes Blair's European history, with many examples such as the literatus Tang Shunzhi 唐順之 (1507–60), from the lower Yangzi delta complaining that too many books were written and printed. At a time when even a well-off butcher claimed a printed obituary, his rough contemporary Zhu Yuanming from Suzhou called for books to be burned because they were too numerous. Concentration here on the lower Yangzi and its literati culture is shaped by these local studies. As recent scholarship has insisted, in distinction to earlier broad-brush studies, it is premature at this stage of research to extend these conclusions across all of China.

Towards Bibliography

The advance of the general market for printed books, together with the destruction and redistribution of ancient collections after the dissolution of the monasteries in England and the religious wars in Continental Europe, generated a new age for the ownership and collection of manuscript and early printed books. A more exacting and technical history of the book, and more particularly of printing, developed from seventeenth-century occasional publications ranging from guides to book collecting and arranging to printers' manuals and sections of works describing different professions. Hieronymus Hornschuch (1573–1616) earned his living as a press corrector, proofreading sheets in Leipzig, where in 1608 he published in Latin his *Orthotypographia*, the first technical manual for printers. Written for other correctors, a version in German by Tobias Heidenreich appeared in 1634, with further editions down to 1744. The manual included correction marks, imposition models and type specimens, while the German version added poems in praise of printing. As Anthony Grafton has commented, even by itself the engraving by Moses Thym accompanying the first edition of Hornschuch offers a fascinating portrayal of the working printing house. In France, Gabriel Naudé's 1627 *Advis*, later translated into English by John Evelyn in 1661, was based on his experience of arranging the library of the President of the Parlement of Paris. Later librarian to Cardinal Mazarin, Naudé sneered at neat bindings and opined that it was absurd to judge books by their covers, but more influential were Naudé's other recommendations of separate subject and author library catalogues. Many other commentaries appeared as incidental to a larger work or argument. In England, Richard Atkyns's single-sheet broadside of 1660, "The original and growth of printing", greatly expanded in 1664, hailed the arrival of the printing press, but he wrote with intent, in this case as a plea for freedom from guild control.

In England, at least, the 'mystery and art' of printing retained its mysteriousness for most of the seventeenth century despite the enlargement of its social and imaginative presence during and after the Civil Wars. As a result, as Henry Woudhuysen suggests, the novelty and breadth of Joseph Moxon's *Mechanick Exercises* needs restating. Moxon's second volume, published in twenty-four numbers between 1683 and 1684, gave an unprecedentedly detailed account of letter-cutting, type-founding and printing.[12] Often cited as the fullest early printers' manual in any language, *Mechanick Exercises* contains the first list in an English book of proofreading marks and includes a twenty-eight page 'Dictionary Alphabetically explaining the abstruse Words and Phrases that are used in Typography'. According to its twentieth-century editors, Herbert Davis and Harry Carter, Moxon the tradesman 'put in writing a knowledge that was wholly traditional',[13] and as Woudhuysen celebrates, the printing part of Moxon's book is cited nearly 600 times in the electronic version of the *Oxford English Dictionary*. *Mechanick Exercises* is the source for first uses of thirty-six words such as frisket, kern, rounce, smoot and unplanished, and even more extraordinarily, nearly 200 instances of the first use in a typographical sense of words such as canon, fount, lower case and shank. Moxon included detailed images of book-making processes, and prefaced his account with 'historical' portraits of Laurens Coster and Johannes Gutenberg, although these seem to have been removed from many surviving copies as trophies to stick in the albums of bibliophiles.

One reason for this interest was that the 'mystery' of printing extended to its origins, so that 'history' equated with disputation and the making and undoing of myths. Debate raged about where and by whom printing began on mainland Europe and in England itself: Gutenberg in Mainz or Coster in Haarlem, and William Caxton in Westminster or Wynkyn de Worde or Frederick Corsellis, one of Gutenberg's workmen, at Oxford. In 1572, Archbishop Matthew Parker, rescuer of so many monastic manuscripts, recorded his uncertainty as to who first introduced printing, which he thought began in about 1461. Within twenty years, many lists of famous Continental printers and claimants to precedent in various ways circulated across Europe. The tributes to Johann Froben, Christophe Plantin, Nicolas Jenson, Aldus Manutius, Lucantonio and Bernardo Giunti, Jodocus Badius, Johannes Oporinus, Robert and Henri Estienne, and Franciscus Raphelengius anticipated a plethora of invented portraits of the various and disputed fathers of printing engraved and collected in the seventeenth century. Popular accounts of Gutenberg date from at least the account of Polydore Vergil (1470?–1555), who told the story of 'Cuthenbergus', a knight who 'found Printyng' and printers' ink and for whom the importance of the craft was that 'one manne may Prynte more in one day, then many men in many yeres could write' (according to the abridgement of Vergil by Thomas Langley in 1546). About a century later, Hieronymus Cardanus apparently first applauded the creation of modernity by that soon clichéd triad of gunpowder, compass and printing press.

In mainland Europe, as Jacqueline Glomski has described, the bibliophile Bernhard von Mallinckrodt issued in 1639 *De ortu et progressu artis typographicae* (On the rise and progress of the typographic art) to mark the alleged bicentenary of the invention of movable type.[14] Von Mallinckrodt defended the claims of Gutenberg against pro-Costerians like Marcus Zuerius Boxhorn. Elsewhere, debate continued for more than two centuries. In Strasbourg, in 1760, Jean-Daniel Schoepflin published *Vindiciae typographicae*, authoritatively championing Gutenberg with the reproduction of extracts from his trial in the town in 1436. Most of these documents disappeared with the burning of Strasbourg city library in 1870, and are today only known from Schoepflin's book. Nonetheless, in 1794 Dr Thomas Cogan in his *The Rhine* visited Mainz and declared for Coster rather than the local Gutenberg as the inventor of movable type. Coster was also claimed for the model for the Englishman who 'stole the art from Holland about 1460'.[15] Being a Costerian or a Corsellian in the eighteenth century was perhaps rather like being a supporter of the Earl of Oxford in modern disputes about the authorship of Shakespeare's plays. It also attests to the absence of clarity in any history of printing and publishing. This was soon to change. In 1841, towards the end of his life, Isaac D'Israeli asked 'How has it happened that such a plain story as that of the art of printing should have sunk into a romance?', although he also observed that there was 'some probability that this art originated in China'.[16]

Already, however, a shared history of printing and publishing had been accumulating even if language and nationalities created barriers. John Fell and colleagues in Oxford in the

1670s wrote about 'the mechanic part of printing',[17] and interest focused on the machinery of book-making processes. The first complete English type specimen surviving is one by Moxon in 1669 and collected by Samuel Pepys. Other bibliophiles collected bookplates and engraved portraits of printers, but the striking increase in the production, circulation and acquisition of books during the eighteenth century brought even greater interest in the attendant publications of the press such as catalogues and type specimen sheets. Alonso Víctor de Paredes's history and compositors' guide, *Institución y origen del arte de la imprenta y reglas generales para los componedores*, written in about 1680, was apparently printed in only a single copy 'para que mi serviesse de memoria'. In 1721, Johann Heinrich Gottfried Ernesti published a much-praised printers' manual, *Die wol eingerichtete Buchdruckerei*. The volume gave the greatest emphasis to language and composition, but included a series of biographies and portraits of celebrated European printers and concluded with Johann Rist's 1677 play about printing, *Depositio cornuti typographici*. In 1722 Johan Olaf Alnander published his manual on printing in Sweden, *Historia artis typographicae in Svecia*, and the manual *La Science pratique de l'imprimérie: Contenant des Instructions Trés-faciles pour se Perfectionner dans cet Art* by Martin-Dominique Fertel was published in 1723, the forerunner of dozens of guides to printing published in Europe in the next century or so.

With greater historical intent, in 1745 Joseph Ames issued his *Catalogue of English printers, from the year 1471 to 1600; most of them at London*, another demonstration of the chronicling urge in the service of the trade. The first English articles on the history of the trade, with accompanying illustrations, appeared in the first issue of the *Universal Magazine* in 1747. They are, however, overshadowed in retrospect by the extensive and still much-reprinted articles and engraved plates in the *Encyclopédie* of Diderot and d'Alembert (1751–72). The French plates include *Imprimerie en lettres*, and images illustrating printers and compositors in a printing house, paper making and allied activity. During these years, Pierre Simon Fournier published his unfinished *Manuel typographique* (1764–6), described by David Pankow as 'one of the monuments of printing history, not only for its thorough account of typefounding techniques and practices, but because it introduced the concept of the point-system to the typographic community'.[18] Significantly, Fournier had not read and did not mention Moxon. Nationally prescribed histories of the book are nothing new.

Increased publication rates throughout Europe also fuelled concerns about bibliomania as well as alarms about the immoral and subversive effects of uncontrolled printing, and these too contributed to essays, letters and more extended assessments of the history and growth of printing and book publication. Ames's partly derivative *Typographical Antiquities: Being an Historical Account of Printing in England* appeared in 1749 and included largely invented portraits of the hallowed fathers of the English trade introducing short testimonials to celebrated printing careers. Ames's compilation, extended by William Herbert between 1785 and 1790 and by the great bibliophile and early bibliographer Thomas Frognall Dibdin between 1810 and 1819, formed only one of many mid and late eighteenth-century European writings on early printing. *The History of Printing in America* by the printer and patriot Isaiah Thomas appeared in 1810. A second edition of 1874 included a catalogue of American publications before 1776 and a memoir of Thomas by his grandson. The more specific *Manuale tipografico* by Giambattista Bodoni was posthumously published in Parma in 1818, nine years before Thomas Curson Hansard's *Typographia*. Such histories and manuals encouraged the study of past book production at the very time that the industry was transformed, but the focus remained on printing rather than manuscripts or publishing, on individuals rather than institutions, and with little cross-border acknowledgement.

The political context is crucial. Ames compiled his history of printing to honour 'a period when Britain roused herself from amid various superstitions, and sat down on the seat of liberty, where she now remains',[19] even though many of England's earliest printers were foreign-born. A newspaper obituary of 1778 similarly praised the pioneering type-founder William Caslon: 'Great Britain is indebted for the improvement she enjoys over every country on the face of the globe in the art of letter-founding; an art obviously and essentially important to a nation, whose great and glorious characteristic is the freedom of the press.'[20] More will be said in the next chapter about the biographical histories of printing and bookselling which increased from the early nineteenth century, but these and other commentaries contributed to a maturing of academic and popular understanding of the contribution of the book – mostly the printed and the European and North American book – to civilization, faith, intellect, science and progress.

Book collectors' clubs, the further outcome of bibliomania, includes most famously the Roxburghe Club, founded in June 1812 after a dinner organized by Dibdin on the eve of the sale of the Duke of Roxburghe's celebrated library. The Duke's copy of the 1471 Valdarfer edition of Boccaccio's *Decameron* sold for a record £2,260, unsurpassed until Bernard Quaritch paid £4,950 for the 1459 Mainz Psalter in 1884. In that same year, New York printing press manufacturer and book collector Robert Hoe and eight fellow bibliophiles founded the Grolier Club, named after the great sixteenth-century French bibliophile. As Kristian Jensen has argued, the new appreciation and sale of rare and antiquarian books created a socially varied marketplace which valued books not simply as sources of textual information but historic commodities capable of shaping a nation's history.[21]

The national and imperial role of books and periodicals, and their authors and journalists, was reinforced by lithography, invented in 1796, and by fresh experiments in printing, typesetting and paper making. In East Asia and India new printing technologies transformed material book production – and bibliographical understanding. Many printers and booksellers now drew on a tradition and repertoire of book publishing history. A landmark publication in England, and one still of use today, was the nine volumes of John Nichols's *The Literary Anecdotes of the Eighteenth Century* of 1812–15, originating from memoirs of the printer William Bowyer in 1782, and Nichols's *Illustrations of the Literary History of the Eighteenth Century*, begun in 1817. Charles Henry Timperley, Manchester and regional printer and writer, gave public lectures on the art of printing. In 1838, after an earlier publication of poems on the art of printing, Timperley published a printers' manual. A year later appeared his *Dictionary of Printers and Printing, With the Progress of Literature, Ancient and Modern*, issued with the manual in 1842 as *Encyclopaedia of Literary and Typographical Anecdote*. In 1845, Henry Stevens, born in Vermont in 1819, arrived in London, where he collected Americana for the British Museum and numerous American libraries and published his *American Bibliographer*, at the same time as his compatriot William F. Poole (b. 1821) pioneered the indexing of periodicals.

Popular curiosity in this activity can be measured by mid-nineteenth-century booksellers' memoirs, essays on book collecting and history, and in particular by renewed interest in Caxton and the founding fathers of printing. As David McKitterick has put it, by the time of the nationalistic trumpeting during the quatercentenary of the printer's arrival in Westminster, 'Caxton himself became difficult to escape.'[22] The much-reproduced 1830s painting by Daniel Maclise has Caxton presenting a specimen of his printing to Edward IV and his family. This romantic and domesticated scene gained huge popularity when engraved in 1858 and then reissued in 1877 as part of the Caxton anniversary celebrations. Nearly 25,000 visitors came to the Caxton exhibition at South Kensington. Caxton now became an imperial figure, with other celebratory exhibitions held in other cities of the empire, each reviewed and extracted in newspapers and periodicals read in the pink parts of the globe.

The exhibitions opened some sixteen years after William Blades's heroic biography of Caxton and his groundbreaking study of his printing office.[23] Blades rejected Ames and Dibdin as reliable sources but praised Moxon as the best early guide on type-founding. In the Caxton anniversary year Henry Bradshaw revisited the life of Caxton and reinterpreted him as a practical printer and historian but one instilled with national pride. In 1885 Blades translated and printed 'as an exercise in photo-lithography' a translation of Rist's 1677 play about printing, adding to the developing national and often anecdotal album of booklore. Disparagement of past chronicling was also common. In his 1896 *The Enemies of Books*, William Blades denounced Ames as a 'biblioclast' who created a 'museum of [torn out] title pages', now residing in the British Library. Other Victorian writers, artists and architects proved adept at inventing traditions and steering history in a national and progressive interest. It is, as we shall see, a prominent characteristic of histories of book production.

3
Description, Enumeration and Modelling

When, in 1932, W. W. Greg declared that 'bibliography, or the study of books, is essentially the science of the transmission of literary documents',[1] such a statement was based on a century's development in bibliographical description. Enumerative (or systematic) bibliography brought together titles sharing commonalities, but with limited bibliographical analysis. A fuller analytical bibliography offered evidence about the book's production from within the book itself. As early as 1818, William Upcott's *Bibliographical Account of the Principal Works Relating to English Topography* advanced the artefactual understanding of a book, although fuller description of the physical composition of books required the work of Henry Bradshaw, Cambridge University Librarian from 1867, and his systematic encoding of the material sequencing of a book's production.

The work that proved instrumental in placing the physical book and its production at the centre of literary studies, R. B. McKerrow's 1927 *Introduction to Bibliography for Literary Students*, began life in *The Library* in 1912–13. It anticipated what was to be known as the 'new bibliography'. In Thomas Tanselle's words, 'what was new...was that it used physical clues present in each book as the basis for trying to identify compositorial stints, the method of proofreading, and other details of a book's printing history that would have a bearing on editorial decisions regarding *the correctness of the text in it*' (emphasis added).[2] As an extension of enumerative bibliography, analytical bibliography studies books as physical objects, their production and textual results and their journey from manuscript to published books, including their paper and bindings. Many bibliographers distinguish further overlapping divisions:

1. Descriptive bibliography, sometimes relating to a copy text, as created for a new edition from the examination of multiple particular copies, but also describing the physical state of any other surviving copies, giving detailed descriptions of the physical state of a book, including format, type, paper and illustrations. This crucially enables the differentiation of one edition from another, the identification of variations within a single edition and an agreed and recognizable means of recording copy-specific descriptions with optimum accuracy and economy. The recorded transcription of long and complex titles, among other aspects of the book, is often problematic. Different conventions are followed in different countries, but the goal is a recognizable formulaic description of collation, including information about a book's format, the register or order of its gatherings, and the number of leaves. Descriptive bibliography, together with the other bibliographical categories, offers an essential foundation for all book study, even though it is often identified as the particular helpmate of literary scholars, cataloguers, collectors and dealers.
2. Textual bibliography, also reliant on the techniques of analytical bibliography and used to understand the transmission of texts from author to printed edition or multiple editions, describing a book's published, material enactment, including handwriting, proofreading and composition, and, traditionally, attempting to recreate the most accurate (usually printed) text as conceived by its author.
3. Historical bibliography, introducing sources external to the actual book and often used in the notes section of formal descriptive bibliography; the history of the processes of individuals and institutions creating books and their ownership and provenance – later expanded to consider copyright, censorship and other control questions, and sometimes therefore regarded as quite separate from

analytical bibliography. It also presaged the more capacious, even sociological reach of 'bibliography' demanded by McKenzie and those who have built on his legacy.

Neil Harris has usefully summarized Fredson Bowers' reordered overview of these distinctions:

> [Bibliographers] begin by gathering together all the information relative to their chosen theme (enumerative bibliography); they explore the historical, social and economic context in which the work or works that interest them were produced (historical bibliography); they study the physical books in order to obtain information about their making (analytical bibliography); if the project warrants, they draw up a report on those same physical features (descriptive bibliography); and, again if the project warrants, they analyse the significance of their discoveries for the transmission of the text and the constitution of a critical version (textual bibliography).[3]

Methods of describing books, however, also evolved from different needs. Long before Upcott, other questions of order, taxonomy and practical access drove the development of diverse library cataloguing codes. Such labours also predated Naudé, but as methods of European and American library cataloguing, still diverse by the end of the eighteenth century, were shared and encoded, they came to greatly assist bibliographical description and provenance research. The earliest standards in the English-speaking world are attributed to Anthony Panizzi, celebrated Keeper of Printed Books at the British Museum, whose ninety-one rules, published in 1841, remained the basis for cataloguing for 150 years. The Prussian government imposed rules for the nation's libraries in 1899, but an Anglo-American focus to this history seems unavoidable. In the United States, as David D. Hall has suggested, the promotion of a 'learned culture' followed from a more rigorous cataloguing and bibliographical identification that also transformed the scale and nature of private book collecting.[4]

Embodying the relationship between library cataloguing and bibliographical description, E. Gordon Duff, librarian and first cataloguer of the John Rylands Library in Manchester, extended descriptive bibliography to the consideration of binding and, more significantly, to 'the collecting and describing of early printed books',[5] giving particular attention to their original physical state and integrity, provenance and copy-specific description. The focus for much of this early attention remained incunables, that is, European books and broadsides printed before 1501 (often in the exact Latin, *incunabulum* and plural *incunabula*). The phrase 'prima typographicae incunabula', or 'the first infancy of printing', first appeared in von Mallinckrodt's 1639 pamphlet which arbitrarily set the still-used end of 1500 as the definitional divide.

Bibliography, as developed in Britain and North America from the late nineteenth century, explained the book in terms beyond those of the messages conveyed by the text. All texts, new bibliographers demonstrated, were understandable as collaborative creations where the 'medium', to anticipate a later characterization of material form, was the product of social interventions, even when restricted to a limited corpus of English classic editions, downplaying the importance of the production of *all* texts. This pioneering work, however, and especially the examination of records beyond the material book itself and its imprint, opened the way for later researchers to expand their range of interests. Thus Edward Arber's *A Transcript of the Registers of the Company of Stationers of London; 1554–1640 A.D.*, first published in 1875, began a long research trajectory that offered a much broader basis for historical bibliography. Arber's efforts inspired historical hand-lists of printers and *The Century of the English Book Trade* by Duff. Dictionaries by H. R. Plomer and others contained entries on printers, booksellers and other members of the British book trades, since subsumed within the online British Book Trades Index, with editions of Stationers' Company and other records completed by Greg, Eleanor Boswell and William A. Jackson. These labours spawned a succession of exemplary studies, including the examination of the Stationers' apprenticeship records by D. F. McKenzie. The Duff and Plomer dictionaries provided models for Mary Pollard's and Charles Benson's capacious guides to printers and booksellers in Dublin, and, with the extension of such detective work to many different archives, for the historical mapping of book trade sites.

Late nineteenth- and early twentieth-century developments in East Asia chimed extraordinarily with book studies in Britain.

A very limited awareness of British and European developments was likely, but more certain was a similar national pride and perspective that encouraged the preservation and cataloguing of old publications in relation to national language, philology and literature. Although new departments and schools of language and literature in both West and East promoted bibliographical and philological investigation, descriptive bibliography of the fuller Anglo-American type remained a foreign notion to Chinese scholarship. The Chinese practice of listing book titles, and most influentially so in dynastic junctures, dates back nearly 2,000 years, accompanied from the twelfth century by *banben*, differentiating editions of an essentially unchanged, usually printed text. Late nineteenth-century Chinese scholars like Ye Dehui 葉德輝 (b. 1864), however, began putting notes together about the history of books and book production. Ye set himself up as the protector of Chinese traditions, having collected, by the time of his death, some 200,000 Chinese rare and old *juan* (卷 chapters).[6] Although widely admired by Chinese scholars for his command of the literary tradition, Ye staunchly defended the social system and political institutions of the Qing dynasty. He believed that Confucianism, in a form shaped by accumulated and politicized commentaries of Ye's lifetime, was to triumph in 'civilized countries of both East and West' because it was the exemplar of 'the supreme expression of justice in the principles of Heaven and the hearts of men'.[7] Ye asserted the unqualified superiority of Chinese culture, although he acknowledged that Europe and America had introduced several beneficial technologies and thereby gives some clue to the extent to which he might also have been aware of current European interests in bibliographical study.

Ye Dehui served as an early consultant for the great lexicographer Morohashi Tetsujirō 諸橋轍次, principal compiler of the Chinese-Japanese *Dai Kan-Wa jiten* 大漢和辭典, completed in 1943, with one volume published and a second in print when the remaining eleven volumes together with all printing types were destroyed by wartime firebombing. Re-editing from surviving proofs needed ten more years to redesign the 50,000 characters and to print the dictionary again by new phototypesetting. In rescuing the writings of the ancient masters, Ye's communications-led objective had been to establish the correct pronunciation, graphic appearance and meanings of words. All contributed to Ye Dehui's bibliographical endeavours, the authentication and rectification of classical texts, as well as the restoration and reconstruction of standard, canonical editions. Ye Dehui's most significant publication, *Shulin qinghua* (书林清话 *Plain Talk on the Forest of Books*, 1911), details the history of the book from the Tang and Song dynasties (617–906) onwards, with painstaking research on technical standards, preservation and collection, and the evolution of designs and technologies. Another work of the same year, the *Ts'ang-shu Shih-yüeh*, translated into English as *The Bookman's Decalogue*, or *Ten Rules for Collecting Books*, by the Harvard Sinologist Achilles Fang, contains Ye's advice about the purchase of books and manuscripts, restoration and display. The work offers rare glimpses of the refined culture of bibliophiles in late imperial China. Joseph McDermott states that Ye's books 'remain today, a full century after their first publication, important first-call reference works for all serious students of Chinese history'[8] – just as McKerrow and even Blades remain essential preliminary reading for students of Western bibliography.

Although working within different traditions, the East Asian pioneers were contemporaries of, or overlapped with, the founders of Anglo-American bibliography. From their youth, these men began making lists and advancing forms of enumerative bibliography: Arber (b. 1836), Charles Evans (b. 1850), Plomer (b. 1856), Alfred W. Pollard (b. 1859), Duff (b. 1863), McKerrow (b. 1872) and Greg (b. 1875). The younger generation of modern Chinese bibliographers included Nagasawa Kikuya 長澤規矩也 (b. 1902), a Japanese scholar of classical Chinese literature, teacher of library science and one of the greatest authorities on Chinese rare books and editions of Chinese classics printed in Japan. At about the same time, Sun Dianqi 孫殿起 (1894–1958) published his *Record of Known Banned Books of the Qing Dynasty 1644–1911* and his *Fanshu ouji* 販書偶記 (*Casual Notes of a Book Monger*, regarded as a supplement to the eighteenth-century catalogue *Siku quanshu zongmu* 四庫全書總目), a bibliographical catalogue first published in 1936 with updated editions in 1959 and 1982. The majority of the 10,000 books listed date from the late Qing, mostly sold in Sun's own publishing house, the Tongxuezhai shudian 通學齋書店. An entry required that each book existed in an individual edition (*danyinben* 單印本), but Sun extended this to include books found within collections and often recorded in a collectanea index. He divided his catalogue into the traditional four categories, of Confucian classics (*jing* 經), historiography (*shi* 史), masters and philosophers (*zi* 子), and belles-lettres (*ji* 集), giving each book's title, size, author and editions, with notes on content, and including not only printed books, but also drafts (*gaoben* 稿本), manuscripts (*chaoben* 抄本) and critically collated editions (*jiaoben* 校本). The catalogue also lists books that had been officially banned (*jinhuishu* 禁毀書), novellas and romances, as well as theatre plays.

In Britain and the United States, as in Asia, the national interest was underscored by broader developments towards the end of the nineteenth century. As McKenzie noted in an anniversary piece, the history of books, if not 'history of the book', was implicit in the work of the Bibliographical Society founded in 1892.[9] Such societies evolved in part from the activities of the earlier literary and antiquarian clubs. The Bibliographical Society, together with the Edinburgh Bibliographical Society, proudly founded two years earlier in 1890, encouraged collaborative understanding of the history of the relationship between the writing, reproduction and circulation of texts by descriptive and analytical bibliography. The Bibliographical Society of America followed in 1904: in its own words, 'the oldest scholarly society in North America dedicated to the study of books and manuscripts as physical objects'. Notable support was given to critical scholarship in the collation of different editions, summarized and extended pre-eminently in Greg's 1951 'The rationale of the copy-text' and then, from the United States, by Fredson Bowers, founder of *Studies in Bibliography* published annually from 1948–9, and author of *Principles of Bibliographical Description*.

Imitative bibliographical societies flourished in Glasgow (founded 1912), Oxford (1922), Canada (1946), University of Virginia (1947), Cambridge (1949), and Australia and New Zealand (1969). As supportive communities of bibliophiles, collectors, book conservators, librarians, university researchers and teachers, printers, publishers, antiquarian booksellers and other members of the book trades, the bibliographical societies sustained an increasingly wide and diverse understanding of what bibliographical matters might be. The constitutions and mission statements of almost all of these societies now prominently include the words 'book history' allied to the originating commitment to bibliographical study. The study encompassed investigations of technologies, labour, professions and process, and the making, distributing and preservation of books, with developing specialist investigations of contributory practices such as G. D. Hobson's and E. P. Goldschmidt's pioneering book-binding research and Percy Simpson's still essential history of proof correction. Despite work on printers and the records of the Stationers' Company, the history of the selling of books in Britain seemed of less interest, at least before a succession of book trade studies authored by Stanley Morison, Theodore Besterman, Graham Pollard and others.

Other European associations of bibliophiles such as the Société des bibliophiles, founded in 1820, and bibliographical societies such as La Società bibliografica italiana (and, since 2015, the Société bibliographique de France) share some overlapping objectives and members but also relationships based on different priorities and perceptions of the value of books.[10] Within societies, emphases on printed and scribal materials often diverged and their activities were also geographically confined. Different structures and traditions in higher education and of learned and local, historical and archaeological societies probably explain the differences between organized bibliographical communities in different countries, together with different emphases of bibliophiles and their clubability.

In France and Italy influential journals such as the *Bulletin du bibliophile* and *La Bibliofilia* carry articles and reviews equivalent to those in *The Library*, *Papers of the Bibliographical Society of America*, *Script and Print*, *Papers of the Bibliographical Society of Canada* and the journals and published papers of other bibliographical societies. Fewer mainland European journals are supported by wider membership societies, although the Association internationale de bibliophilie publishes annual and occasional papers, as do professional library organizations such as the Associazione italiana biblioteche. The patronage of publishers such as Leo S. Olschki Editore for *La Bibliofilia* is the more important, while other journals and activities worldwide are sustained by specific libraries, universities and local learned societies (or, like *The Book Collector*, by a loyal subscription membership and an indefatigable editor). Other journals, some hosting lively debates, include *Revue française d'histoire du livre*, *Publishing History*, *Book History*, *Histoire et civilisation du livre*, *Quærendo*, *Wen xian* (*Documents*) 文献, and, more recently, as edited by Peter Kornicki, *East Asian Publishing and Society*. In Germany, the annual Gutenberg-Jahrbuch has been published since 1926 by the Internationale Gutenberg-Gesellschaft, with an annual Gutenberg prize awarded by the city of Leipzig since 1987, emulating the occasional gold medal awarded since 1929 by the Bibliographical Society. For Martin Boghardt, however, the absence of a unifying bibliographical society contributed to the stunting of bibliographical studies in Germany, despite foundational work and individual publications, for 'the bibliophiles were too esoteric, the incunabulists were not disposed to go beyond the year 1500, and the textual critics confined themselves to particular editions'.[11]

The division between early print and manuscript studies continued elsewhere, and although much recent scholarship acknowledges the role of modern manuscript circulation, research techniques still create professional distance. To burgeoning studies of the early and modern manuscript have been added new studies of paper making, binding, scriptoria, labour and commercial techniques, different productive processes and the history of manuscript sales and collection, much intersecting with the development of library history. Certain non-European and European contributions found limited audiences. A pioneering study by Johannes Pedersen, *Arabiske bog* (*The Arabic Book*), appeared in Danish in 1946; like many non-English books, it took until its 1984 translation into English to gain much attention. Many important studies, such as the history of Swedish book booty, stolen in the Thirty Years War, *Storhetstidens litterära krigsbyten* (1916 and 1920), by Otto Walde, librarian of Uppsala, still await their translator. In Japan, those expanding bibliographical studies beyond their early twentieth-century foundation, such as Chiyoji Nagatomo and Toshiyuki Suzuki, benefited from the 1998 English account of Japanese book history by Peter Kornicki, extending the reach of the research on material book forms and communication networks in premodern Japan.

The modern study of Western manuscripts advanced from the early twentieth century with the scholarship and cataloguing heroism of Falconer Madan and the palaeographical devotions of M. R. James, Sydney Cockerell, Neil Ker and Albinia de la Mare, among many others. The early labours of Ludwig Traube (1861–1907), palaeographer and first holder of a chair in medieval Latin in Germany, contributed to dividing manuscripts into families according to characteristic scribal errors when copying from a text or writing from dictation. Further detective work derived from interventionist emendation of the texts themselves. In Britain, Ker's collaborative work from the 1930s collected evidence of provenance from medieval books and promoted the notion of a Corpus of British Medieval Library Catalogues. Palaeographical determination of a manuscript's date and origins and the hands through which it passed, whether or not this helps to reconstruct its original form, contributes to the history of the text or what Traube called *Überlieferungsgeschichte*. The uniting of textual criticism and palaeography in this particular form of literary and book history reveals textual routes of transmission from historical communities to present times and further knowledge of the history of scholarship and thought. Catalogues of Dated and Datable Manuscripts derive from the pan-European, Paris-based Comité international de paléographie latine (CIPL), funded in the 1960s, together with the Association paléographique internationale: culture, écriture, société (APICES). At the same time, digital comparison of manuscript copies of texts held in repositories in different parts of the world has been transformative. Digital Scriptorium supported at Berkeley, California, is a consortium of libraries and museums offering free online access to images of their premodern manuscripts, and the Folger Library, Washington, aims to offer its early modern manuscripts online as EMMO. Many forms and formulae of bibliographical description have yet to catch up – having been driven not just by printing but by *letterpress* printing and its composition and physical arrangements. The enhancement of digital inspection *and* recording resources is, however, transforming a digital bibliographical study of manuscripts.

Particularly for incunables and early printed books, analytical bibliography and more sophisticated collational formulae were developed by use of such aids as the Hinman

Collator. Invented in 1963 by the Shakespeare scholar Charlton Hinman, the Collator projected side-by-side images from the pages of surviving copies to identify printed textual variants between them. The Collator was later refined and reduced in size as Carter Hailey's Comet Portable Optical Collator. Pre-eminently for the examination of manuscripts, early photographic techniques from 1839 allowed the enhancement of faded writing, and from 1894 the decipherment of palimpsests where manuscripts were not simply illegible, but had been deliberately erased and then written over. Ultraviolet radiation (UV), first used in Germany in 1914, revolutionized this study to examine watermarks, paper fibres, ink, impression techniques, re-engraving and woodcut positioning, but is now itself superseded in many cases by hyperspectral imaging equipment. This combines high-resolution photography with multispectral imaging to allow selective light modifications such as filtration to isolate fluorescence in concert with UV illumination and offers unprecedented examination of parchments, papyrus, papers, other fibres and inks.

Digital images such as the resources of the binding inventory of the Einbanddatenbank (German Database of Book Bindings) further extend recording possibilities for incunables and early printed books, and the often still inadequate means of recording the stages and configuration of lithography and intaglio. The history of type design and of the design and disposition of type on the page, from the pioneering 'display' research of the American graphic designer Douglas McMurtrie to the more recent insights of Roger Stoddard and Michael Twyman, can also now benefit from digital comparative projects. Taken to its furthest level, no copy of even a printed book from a large edition will ever be the same as any other copy, or as Bettina Wagner concludes, 'every copy of an early printed book is an individual object with characteristic features that distinguish it from all other copies of the same edition'.[12]

Such study extends the enumerative to the fuller description of the processes, deliberate or accidental, that made books and helped determine their use – and gives us evidence of it, including personal binding preferences, marks of ownership and handwritten annotations. Enumerative bibliography, sometimes referred to as 'systematic bibliography', lists rather than describes collations and copy-specific features minutely, but in recent years more expansive listing and recreative projects have also been developed. Historical bibliographies of specific genres such as that of the late eighteenth- and early nineteenth-century novel incorporate sources designed to establish print runs, date of publication, critical reviews, provenance locations for extant copies and authorship attributions. Importantly, reviews and business records – but not advertisements or publishers' catalogues, which can be false promotions – offer details and certainty of the publication of books no longer surviving and therefore without the possibility of full physical description. The use of contemporary descriptors such as 'novels' taken from catalogue headings in periodicals also assists clearer historical demarcation of popular and non-canonical genres.

Retrospective Catalogues and Bibliometrics

Fundamental to the identification and study of past printed publications has been the construction of national retrospective short-title catalogues (STCs), creating a systematic record of printed books surviving in libraries and collections across the world. The first of these STCs, for books printed in Britain to the end of 1640, was intended – it is important to recall – to allow a rigorous understanding of the transmission of Britain's pre-eminent literary texts from manuscript to print.[13] Significantly for book history, these catalogues thereby took no interest in lost books or, generally, small productions of a page or less, and worked to the detriment of any appreciation of the circulation at any particular date or period of pre-existing older texts as well as of manuscripts.

Nation-states frame European and Western bibliographical studies, and continue to do so in eastern and central Europe where many bibliographical archives have become newly available or have received fresh attention in recent years. A national focus is understandable in terms of at least more traditional literary and linguistic interests and of practicalities ranging from funding and labour to institutional support and linguistic expertise, but the framework remains a problem for historians. However much print is identified with the cultivation of different vernacular languages and with campaigns and protests that helped advance early modern state formation, in many other ways, the nation is a misleading geographical unit for the history of print. The political, but not always linguistic, unit was the obvious enabler for the retrospective national STCs, but books circulating within that unit were and are international commodities.

The increasing influence of STC projects promoted interest in national library collections and helped advance bibliometric, or book-counting, surveys along national lines. A primary objective of the Bibliographical Society was to support this creation of sequentially ordered records of all surviving printed books before and including 1640. The aim could be viewed as shadowing great Victorian heritage enterprises such as the Historical Manuscripts Commission, the National Gallery and National Portrait Gallery. The first edition of the STC to 1640 under the editorship of A. W. Pollard and G. R. Redgrave was published in 1926, with Donald Wing's eponymous continuation to 1700 published between 1945 and 1951. The development of STCs through the twentieth century provided a secure and distinctive base for ambitious historical bibliography, especially given the additional labours by Wing and Katharine Pantzer, whose revision of STC to 1640 offered numerous historical and derivative appendices, which included locations, printers and trade signs. Other extensions ranged from Paul G. Morrison's *Index of Printers and Publishers* and Carolyn Nelson and M. Seccombe's catalogue of *British Newspapers and Periodicals, 1641–1700* to David Foxon's *English Verse 1701–1750*.

Separate but associated undertakings included the detailed published guides, indexes and reproductions of printers' archives, most notably of the eighteenth-century London ledgers of the Bowyer firm by Keith Maslen and John Lancaster, published in 1991, and the cataloguing of special collections such as the Thomason Collection of Civil War Tracts held at the British Library. A projected STC of items printed in territories of the United States between 1639 and 1820, with debate about which pre-1776 territories might be included, was published between 1903 and 1934 as Charles Evans's *American Bibliography: A Chronological Dictionary of All Books, Pamphlets, and Periodical Publications Printed in the United States of America*. With Melvil Dewey, Evans was also founder of the American Library Association. Studies of this early American print period similarly benefited from Robert B. Winans's *Descriptive Checklist of Book Catalogues Separately Printed in America 1693–1800* (1981) and Robert Singerman's *American Library Book Catalogues, 1801–1875: A National Bibliography* (1996). Cautions about STCs and bibliometrics are reconsidered later, but the immense labours on the retrospective catalogues and catalogues of allied sources created grounding and indispensable resources for the history of the book. Although evidently restricted to printed and indeed largely letterpress items of more than one page, the STCs offer unrivalled bibliographical resources and the basis for extension to 1801. The continued planning of a nineteenth-century English language equivalent is currently best embodied by a published and now online subscription Nineteenth-Century Short Title Catalogue (NSTC), but it is restricted to the holdings of eight major libraries. New technologies overtook former productions and offered new search possibilities, albeit having to solve incompatibilities between different machine-readable cataloguing systems. The Eighteenth Century Short Title Catalogue, then known as the ESTC, was released commercially on CD-Rom in 1992 and then online four years later, including from the outset material identified by the North American Imprints Project, itself reaching to 1876. It was at this point, in 1991, that Marcus McCorison, one of the most distinguished of North American librarians, asked the academic community to rejoice in 'book history' but with a significant emphasis upon collection, the conserving repository and a sort of service economy:

> I represent the ghost of bibliography past, the wretched piler-up of lists, the antiquarian and collector of books. I come to celebrate book history – the book history that includes the building of great collections, generation after generation, to endow a field of study with its literature, perhaps before the topic exists; book history that compiles the record and describes the output of a printer or of a publisher...a book history done in the grand manner...[providing] the basic data that literary scholars, economic historians, other bibliographers, or intellectual scholars use with profit.[14]

The original ESTC was within a few years subsumed within the much more ambitious English Short Title Catalogue, happily able to retain the same acronym. It considerably revised the

STCs already published, now searchable online and covering letterpress books, pamphlets, newspapers, serials and a variety of ephemera printed in all languages before 1801 in the British Isles, Colonial America, United States of America (1776–1800), Canada and territories governed by England or Britain before 1801. To illustrate the expansion in coverage we should note that ESTC includes items printed in any other part of the world, wholly or partly in English or other British vernaculars or with false imprints claiming publication in Britain or its territories, in any language. The enhanced resource therefore includes, for example, certain printing in Portuguese from India, in German from North America, in Gaelic from Scotland and in French from both France and the Netherlands. Included are atlases and texts which are wholly engraved, but not engraved music and separate maps and prints, apart from engraved items included in earlier STCs. Certain advertisements, including slip-songs and election handbills, are now also included, but not small printed items such as trade cards, labels, invitations, bookplates, currency, playbills, concert and theatre programmes, playing cards, games and puzzles.

The questions and challenges that STCs were designed to address had therefore changed. Technically begun as enumerative bibliographies, the catalogues now also evolved through ESTC as something much more descriptive. Titles were no longer 'short', and entries provided copy locations, further historical notes and even links within individual entries to other resources and websites. The ISTC (Incunabula Short Title Catalogue), coordinated by the British Library, records some 30,400 editions printed in the first fifty years of European letterpress, but excludes material printed entirely from woodblocks or engraved plates. Information on each item includes authors, short titles, the language of the text, printer, place and date of printing and format. Locations for copies have been confirmed from libraries worldwide and links are provided to online digital facsimiles and online catalogues of incunables such as the Gesamtkatalog der Wiegendrucke and the Bayerische Staatsbibliothek Inkunabelkatalog.

Significantly, all these STCs continue to recalibrate the rarity of books and editions. The additional specialist work of a new generation of historical bibliographers has provided clearer historical profiles of title outputs, and notwithstanding cautions which follow, the fog over the timing and dimensions of publication is lifting. There are, however, many blanks. Many particulars such as newspaper publication, subscription lists, booksellers' trade sales and the production and distribution of chapbooks and popular ephemera remain highly problematic. Publications such as the massive index to the eighteenth-century printing ledgers of William Bowyer and son are making speculation less hazardous,[15] but the exact print run of most editions is unknown. We have to accept that most survival rates are beyond calculation and that the number of copies printed for the great majority of editions can only be guessed at from entries for similar material in the few surviving printing ledgers and business letters. A serious failing of the majority of European STCs was to exclude in their early stages single-leaf items, that is a stand-alone page printed on both sides, such as a ballad, and even items such as chapbooks of twenty-four pages printed from a single, then folded sheet. Ballads, chapbooks and many notable miscellanies circulated in their tens of thousands across the Continent.

More positively, ESTC encouraged the continuation of retrospective cataloguing elsewhere in the world, even if compounding the national biases. The online Short Title Catalogue Netherlands, 1540–1800 (STCN) contains bibliographical descriptions of all surviving books published in the Netherlands and those in Dutch published abroad between those dates. STCN complements the companion Short Title Catalogus Vlaanderen (Short Title Catalogue Flanders, STCV) of surviving Dutch language materials printed between 1601 and 1700 within the present-day boundaries of Flanders, including Brussels, and, in the catalogue's second working phase, works printed in Flanders in other languages than Dutch – notably Latin, Spanish and French. Again, titles are no longer 'short'. French and German STCs are ongoing but currently limited by chronological range and by the collections consulted. The Catalogue Collectif de France (CCFr), accessible via the website of the Bibliothèque nationale de France, is more advanced, but limited to pre-1701 imprints, as are the German Verzeichnis der im deutschen Sprachraum erschienenen Drucke des 16./17. Jahrhunderts (VD16 and VD17, or the Bibliography of Books Printed in the German-Speaking Countries from 1501 to 1600 and from 1601 to 1700 respectively) but now supported by VD18 (to 1800), ongoing since 2009.

Nothing as accessible or comprehensive yet exists for those attempting to identify the titles of books and pamphlets originating from Spanish, Portuguese or Italian territories. Biblioteca Nacional de España hosts an online STC of fifteenth- and sixteenth-century Spanish imprints. Ongoing in Italy is EDIT 16 Censimento nazionale delle edizioni italiane del XVI secolo, an online initiative of the Laboratorio per la bibliografia retrospettiva of the Istituto Centrale per il Catalogo Unico (ICCU). The Centre for the History of the Media at University College Dublin is undertaking The Iberian Book Project, a catalogue of all books printed in Spanish or Portuguese or printed in Spain, Portugal, Mexico or Peru, 1472–1700. The USTC (Universal Short-Title Catalogue) Project at the University of St Andrews comprises 52,000 pre-1601 entries and has sponsored supplementary projects including *French Vernacular Books: Books Published in the French Language before 1601* (2007). One of its editors, Alexander Wilkinson, also compiled a reconstructive catalogue of titles apparently no longer surviving. Much broader, if less refined, support is offered by the Online Computer Library Center (OCLC) and 'The European Library' hosted since 1997 on the Gabriel (Gateway and Bridge to Europe's National Libraries), a searchable site with 200 million entries of the holdings of forty-eight European national and research libraries. A further Heritage of the Printed Book Database, previously called the Hand Press Book Database, collects in one file the catalogue records of major European and North American research libraries covering items of European printing $c.1455$–$c.1830$.

Catalogue-based study of extant manuscripts, such as the printed volumes of the *Index of English Literary Manuscripts 1800–1900*, confronts many more difficulties of selection and definition. Even so, major projects have encouraged innovative research, such as the *Catalogue of English Literary Manuscripts 1450–1700* based at Senate House, University of London, which offers an online record of manuscript sources for over 200 major British authors of the period 1450–1700. Other freely accessible sites include image digitizations of all pages, such as Gallica from the Bibliothèque nationale de France, with manuscripts among the 250,000 post-1500 items accessible for optical character recognition (OCR) research, by which computers take the pixels of a scanned book and convert these into searchable and editable text. The Münchener DigitalisierungsZentrum (MDZ) or Munich Digitization Centre currently hosts more than 900,000 titles online. The many and rapidly increasing interactive sites for digitally imaged manuscripts include the ongoing Mandragore, base des manuscrits enluminés, for medieval books and the Parker Library on the Web, completed in 2009. The Wren Digital Library continues at Trinity College, Cambridge. Elsewhere huge labours and funding grants support similarly ambitious digitizing projects.

The most surprising contrast with Asian and in particular Chinese retrospective bibliography is less its different development than the modest survival rates of books published before the mid-nineteenth century. According to best estimates, about 277,000 titles survive from pre-1912 China and about 400,000 from pre-1868 Japan (although this excludes non-classical Chinese texts in both countries). By comparison, Eltjo Buringh and Jan Luiten van Zanden have calculated that over 1.7 million different printed titles survive from pre-1801 Europe. The general scale of difference is impressive, despite numerous flaws and variations in the methods of counting. David McKitterick and others have severely criticized the basis for the European estimates,[16] and the Asian tallies are curtailed not only by the destruction and poorer preservation of old books, but also by different bibliographical practices and the subsumption of multiple issues within Chinese bibliographical entry titles. The 400,000 titles surviving from pre-1868 Japan, representing about two-thirds of all known surviving imprints of the much larger and more ancient Chinese territories, suggest how much of the Chinese imprint and manuscript record has been lost, or remains unsatisfactorily catalogued or simply uncatalogued. In an empire larger than multilingual western Europe, most Chinese titles were also published in a single language and thus a repeated title commanded a comparatively greater number of copies than a European language equivalent.

A further caution concerns derivative enumeration. Counting of title entries requires restraint, as exponents of statistical bibliographical enquiry attest, from Daniel Mornet in 1910 (discussed in the next section) to Michael Suarez in his compendious introduction to volume 5 of the *Cambridge History of the Book in Britain* ninety years later. Many have delivered stern warnings to users of statistics, but not everyone attends to them. The enlargement of the book trade, for example, can be very generally plotted by the increase in the publication of separate titles or of editions, but estimates based on such counts cannot take account of the varying number of printings for each edition nor the continuing trade in all books, including imported and second-hand books. Many graphs of changing published output are based on title counts, but this is no guide to the volume of production when edition sizes ranged from print runs of 10,000 or more for bibles and prayer books to the more usual 500 or 750 for novels. Only where archival evidence of print runs survives (as will be discussed) can some measure of the volume of production be gauged. Such records survive for a minority of titles only. Most printing accounts are lost. Moreover, if it were possible to produce a snapshot of all books and magazines circulating in any given year, it would reveal a mix of new and old, foreign and home-produced, bound or unbound, incomplete and damaged.

Equally dangerous is the use of component parts of STCs to construct specific histories. ESTC lists imprint information, but entries for books published and printed by large consortia do not list all the publishers or other booksellers given in the original imprint. After the first five or so contributing booksellers, ESTC then states the number of 'others'. Typically, for example, the 1790–1 edition of Samuel Johnson's *The Lives of the Most Eminent English Poets* is entered in ESTC with the first five named contributing publishing booksellers followed by the note 'and 35 others'. There are, at the date of writing, nearly 3,000 ESTC entries that append 'and others' to what are incomplete imprint lists. Here, ESTC tallies have also been complicated by revisions to its display mode so that otherwise non-limited searches must be extended to a full 'list' to reveal all catalogue entries. To confuse matters more, some of these imprint lists, especially before 1700, include signatories to prefaces. Searches on imprint words to identify contributing booksellers also disclose names of those merely listed for promotional effect, as, for example, a bookseller's predecessor.

Notwithstanding such cautions in using STCs, photographic, electronic scanning and digital advances have transformed the catalogues as launch pads to further resources, and have offered, in two stages, a glorious variety of online images, searchable databases and metadata. The first stage involved the photographing, microfiching and then scanning and digital reproduction of extant texts, although much was scanned from the original photographing and the arrangement often remains within the guiding framework of the STC. The impact of these resources can overwhelm. Coordinated by the American Antiquarian Society (AAS), Evans's *American Bibliography* also spawned reproductions on the Readex Microprint-AAS Early American Imprints series. Bibliographical entries in Evans 1640–1800, but not most of the 1801–19 continuation by Shaw-Shoemaker, are now subsumed within ESTC. The reproduction of the texts themselves cannot replace their physical examination or even copy-specific recording offered by sophisticated comparative bibliography, but the images do allow unprecedented and comparative access to rare, sometimes unique copies of editions scattered across the world. Perhaps the two most important derivative online collections, Early English Books Online (EEBO) and Eighteenth Century Collections Online (ECCO), replace hundreds of reels of microfilms.

In a further and often challenging procedure, digital scanning includes OCR. ECCO is thus searchable, although not EEBO, despite continuing experiments to 'read' the original photography. Searching confronts obstacles such as the obvious confusion between the lower case f and the long s, but also problems in identifying letters printed in broken type or smudged ink or otherwise damaged or imperfectly printed. The advanced word and phrase searching on resources such as ECCO nonetheless allows text-mining and language use research that supports studies such as that by Peter de Bolla investigating the eighteenth-century conceptualization of human rights. The extreme enumerative plotting of numerous trajectories of the European novel by Franco Moretti coalesces around his term 'distant reading' and sits fully within progressive digital humanities research. It propels bibliometric labours still further to 'computational criticism' that aspires, from computer-led interrogation of thousands of texts, to reveal hidden literary patterns and structures in world literature. It is even more vulnerable to methodological criticism.

Other digitally enabled text-trawling interrogates individual, and often very large, collections or compares specific elements such as woodcuts, ballads or genre across collections. Such activity invites questions of access, subscription costs, security and integrity, but the larger questions remain those of methodology and avoiding misplaced ambition. Among broader collaborations, the HathiTrust Digital Library is developing research facilities to 'enable advanced computational access to the growing digital record of human knowledge'. Google Books has scanned some 30 million books, with varying accessibility according to copyright, commercial and other issues, but derivative metadata developments include Google's Ngram, developed since 2010 and allowing the interrogation of digitized texts published since 1800 and held in over a dozen university libraries. Searches on words or phrases 'tracks their popularity in books – millions of books, 450 million words – suddenly accessible with just a few keystrokes'.[17] The outcome is often more party game than book history, but results can be suggestive.

More serious limits are linguistic, morphological and geographical. Little, and nothing comparable to ECCO, is available for Asia – or indeed Central and South America, Africa and central and eastern Europe. With finding aids and catalogues moving beyond Europe, international digital library collaborations include the France-Japan and France-China projects, and the International Dunhuang Project (IDP) presents numerous resources, including manuscripts, paintings, textiles and art objects, from Dunhuang and the archaeological sites of the Central Asian Silk Road. The World Digital Library was launched by UNESCO in 2007 and the Europeana digital heritage portal provides access to more than 53 million items partly or wholly digitally imaged from (currently) 3,300 libraries, archives, museums and audiovisual collections. Historians of nineteenth- and twentieth-century printed books will also remain less well served than historians of earlier centuries, where the relatively smaller numbers of publications have made well-ordered STCs, photographing and digitization more manageable, for all the methodological reservations. This serious imbalance in research possibilities between periods is compounded by false dividing timelines: in Britain, 1640, but even more so 1700 and 1801. It is also needs reasserting that STC-based understanding of book publication, and the interrogation of the photographed, digitally imaged and searchable digitized texts, concern new production and not the history of books in circulation or consultable at any one time. It is not simply that most of this work gives no sense of popularity in terms of edition sizes or of reader response, but it privileges new publications above those then also in circulation (deducible if not quantifiable by other sources).

New Perspectives and Projects

The challenge of historical discrimination between published and circulating texts is nothing new. Earlier contributions in book history derived from explorations of that most perplexing question of French history, what caused the Revolution? Although their consequences were not fully appreciated at the time, early twentieth-century studies of library holdings and popular literature of eighteenth-century France, and notably of the *bibliothèques bleues*,[18] introduced methodologies and problematics that were to transform cultural history and the history of ideas. The work of Daniel Mornet, Marc Bloch, Lucien Febvre and later Robert Mandrou and others, many associated with the Annales school of social, economic and cultural historians, introduced strategies and a widely cast *bibliologie* that invited broader conceptual studies. Here, bibliometrics taken from enumerative and statistical work sought to interpret what the French Revolution meant to common people and readers, even though this rich tradition of French bibliographical and sociological historical work and 'histoire du livre' was for long relatively unknown to English-speaking readers.

Mornet primarily studied the literary history of the eighteenth century, with a seminal article in 1910, later developed into his better-known *The Intellectual Origins of the French Revolution 1715–1787* (1933). In attempting to identify what was *actually* read, Mornet questioned the intellectual and ideological origins of the Revolution by analysing 712 catalogues of private libraries auctioned between 1750 and

1780 and now held at Toulouse city library. The problems of such approaches will be reassessed in chapter 5. Mornet constructed statistical tables which astonished Enlightenment historians not simply by recovering forgotten works that were the most popular titles in about 500 contemporary libraries, but by his finding that among the 20,000 books in question there was only one copy of Jean-Jacques Rousseau's *Social Contract*. In one of those many cautions that all book historians must digest, Mornet's deductions have been charged with a failure to account for censorship regulations which removed polemical titles from the book and auction lists and catalogues he studied. Nonetheless, in Robert Darnton's words, 'the conclusion seemed self-evident: the book which posterity had consecrated as the Bible of the French Revolution had hardly been read before 1789'.[19]

French and Continental contributions and their particular theoretical and bibliometric emphases contrast with the long tradition of bibliographical and empirical scholarship in the Anglo-Saxon world, where British retrospective national bibliography combines with analytical and textual bibliography and an emphasis on economic and material conditions in 'book history'. But new thinking also derived from the challenges of both early transnational study and progressive national endeavours in book history. After the Second World War, and following from Mornet and others, two landmark but challenging histories transformed the understanding of the early modern book in the context of the social, political, intellectual and scientific history of Europe as a whole. In 1958, in *L'Apparition du livre*, Henri-Jean Martin and Lucien Febvre chronicled the astonishing rapidity of a pan-European adoption of printing by towns, religious institutions and universities. This magisterial account, with a slow-burning influence over the next decades, drew partly on broad enumerative conclusions and implicitly reinforced a sense of the otherness and of the abandonment in the first age of print of scribal culture (perceptions to be challenged by later critics). Twenty years later, and shortly after *L'Apparition du livre* first appeared in English as *The Coming of the Book*, Elizabeth Eisenstein radically extended this narration of the modernizing impact of printing by arguing that the sixteenth-century press fomented intellectual, scientific, political and religious revolution. The history of the books is fundamentally, and for some essentially, concerned with the transformation of knowledge but the impact of printing has been elevated to an especial historical potency. The Eisenstein thesis rested on three main propositions: that the printing press revolutionized, first, the volume of textual production, second, the speed of that production, and third, the nature of the text itself. The volume of printing was palpably far greater than the written output of scriptoria, as was the rapidity of printed manufacture that enabled faster dissemination and more effective and often vituperative debate.

Such arguments hinge on the transformative power of print technology and are widely labelled as 'technologically determinist'. The third claim in the Eisenstein thesis proved the most far-reaching and contentious. According to Eisenstein and her many – and often astutely engaged – adherents, the reproductive quality of printing that effected the communications revolution resided in an exceptional textual fixity that gave new authority to the published word and new certainty to debate. The not unhelpful contention was that a reader in, say, Prague might read and discuss a near-identical text with a reader in Lisbon in possession of a copy of the same printed edition. No longer might the text vary according to the style and aptitude of the scribe and suffer from a real or presumed unverifiability. Reliance on oral transmission was lessened in a 'communications shift' that codified signs and images and created what she called influentially but not unprecedentedly, 'print culture'. The most obvious objections here are that printed copies of books, and especially products of the early letterpress, are not particularly uniform and vary greatly between individual printings, and also that copies of an edition – and even the same individual copy – are read very differently by each and every reader.

There will be much more to argue about 'print culture' in this volume, but the 'printing revolution' that was here given such historical prominence was one of standardization, linguistic fixity, translation into vernacular languages and the revival of classical scholarship and ancient languages. Most significantly, perhaps, the new technology and industry underpinned the success of biblical translation into the language of common men and women. Technology interacted with new forces in religion, politics and science to produce, among vast and prolific publications, the popular and the learned, including Lutheran and Calvinist tracts, Copernican treatises and printed editions of Pliny, Galen and Aristotle. As discussed in the next chapters, intimate social histories, effectively 'micro-histories', most pertinently question emphasis on the 'fixity' of these printed texts, and they do so by evaluating the experience of reading. While printing technology unquestionably allowed texts to be replicated more quickly, in greater numbers and with unprecedented technical stability, no meaning is given to a text until it is read. In this sense a text is an unstable cultural object.

Between the publication of *L'Apparition du livre* and Eisenstein's thesis, interest and expertise in the history of books continued to deepen with the support of bibliographical societies and the increasing influence and inclusivity of their projects, publications and journals. The Printing Historical Society was established in London in 1964, followed soon after by the American Printing History Association. Numerous museums of printing opened in Europe, North America and many other parts of the world. These are scholarly resources but also inspire public interest. Redundant or partly revived paper mills and printing works have also welcomed visitors and students, encouraging participation, learning and research (table 1).

Together with public and national library and literacy initiatives, the early museums foreshadowed institutional and university centres for book history and a greater public engagement in the history of a medium soon to be eclipsed in the minds of most citizens by digital technologies. In 1977, Daniel Boorstin, then Librarian of Congress in the United States, officially established a Center for the Book to promote books, reading, literacy, libraries and wide-ranging historical scholarship, with John Y. Cole as founding director. From 1984 the Center supported state affiliate centres for the book, now established, with varying activity, in all fifty states. Other centres, large and small, followed (table 2). From the 1980s, long-established research institutions also expressed interest in developments in book history, hosting lectures, research posts, publications and summer schools and seminars. In 1983, for example, the American Antiquarian Society, Worcester,

Table 1 Printing, paper and allied museums

Selected printing museums

Museum Plantin-Moretus, Antwerp	1877
Gutenberg-Museum, Mainz	1900
Musée de l'Imprimerie, Lyon	1963
Museo Bodoniano, Parma	1963
Melbourne Museum of Printing, Footscray, Victoria (formerly the Australian Type Company)	1977
Museum of Printing, Haverhill, Massachusetts	1978
Bogtrykmuseet, Esbjerg, Denmark	1979
Mediemuseet (formerly Danmarks Grafiske Museum), Odense, Denmark	1984
Casa da xilogravura, Campos do Jordão, Brazil	1987
Musée des arts et métiers du livre, Montolieu, Aude, France	1989
Robert Smail's Printing Works, Innerleithen, Scotland	1990
Cheongju Early Printing Museum, Unchon-dong, Cheongju, South Korea 청주 고인쇄박물관	1992
Type Museum, Oval, London, 1992–2006, now the online Type Archive	
Crandall Historical Printing Museum, Provo, Utah	1994
National Print Museum, Dublin	1996
The China Printing Museum 中国印刷博物馆 Huangcun Town, Daxing District, Beijing	1996
Printing Museum, Bunkyo-ku, Tokyo 印刷博物館	2000
Genadendal Museum and Printing Works, South Africa; works active 1857–2002	2004
Museum of Typography, Μουσείων Τυπογραφίας, Souda, Greece	2005
Eesti Trükimuuseum,Tartu, Estonia	2010

More than 100 others belong to the Association of European Printing Museums

Selected paper mills and museums

Museo della Carta, Amalfi, Italy	1971
Baseler Papiermühle, Basel, Switzerland	1980
Museo della Carta e della Filigrana, Fabriano, Italy	1985
Jeonju Hanji Museum 전주한지박물관, formerly Hansol Paper Museum, South Korea	1989
Moulin à Papier de Brousses, Brousses-et-Villaret, Aude, France	1994
Suho (Shuhuo) Memorial Paper Museum, Taipei, Taiwan 樹火紀念紙博物館	1995
Osterreichisches Papiermachermuseum, Laakirchen-Steyrermühl, Austria	1997
Museu do Papel Terras de Santa Maria, Porto, Portugal	2001
İbrahim Müteferrika Kağıt Müzesi, Yalova, Turkey	2013

Selected allied museums

Deutsches Schreibmaschinenmuseum (Museum of Historic Typewriters), Bayreuth, Germany	1934
Museo de artes gráficas, Bogota, Colombia	1964
The American Bookbinders Museum, San Francisco	2008

Table 2 Centres for the history of the book

Center for the Book, Library of Congress, Washington, DC with affiliate Centers in US states	1977 from 1984
Cambridge Project for the Book Trust, Cambridge (hosting conferences and publications)	1990
Centre for Manuscript and Print Studies, Institute of Advanced Studies, University of London	1994
Scottish Centre for the Book, Napier University, Edinburgh	1995
Centre for the History of the Book, University of Edinburgh	1995
Leiden Centre for the Book, Leiden University	1997
Institut d'Histoire du Livre, École Nationale Supérieure des Sciences de l'Information et des Bibliothèques, Lyon	2001
Centre for the Study of the Book, University of Oxford	2002
Center for the Study of Books and Media, Princeton University	2002
Centre for Material Texts, University of Cambridge	2009

Massachusetts, introduced its Program in the History of the Book in American Culture, followed by similar initiatives at the William Andrews Clark Memorial Library at the University of California at Los Angeles (UCLA) and the Harry Ransom Center at the University of Texas at Austin.

One of the most effective networks developing book history has been the Society for the History of Authorship, Reading and Publishing (SHARP). First convened in 1991 as an international association and from 1992 as an online discussion group, SHARP encouraged greater interdisciplinary academic participation, convening annual international conferences and encouraging affiliate 'panels' to promote book history at major humanities gatherings and hiring fairs such as the Modern Language Association, the American Historical Association, the International (and American) Society for Eighteenth-Century Studies and the Renaissance Society of America. SHARP also hosts an archive of past online discussion among a worldwide community of scholars and enthusiasts. SHARP's core activities have concerned the printed book, and its North American orientation separated it from non-English-speakers for some years, but it has more recently reached out to continental

European and Asian scholars, with the promotion of regional subgroups in Australasia and South America. Although not unmindful of history, other 'centres for the book' pursue missions allied to contemporary politics and culture. The National Library of South Africa in Pretoria, for example, supports a centre which 'advocates the importance of reading, writing and publishing for development and nation building', while at the same time the history of the book in Africa is the focus of much new and pioneering comparative research.

Rare book(s) schools mostly developed separately from the centres for the book, and some predate them. In addition to their pedagogic and collegial importance, the schools, summer seminars and taught courses have greatly assisted in breaking down national as well as disciplinary boundaries. The Rare Book School founded by Terry Belanger at Columbia University in 1983, and which moved to the University of Virginia in 1992, pioneered collaborative and specialist bibliographical courses, successfully emulated by similar schools in London, Edinburgh, UCLA, Lyon, and peripatetically in New Zealand and Australia. Importantly, the schools, together with permanent seminars at the universities of Pennsylvania, Harvard, Princeton, Yale (at the Beinecke Library), Stanford and elsewhere (including in Washington, Paris and London), expanded geographical, temporal and interdisciplinary interests within bibliography, bibliophily and book studies. Formal book history degree courses, now offered in more than forty universities worldwide, extend the ambit of rare book schools, and many operate partnerships with libraries, museums, galleries and university humanities departments. Many host or liaise with book and book history exhibitions and bibliographical lecture series. Several of the named lectures are of long and celebrated standing and carry endowed Readerships (table 3).

Advancing academic specialization, much in evidence in rare books schools and book history programmes, has also brought constructive dialogue between different methodological approaches, even between those who have tended to dismiss each other either as theorists or as antiquarians. Bibliographical progress in, for example, collation techniques and encoding, international cataloguing rules and the study of signatures, *mise-en-page*, factotums,[20] and much more besides, encountered different and often incompatible linguistic and scholarly

Table 3 International lecture series in bibliography, and the history of the book

Sandars Lectures (and Readership) in Bibliography, University of Cambridge	1895
A. S. W. Rosenbach Lectures in Bibliography, University of Pennsylvania	1931
J. P. R. Lyell Lectures (and Readership) in Bibliography, University of Oxford	1952
James Russell Wiggins Lectures in the History of the Book in American Culture, American Antiquarian Society, Worcester, MA	1983
Panizzi Lectures, British Library, London	1985
McKenzie Lectures, University of Oxford	1996
Kenneth Karmiole Lectures on the History of the Book Trade, Clark Library, University of California at Los Angeles	2004
J. R. de J. Jackson Lectures, University of Toronto	2011

conventions. Different interpretations exist, for example, of the word 'typography' and 'jobbing printing', and of difficulties in translating between languages.

Other projects advanced the history of authorship, publication and reception, of which the most prominent are multivolume and multi-author histories of the book in France, Britain, the United States, Canada, Scotland, Australia and Ireland, listed separately at the end of the Bibliography.[21] The multivolume national histories are signal achievements, the culmination of important collaborative discussion and research. The volumes contain many unrivalled essays, but they also embody the framing and division of much European and Western bibliographical and book history by nation-states – when, in so many ways, the nation is a misleading geographical unit for such research. As noted, STCs are far more advanced in some nations than others, aggravating national biases, but while the political (not always linguistic) unit is the obvious enabler for retrospective national bibliographies, books circulating within that unit were and are international commodities.

Any national history of the book and print needs to be a history of book exchange in and out, of the trade in books, of the different books in circulation and read at any one time, irrespective of where they were originally printed or first sold. Even the identification of origins is beset by nightmarish bibliographical problems. For example, the imprints of many editions declared that they were printed in the Netherlands when they were not, and many that *were* printed in the Netherlands stated that they were printed in France or Germany, or elsewhere. But the greater issue is the travel of the books and print. The analogy with histories of letter writing is useful – and we shall return to the relationship between script and print again. Projects recovering correspondence such as 'Electronic Enlightenment' at the University of Oxford provide invaluable and revelatory support to ongoing book history research collaborations engaged in transnational book circulation. That led by Otto Lankhorst, for example, traces the Russian and Eastern destinations of books from the Netherlands, Amsterdam and The Hague, and the German links forged with St Petersburg and the Baltic towns.[22]

The greater analysis of distribution but also of reception and reading offers a critical means of crossing national boundaries in book history, and underpins, in the remainder of this book, the wider lens that epitomized the development of book history from the 1980s. Just as new attention is given to the global or transnational, a key consideration is study of the transmission of texts, of how bibliometrics might move from production to circulation. The distribution of books, one of the mechanics of cultural transaction, both created and breached frontiers for the written and printed word, vernacular and otherwise. Distribution entailed confrontation and misapprehension as much as collaboration and understanding. In the past thirty years or so, however, resurgent interest in a broader historical bibliography has inspired dozens of studies of literary transmission in an early modern republic of letters or a modern European, transatlantic, transoceanic and global realm of popular, scientific, religious or scholarly literature. An unavoidable aspect of this scholarship has been its framing within the influential modelling of different agents of communication, much borrowed from media studies. The celebrated invocation by Marshall McLuhan of the medium as the message was developed from Innes and also much influenced by Walter Ong's analysis of the cultural and educational impact of the shift from orality to literacy.[23] McLuhan's *Gutenberg's Galaxy* (1962) and *Understanding Media*

(1964), among other works, famously and controversially extended media theory by associating technological change from alphabetic writing and printing to the electronic with changing cognitive organization and hence social life. This included, he predicted, the 'electronic interdependence' of the 'global village'.

Circuits and Diagrams

Many foundational accounts of book history incorporate illustrative diagrams. As archival and bibliographical case studies developed and contributed to more extensive histories of authorship, book manufacture and publishing, broader questions demanded answers. Was it possible to develop explanatory models, or at least helpful pointers to the complex historical relationships between the different agencies involved? A special attractiveness of such modelling was its appeal in crossing traditional disciplinary boundaries, prefiguring larger claims for the subject of book history itself.

A decade or more after the adages of McLuhan, Robert Darnton proposed what was to be a highly influential 'communications circuit' model As he explained, the model assumed that 'printed books generally pass through roughly the same life cycle', his goal being to show 'how its disparate segments can be brought together within a single conceptual scheme'.[24] His identified stages in the production, circulation and reception of the text also defined historical relationships between people as mediated by book trade practices and communication. Subsequent modification by Nicolas Barker and Thomas Adams of what was essentially a materially driven circulation of ideas model invited more investigation of its intersection with book preservation, textual and descriptive bibliography, the continuing circulation of older books and library development and use. Bibliographers, Barker and Adams wrote, reacted to Darnton 'with mingled fascination and alarm', restating McKenzie that 'the essential task of the bibliographer is to establish the facts of transmission for a particular text'.[25] As we shall see, however, it was the interpretation of the history of reading that remained the most challenging and important of the mapped-out circuit stages.

Overall, such modelling, often called agent-based modelling (or AGM), hugely affected the early conceptualization of the history of the book as a field of study, even though models are always more contingent and modifiable than prescriptive. As Darnton was the first to acknowledge, models are nothing but the servant of new thinking, even though they are servants who organize thought, directly assist in archival and evidential interpretation and encourage other, bold and provocative conceptualizations. Thus Peter McDonald offered another model, from the perspective of literary studies, which sought to refine the functions-based circuit of Darnton and deepen our understanding of historic literary culture by engaging with the broader propositions of the sociologist Pierre Bourdieu, who was fascinated by modes of cultural reproduction and conceived of a literary field as a social microcosm embodying its own structure and dynamic laws. With simple lines rather than graphics, McDonald's model reconstructs the 'predicament' of the text as forcefully shaped by publisher and market as much as by author.[26] A further intersection might be found with Bourdieu's 'habitus' or the physical incarnation of cultural capital by the deep-rooted habits and skills of life experiences.

McDonald's model usefully demonstrated the value of engagement with theoretical constructs, while other models attempted to sketch in the multiple agents complicating the pared-down circuits. Among others, Elizabeth Le Roux has borrowed models from political science and sociology to examine production under strict external control – in her case South African university presses during apartheid. More mathematical modelling based on least square regressions tested the robustness of the relationship between different variables in simple demand equations interrogating the historical market for books. Such exercises ultimately depended on the often questionable nature of inputted series of historic economic data. Perhaps the plainest economic model of all was William St Clair's emphasis on tranching down, or dividing financing by varying degrees of risk and returns, to explain book production preferences under a monopoly regime in eighteenth-century England. This accompanied his critique of Darnton's apparent neglect of *anticipated* readers and of how readers' preferences influenced the decisions of printers and booksellers.

St Clair has publicly expressed irritation that his modelling has been accepted more by literary scholars and economic historians than by bibliographers and historians of the book, but all modelling, however stimulating, has been subject to the tut-tutting of scholars expert in the nuances of bibliographic description and reconstruction, Again, although existing models have encouraged productive questioning, including of localities and the sites of production (the 'where' much discussed in this volume), the models also highlight the extent to which they are centred on Europe and America and apply to periods no earlier than the early modern – and often only to printed productions. Most existing models hinder our understanding of the relationship between the very varied production, distribution and markets elsewhere in the world, and particularly in early modern Asia and China, and everywhere in ancient and very modern times.

Even so, the most interesting aspect of the use of such explanatory diagrams is the resulting tension between modelling and theory which has encouraged others to reach out for new inspiration and methodological novelty. The adaptation by William Warner and others of actor-network theory (ANT), which treats objects as part of social networks and maps relations between materials (or 'things') and concepts, has plotted anew and for specific case studies the relationship between communicators and communicated. The adoption of geographic information systems (GIS) by Fiona Black and Bertrum MacDonald to superimpose variegated book data over geographic information has inspired many to investigate this additional digital application to book history modelling. The highly sophisticated modelling by Michael Werner and Bénédicte Zimmermann has exposed book history to entangled history or *histoire croisée*, a reminder also that different sources and archives, as well as different foundational disciplinary approaches, encourage different models. The creators and revisers of book history models are, after all, labourers in archives ranging from the Société typographique de Neuchâtel, the special collections of the British Library, publishers' business ledgers, shipping registers, apprenticeship records of the Stationers' Company in London, civic taxation and notarial records in London and Paris, and many more besides.

One further point should not be neglected. Although unacknowledged directly in these models, their typologies were shaped by the development of media studies from the late 1940s. Accumulating mass communications studies, in tandem with the burgeoning of film, television and digital communications, insisted that media were the prime moulders of society, studies best summarized in the guide *Mass Communication Theory* by Denis McQuail. Usefully for students of book history, McQuail makes special mention of the difficulty of identifying specific uses of media, and the problems in understanding the reception given to any specific medium.

In the early 1980s McQuail and Sven Windahl published *Communication Models* and brought to a much larger academic audience the communication models of Claude Shannon which, as popularized by Warren Weaver, integrated ideas of information source, message, transmitter, channel, receiver and destination, error, decoding or translation, and much more besides. At the same time, with Shannon-Weaver often disparaged for an apparent neglect of human and historical contexts, George Gerbner, who directed the increasingly influential Annenberg School for Communication and Journalism at the University of Pennsylvania, successfully promoted communication theory across different university disciplines. There were many challenges here, including the mapping of relatively specific cultural and economic models onto more ambitious macro 'world-system' models. The most famous of these was developed by Immanuel Wallerstein, with its emphasis on world empires and world economies, dividing the world between dominant high-skill, capital-intensive core countries, and lower skill, labour-intensive semi-periphery and periphery countries, whose identities and relationship to one another change as a result of transport revolutions and economic intensification. The global expansion of the book itself demands new modelling to capture, among many variables, international labour division and imperial and economic systems based on multinational, highly capitalized global publishing conglomerates.

The real precursor to later communications models was the work of the American political scientist Harold Dwight Lasswell, an assailant of disciplinary boundaries, anticipating in spirit the cross-disciplinary energy of the history of the book. Lasswell proposed five important questions of communication and its conveyance: the Who, Says What, In Which Channel, To Whom, With What Effect? interrogations in the historical understanding of communication, including material texts. First espoused in 1948, Lasswell's five-question model of communication led to the emphasis in communication studies on determining effects. The focus of the model is broken down by each element of communication: 'who' refers to the communicator who formulates the message; 'what' is the content of message; 'channel' indicates the medium of transmission; 'whom' describes either an individual recipient or the audience of mass communication; 'effect' is the outcome of the message. The movement of the message travels from the communicator to the audience. Although this model represents a one-way flow of communication, the 'effect' also refers to feedback in public relations.

Lasswell's contemporary Paul Lazarsfeld did even more to crystallize the focus on communication effects, while Gerbner expanded Lasswell's model to focus 'attention on perception and reaction by the perceiver and the consequences of the communication'. In 1958, Richard Braddock suggested that the model be expanded to consider two additional and formerly neglected elements: 'for what purpose' and 'under what circumstances'. Criticism still followed, however: that Lasswell's model attended to key elements in the mass communication process but did not link elements together with either specificity or a sense of active process. Yet with further refinements, Lasswell, Richard Braddock and others form the basis of comparative critiques that also allow easy summary of the type of sources available for answering, in different time periods, different leading questions that form the basis of theories of book history.

As the following two chapters elaborate, of Lasswell's questions, the final two were by far the most challenging when transferred to 'books'. The 'to whom' (the identity of readers) was difficult enough, demanding, among other things, the measurement of literacies and the economic constraints upon access to books and print that might be as great as the limits to reading skills and comprehension. Far more problematic was the evidential basis of 'what effect?', of ascertaining how and why reading was done. Questions of reading abilities and aptitudes relate to age, gender, social and economic circumstances, environment and even light and posture, but the history of reading practice also requires an understanding of motivation. As is engagingly and repeatedly argued in many histories of books, consumers revisited texts and effectively remade them by their different readings. Differences in interpretation were made not only between different people of different gender and different competences, as affected by intelligence, education, skill and incentive, but by the same person revisiting the text on different occasions, at different ages or for different reasons.

4
Who, What and How?

Questioning of the who, what and how underpins the astonishing development of the history of the book in the last thirty years. Crucially, however, these questions have been posed in relation to one another, ensuring that the agents and agencies determining and controlling production and transmission were not analysed in isolation. Judicious questioners, often resisting pigeonholing as 'historians of the book', ensured that the focus of study was not divorced from the historical circumstances of production, circulation and use, whether that focus was the identification of authorship, editorial annotation and the recovery of authorial intent, censorship and copyright evasion, or the cataloguing procedures of an ancient library.

Few of those recovering a printer's copy-text or establishing a copy-text for an 'ideal' edition for literary evaluation ignored new possibilities for understanding the historical context of the manufacture and reproduction of the text. D. F McKenzie and Jerome J. McGann were among the most influential of those who, in different ways, re-examined evidence relating to the physical text, from its composition, typographical presentation and material form, to the social, economic and political circumstances of its publication. McKenzie, for example, in establishing the first full critical edition of the works of William Congreve, in the absence of surviving manuscripts for any of the key texts, reimagined the playwright's intentions by a rigorous and close analysis of early printings coupled with a vast range of historical sources. The bibliographical revisionism they inspired focused on the recovery of scribal and printers' working practices and of the meaning of texts within the particularities of their publication, transmission and reception. McKenzie's later work built upon his earlier pioneering research, which recovered evidence of the payments to compositors and pressmen and established that concurrent printing, that is the use of more than printing press and even printing house to complete an edition, was a common early modern practice. Such research not only reinforced the importance of archival evidence as a necessary adjunct to an examination of the material book, but advanced the argument that every text contained interventions that could not and should not be suppressed by modern editorial processes.

Fresh insights offered a means of conceptualizing change over time: of materials, of the different personnel, of different techniques, of transport and of acquisition and response. The pursuit of a more historical agenda, of agency and causation, inevitably urged new questioning of the economics of production, supply and investment, including, notably, the protection of literary property by copyright and other controls such as guild supervision. How, for example, were expansion and contraction related to patronage, market or distributive conditions and to the intervention of external checks in the form of pre- and post-publication censorship, licensing and political and judicial sanctions against literary content?

By the final decade of the twentieth century, diverse scholars, pursuing different interests, and many free of the constraints of university departments, addressed what were now increasingly labelled 'book history' questions in relation to authors, scribes, printers and financing publishers and to many different types of product from the luxury and celebrated to the cheap or ephemeral, manuscript or print, pamphlet, newspaper or periodical. Study of distributors, from merchants and booksellers to librarians and private lenders, accompanied investigation of guild and state intervention, censorship, privileges and issues of copyright and piracy.

The result was a formidable reassessment of what books were and did, moving forward a rich and varied agenda. David D. Hall and Hugh Amory pioneered new study of religion and publication in early New England. Anthony Grafton and

Ian Maclean transformed the intellectual and social history of early modern scholarship and education. In Germany numerous literary scholars coalesced around a Sozialgeschichte der deutschen Literatur (a social history of German literature), mostly investigating the genesis and reception of bestsellers and critical literature. The suggestions for further reading in the Bibliography at the end of this volume offer leading examples of those who have reinvigorated the longstanding publishing history of Enlightenment France and Germany, reassessed the authority and instability of print and information management, rewritten the social history of cheap print, peddling, politics and popular piety, and reworked our understanding of literary authorship in relation to publishing and print and manuscript circulation and preservation. Others extended this study to the operations of copyright and censorship and the social and political history of news, journalism, newspapers and periodicals.

Structural aspects of the book trade enjoyed fresh scrutiny from research groups interested in both provincial and metropolitan publication. Study of twentieth-century book production and reception ranged from the advance of international conglomerates and bestsellers to the sociology of electronic media, with different perspectives. Others researched the fundamental economics of Georgian and Victorian publishing practices and undertook major incursions in printing history, advancing the bibliographical study of Bible publication and the creative concept of the transaction between producer, donor and recipient. Fresh reviews of anthologies accompanied reassessment of past forms of media and the manifold contribution of women to writing, reviewing, publishing and the book trades. Although such collaborative work seemed more concerned with printing, numerous scholars of medieval Europe published seminal works that relocated manuscript production and palaeography within broader historical parameters, and others revitalized the study of incunables.

Much of this activity extended or reshaped studies which for many years had been heavy-duty staples of the curriculum, from new explorations of literacy and working-class writing and reading that re-evaluated the foundational 1957 *The English Common Reader* of Richard D. Altick, to Peter Blayney's forensic research revising, among other studies,

Cyprian Blagden's sallies into the history of the Stationers' Company. Many also contributed to a very different bibliographical interpretation from Ian Watt's iconic and seemingly imperishable 'rise of the novel', including its development in North America. Just as broadly, a new generation of historical bibliographers revisited the social, economic and political history of publishing and republishing in the United States. An assorted and widely scattered group completed studies of publishers and their relations with authors, house histories of printing firms, and accounts of other, important products of the press like ballads and chapbooks, children's books, maps, prints, and music that together replaced standard surveys like H. S. Bennett's three-volume *English Books and Readers* of 1952–70.

What is striking is the diversity of research activity and approach, and also the key areas of intersection. Peter Kornicki was one of the first to bring an understanding of Japanese book history to the English-speaking world, and to do so with comparative insight. James Secord and others brought new insights from publishing and reception history to bear radically upon the writing of the history of science. New histories of engraving, intaglio and photogravure contributed to fresh understanding of map production, the publication and reception of musical notation and printed scores, and the illustration of books, periodicals and newspaper. Committed archivists and academic librarians radically revised accounts of library and collecting history, quite in addition to the pioneering contributions of multivolume national publications. The contribution of Michael Twyman and others to printing and lithography and of John Bidwell and others to paper history underpinned many of these advances. Notably, researchers and conservationists such as Nicholas Pickwood and Mirjam Foot worked to advance the understanding of binding as integral to the history of books rather than a division of connoisseurship or art and collecting history.

At the same time, other historians and sociologists responded to this research with prominent seminars and histories devoted to modern publishing and communication, transoceanic information networks, and belief and religious publication, led by Asa Briggs, Jean-Yves Mollier, John Thompson, Christopher Bayly and Bernard Bailyn, among others. Among their other seminal and hugely influential studies, Peter Burke, Roger Chartier and Daniel Roche organized seminars that in different ways addressed the social history of knowledge. These contributors, with different emphases and approaches but sharing common objectives, were overwhelmingly British, French and North American, but with the isolated companionship of scholars elsewhere and often trained also in different bibliographical and conservation traditions. Within a decade, however, the growing body of work included monographs and essays from Australasia, with its distinguished tradition in British and French bibliographical scholarship, Russia and central Europe. There followed notable published work from India, Mexico, Brazil, Japan and South Africa, and developing exchanges with historians and literary scholars in China and elsewhere in Asia. By the 2010s, scores of monographs and articles were published annually to which the authors or their publishers attached, centrally or tangentially, the label 'history of the book'. The majority of these still concerned Europe and North America and the age of print, but with increasing attention to the twentieth century and to the interplay between script and press. As earlier chapters have made clear, geographical broadening of interests as well as greater exploration of ancient forms of books usually required fundamental requestioning of the inception of and relations between the material objects, their manufacturers and their mode of transmission.

What was also most innovative about these new histories was their combination of different sources and the ingenuity required in locating new types of evidential record, many of which also demanded new tactics and caution in interpretation. Textual interrogation combined with extensive paratextual and material analysis – of palaeographical and codicological variation, illumination, rubrication, appendices, notes, indexes, *mise-en-page*, illustrations and typographical design, together with format, binding and broader physical aspects of the text. Just as fruitful, however, was the exploitation of a much greater range of extra-textual evidence, notably including provenance research.

New histories of European medieval books necessarily analysed the many and changing operations involved in their manufacture, especially the division of labour and the involvement of several different craftsmen working on the same production. Transcribing, or the carrying over of a text from exemplar to apograph (or transcript) and imitating contents, style of script and page layout, are part of the creation of every book. This, nevertheless, differs from the modern concept and accuracy of a facsimile or a fake. In mainland Europe, the term 'diplomatic' extends to all aspects of documents and records, including study of the exactitude of copying. 'Codicology' has been applied widely to all aspects of manuscript books besides the study of handwriting, for which Handschriftenkunde is more technically reserved in German-speaking lands. In Britain and the United States, codicology is more inclusive, and knowledge of handwriting – palaeography in the strict sense – is incorporated into an understanding of the composition of the codex, its writing, correction, annotation, rubrication, binding, marks of ownership, paste-ins or other additions, and provenance, including sales and cataloguing.

The recovery of copying errors and corrections from manuscripts and early printed copies reveals much about writing and reading habits, but the diverse locations of so many survivals can overwhelm, so that classification and logging is essential. The *Revue d'histoire ecclésiastique* has been doing this since 1900 and *Scriptorium* since 1946. *Medioevo Latino*, a bibliography published annually since 1978, is now online and focuses on texts written in Latin between 457 CE and the beginning of the sixteenth century. Technical research on extant codices, some very fragile and fragmentary, spans very different expertise. New advances in Greek and Byzantine palaeography retrace textual transmission by new classification and digital comparison. Many Greek manuscripts in Paris, for example, are now fully available from the Gallica portal, and the Paris-based Pinakes database of Greek manuscripts supported by the Centre national de la recherche scientifique (CNRS) compares new digitizations of codices physically scattered around the globe. The Digita Vaticana Onlus, founded in 2013 to digitize the 80,000 manuscripts in the Vatican Library, is another among the many digitizing projects under way around the world.

In Britain, identification of later hands has also been much advanced by online compendia such as Late Medieval English Scribes, a catalogue of all identified and unidentified scribal hands in the manuscripts of the English writings of the five major Middle English authors. Among different but allied studies, Heather Wolfe and Daniel Bellingradt have reassessed the availability of late medieval and early modern paper in Europe, and Alexandra Gillespie and others have investigated the production history of Sammelbände (composite volumes of two or more works). Debates continue about what was split and rejoined in the age of incunables and in the early sixteenth century and what was put together and destroyed as a result of collecting manias from the late sixteenth century. An assessment of loss is again important. Rosamond McKitterick, among others, relates early medieval European library catalogues to the organization of knowledge, while Richard Sharpe's British project on medieval library catalogues, extending the labours of Ker, has put into print the library catalogues and booklists known to survive from British institutions of the Middle Ages, thereby elucidating the range of authors and works that were in circulation. His *Handlist of the Latin Writers of Great Britain and Ireland before 1540* draws also on the understanding of sixteenth- and seventeenth-century recorders of books.

In many such studies using wide-ranging archival materials, ancient and modern, the 'who' concerned not just the identity of the different book manufacturers but the originator, the author. Recent histories of the book have revisited scribal production, author–publisher relations, anonymity (apparently and often deliberately *livres sans auteurs*) and the identity of the author, translation and the translator, professionalization, and many other aspects of the historical circumstances of authorship.[1] Ideas of authorship derive from broader historical contexts. The identification of a corpus of popular but non-canonical authors has challenged the definition of Literature (with the canonical or critical L), and fresh research on questions of handwritten culture, copyright, self-publishing, subscription schemes and royalties has reassessed what it meant to be a writer. Chinese comparisons also invite questions about authors and audience. Many East Asian authors steered the process of production and distribution of their work through family and publishing 'jiake' to a degree unmatched in early modern and modern Europe. The early East Asian author is often a composite figure in the sense that texts are linked up and given just one authorial name. Chinese processes, however, also bore, in some specific ways, similarity to Western private manuscript distribution, later 'printed for the author' self-financed publication and modern digital self-publishing. East Asian authors' expectations of audience appear extremely variable – and also to intersect in unexpected ways with gender profiles.

Authors' letters and personal records, book and library catalogues, publishers' advertisements, printing manuals, auction records, and many more examples, are sometimes identifiable in foundational bibliographies to major authors or genres. There remains, however, an abundant need in book history for archival digging and the sort of detective work and lateral thinking that appeals to the more empirical historian. And new archival retrieval systems serve a crucial role, The most valuable but often the most elusive records are those from the original businesses detailing exact production costs – of materials and labour – and of timings and pricing calculations, so that other, sometimes ancillary, business records had to be used in compensation, although even these rarely survive for pre-early modern activity. The identification and interpretation of a great range of different archives, some public, some private, supported and supports the development of the history of the book. Evidence derives from business records and ledgers, apprenticeship records, probate, legal, notarial, police and court records, government, parliamentary and local authority papers, customs and shipping records and dockets, taxation and census returns, insurance records, leases and other property records, and much more besides. Such records, many particular to the persons, processes and sites involved, continue to reward ingenuity in recovering the history of operations – of the who, what, and how, but also the where and why.

Economics

The who, what and how of book history are ultimately inexplicable without investigation of materials and labour costs, print runs, sales and prices. The goal reaches beyond the celebratory histories of individual publishing firms to a more rigorous history of the economics of knowledge producers and consumers who may or may not be purchasers. Economic book history requires the retrieval of runs of business records, a task encountering obstacles of survival and access. Modern firms appear to offer richer archival resources, but they also often require imaginative compensatory modelling to account for irrecoverable data. The application of economic history has been an underdeveloped resource in most histories of the book, despite statistical and interpretative advances. The analyses of individual firms by Aileen Fyfe, Jean-Yves Mollier and others are archivally grounded, while William St Clair's call-to-arms in modelling a 'political economy of reading' is based upon sustained assessment of production, pricing and consumer data in relation to intellectual property regimes. In premodern China, Japan and many other parts of the world, however, non-commercial or private book production and publishing predominated, challenging us to understand different economic assumptions explaining the way in which domestic groups and authors funded book production and textual transmission. Even in ancient times, the supplanting of traditional papyrus, waxed boards and parchment by paper essentially resulted from economic considerations.

From the comparative perspective especially, numerous economic issues demand attention. Among these are the under-researched economy of the closed patronage and compound costings of medieval book production, the increasingly debated question of undercapacity in early modern printing houses, and the alignment or misalignment of productive resources with demand. As will be discussed, further research requires an appreciation of non-book printing supply and demand. Extensive business records, ledgers and letters, stretching over many generations, miraculously survive for several great European printing and publishing firms. These archives include those of the Crombergers of Seville in the early sixteenth century, Plantin-Moretus in Antwerp from 1555 to 1876, the Luchtmans in Amsterdam, Strahan and John Murray I in London in the eighteenth century. In later centuries, the archives survive of Macmillans, Longmans and the later Murrays, together with those of other printing and publishing firms whose records are preserved at the University of Reading, and certain accessible private archives across Europe and the Americas. Given their magnitude, these records will benefit from new searchable, online cataloguing. The Plantin-Moretus ledgers and papers, for example, sit on 113 metres of shelving, accessed via the 1926 inventory of Jan Denucé, but with online inventorying and access in progress.

Even more challenging is the bibliometric examination of mass production in the nineteenth and twentieth centuries, whether transnationally or of particular sectors of the trade, as begun by Simon Eliot, Alistair McCleery, Alexis Weedon and many others. As John Thompson and Eva Hemmungs Wirtén also demonstrate in different ways, recovery and explanation of the complexity and volume of change is daunting. The revolution brought by stereotyping (fixing hand-assembled type in metal), the automation of punch-cutting and typecasting and mechanization of typesetting, including Linotype and Monotype, ensured waves of mass and cheap book publication and the surge in newspaper and periodical production. By 1890, for example, some 650 periodical and 500 newspaper titles were published in London alone. Broader business issues in the history of the book concern finance, labour history and transport, and offer particular problems of comparison across periods and societies. New histories are currently seeking to understand the consequences of international trade agreements and mergers such as Bertelsmann's takeover of Random House and Penguin, and the transnational publishing policies of multinationals such as Reed International, Pearson and Springer Verlag. Thompson's authoritative *Merchants of Culture*, a study of the modern publishing business, shrewdly circumvents closed business archives by an assessment based on 280 interviews.

Global perspectives demand new approaches. The popularity of distinctive non-commercial publishing in premodern East Asia resists Western associations of the expansion of printing with the rise of capitalism and suggests a reformulation of the propositions of Jürgen Habermas and the linkage of market expansion with the public expression of private opinion on public matters. In China, Korea and Japan, government, religious institutions, private individuals, families and commercial publishers all sponsored book production, and the working economics of different technologies responding to these different types of demand and patronage also offer instructive contrasts. The comparative perspective is also illuminating.

As Beth McKillop has suggested, Korean and Chinese use of movable type looked clumsy and inefficient to Europeans, and yet East Asian appreciation of printing by movable type in Europe was similarly limited. Such printing required great capital outlay and overheads, and its use of printing types that benefited from being limited to twenty-six alphabetic letters appeared quite inappropriate to any attempt to replicate over 50,000 Chinese characters.

The comparison invites fundamental questions about production efficiencies, replication processes, audience size and perceptions of technology and progress. Under the Song dynasty from 960, China sustained a woodblock printing boom, with increasing availability of cheaper texts, and by the years when printing presses were set up in European towns and cities, most printed books in China were less expensive and already more widely distributed both socially and geographically. Western movable type and paper cost more than woodblock printing in China, where cheap family labour also generally reduced expenses further. Emphasis upon the technical efficiency of the early European printing press, therefore, must be qualified by emerging histories of printing-house practices that emphasize how costly and time-consuming was the casting of type and its composition and recomposition for successive editions of the same book. Comparative studies of early modern Asian printing practices and the intricate and correctable xylography of China, Korea and Japan will be rewarding, especially in studying the interplay between the commercial and the intellectual, between city production and country distribution.

Woodblock printing did not spread as fast in East Asia as letterpress printing in early modern Europe. However, from the seventeenth century, woodblock printing, much privately undertaken by publishers with greatly varied backgrounds, flourished in rural and urban areas in East Asia and both the state and private individuals set publishing standards of paper, calligraphy and editing, often far higher than those of commercial publishers in Europe. Chinese schoolteachers and graduates contributed to commercial publishing activities, even though some did not consider full-time publishing as an honourable activity. Conversely, by the seventeenth and eighteenth centuries, many collectors attempted to publish their own copies of rare and famous titles in their collection.

94 Who, What and How?

Distribution was as important for non-commercial as commercial publications, but involved different originating motivations and effects. Chinese commercial printing developed some 200 years after the first known printing in China in the early seventh century. Just as in Europe, non-commercial, private publication tended to privilege questions of impact, of how an audience might react to a text, with means of distribution as assured as the identity of the recipients. By comparison, in commercial printing and publishing, distribution might determine the economic survival of the originator producer in a more uncertain marketplace. Dissemination is crucial in both scenarios, but economic imperatives are variable. As Ian Maclean has observed of the early modern European book trade, and notably from the perspective of the often impoverished scholar, profit did not necessarily correspond to monetary surplus or mercantile expansion. We often need to refine twenty-first-century models that privilege business strategies and supply-side economics over other early modern concerns. Greater appreciation is required, for example, of scholarly and intellectual enterprise that depended upon enduring forms of patronage, subsidy and commerce that were driven by social, political and ideological objectives.

Wider Horizons

The obvious and fascinating challenge is to extend the search for new sources that reveal book production, transmission and reception in other parts of the world where research on books is neglected, sometimes with gaps of centuries. The understanding of what often appears to the West to be material in unusual forms is also limited by language barriers. We can at least take advantage of new means of digital reproduction and exacting textual comparison from far-flung sites, although direct, physical examination will remain the *sine qua non* of definitive interpretation.

Such adventurous *comparative* scholarship is embryonic, but offers opportunities to relate broader concepts and to pose different questions across very diverse areas. To give one striking example, what Joseph McDermott has called an 'explosion of Chinese and non-Chinese research' on the Chinese book in imperial China after the tenth century has transformed scholarship on canon formation, manuscript culture, textual transmission and knowledge formation. New research taps into traditional Chinese strengths in bibliography and revisits questions of production (woodblock as well as movable type), distribution (buying, giving, lending, and even stealing), and the consumption of books (reading practices, private and public libraries, and collectors). As both Christopher Reed and McDermott have argued, economics, culture and technology explain the Chinese millennium-long preference for simpler and more portable woodblocks and then, after its invention in 1796 by the German author and actor Alois Senefelder, for lithography, rather than for movable type and letterpress.[2] But the meaning conveyed by Asian portable and differently produced texts was equally mutable. As Cynthia Brokaw insists, we must ask how 'book' was understood. Before the twentieth century, many Chinese books comprised miscellanies of collected and usually unattributed excerpts from other texts, and deleted or exchanged excerpts in new printings of the same title. This continuous republishing style reworks our understanding of authorship and destabilizes Western notions of the book.[3]

Similar questions might be asked of the production of Sanskrit texts in India, studied in Europe since the seventeenth century but currently benefiting from resurgent interest, particularly in German research centres. The success of lithography in India from the mid-nineteenth century, as Graham Shaw has shown, requires further economic questioning. In China, a few decades later, lithographic production outsold both Chinese publishers' woodblock titles and the same titles from Christian missionaries' letterpresses. In turn, lithography was challenged from the 1880s by improved letterpress machinery, advancing mass production to an even higher scale. At issue, however, is the availability of and access to the sort of sources that transformed the history of books in the West. Nonetheless, the deepening understanding of the 'what' and 'who', if not always the how, is advancing, not least in studies of genre and authorship. What we might now deem a book history perspective is evident in studies of Chinese women authors and publishers by European and North American scholars such as Susan Mann, studying the editing and publishing activities of women like Yun Zhu (1771–1833), and Ellen Widmer, exploring a Beijing–Hangzhou alignment of women authors.

The redefinition of what was printed, when and where, and the exploration of the multifarious consequences of the establishment of printing – and of lithography and successor technological developments – have been the central and continuing achievements since Febvre and Martin's mapping. These also revise the standard 1959 account of 'five hundred years of printing' by S. H. Steinberg, even as updated by John Trevitt.[4] Greater understanding of the role of the printing press has informed numerous influential histories of vernacular traditions, linguistic variation and political, religious and economic transformation, notably European revolutions and the Reformation, and less popularly, commercial, financial and industrial expansion. Hebrew typographic printing began in the Ottoman Empire in 1493 and in Morocco in 1515. Armenian type was used from 1567 in Constantinople and from 1638 in Iran. Syriac and Arabic type printed the first Arabic book in the Middle East in Lebanon in 1610. Greek books were printed in Constantinople in 1627. Table 4 offers a selective listing of the arrival of European printing presses and type in different towns and cities, including many outside

Table 4 Earliest known printing by metal type cast in Europe and North America in selected towns and cities worldwide

Mainz	before 1452	Vilnius	1543
Bamberg	before 1457	Moscow	1553
Rome	1465	Constantinople	1567
Basel	before 1468	Peru	1581
Venice	1468	Cambridge, Massachusetts	1638
Paris	1470		
Milan	1470	Philadelphia	1685
Seville	before 1472	Madras	1772
Lyon	1473	Buenos Aires	1780
Cracow	1473	Bombay	1792
Westminster	1475	Cape Town	1795
Antwerp	1481	Sydney	1802
Stockholm	1483	Brazil	1808
Istanbul	1493	Tehran	1820
Salonika	1515	New Zealand	1835
Mexico City	1539		

Europe. Movable type, in varying forms, arrived in East Asian settlements more than two centuries before 1452, while North American presses and type pioneered printing in such locations as Hawaii in 1821, Liberia in 1826 and Oregon in 1853. Early modern European history has been particularly exposed to the application of new bibliographical research to familiar contours. By about 1480, presses operated in at least 121 towns and cities across Europe. The number of towns with printing presses increased to some 270 by 1500 (but also with some consolidation of adjacent centres). Jean-François Gilmont estimates a total publication of the pre-1501 incunables of 30,000 titles in 9 million volumes. Printers in the Baltic lands were among many examples of those contributing to the shaping of language by the design and founding of type. Much of this activity was led by biblical translation and publication. The migration of foreign printers proved significant. Nikolajs Mollīns, the first great printer in Riga, arrived from Antwerp just as Caxton was succeeded by the Flemish de Worde, all of these early printers standardizing dialects and developing a written language by print.

As Lotte Hellinga observes, 'In vernacular texts written in the Middle Ages (and much later), one can immediately perceive script-features linked to the use of a particular language, which express its identity, in graphic form, almost as strongly as the language itself.'[5] That identity bifurcated when print offered an alternative to continuing scribal forms, but also (in riposte to Eisenstein's critique), in standardizing, print also constrained differences. Lithography, and perhaps even more, in the early nineteenth century, stereotyping, brought further changes. A Syriac New Testament had been produced by stereotyping in the Netherlands early in the eighteenth century, as was recorded by Timperley in 1839. Very largely, however, typeface conventions had been set, and stereotyping quality was judged by the accuracy of its reproduction of existing, familiar letter forms. Lithography proved especially successful in printing South Asian languages. Compared to Europe, where it was often marginalized, lithography became a mainstream Asian printing technology, allowing a certain democratization of print. Theological subjects comprised the most frequently published titles, followed by educational textbooks and belles-lettres.

Study of lithography relates also to the history of the book in Islamic lands, with its own distinguished tradition but where leading scholars such as Sheila Blair and Jonathan Bloom have long called for more comparative research. The first books in Arabic type were printed by non-Muslims first in Venice in 1514, and the Qu'ran itself was printed there in 1537. The text in ḥijāzī script was established soon after the Prophet Muhammad's death in 632 CE, but this first Venetian and commercially unsuccessful attempt in movable type carried many typographical shortcomings which made much of it unreadable. The next attempt at printing a full edition was not until 1694 at Hamburg. In Asia in the nineteenth century, however, lithography became the printing technique of choice for Muslim communities because it assured a mass and more accurate replication of manuscript, considered the norm for textual authority rather than wanton print. Lithography also offered easier script-type reading than European cast letter-types of Arabic and Indian language scripts. Like Greek and Roman scripts, Arabic script is written with individual symbols for letters, and can be adapted for related languages by adding diacritical marks to its eighteen graphemes.

Persia did not even support printing by woodblock or movable type until the early nineteenth century, while the first state-run Muslim printing press in the Arab world began in Cairo in 1819, with commercial presses, even then tightly regulated, only in the late nineteenth century. Early manuscript Qu'rans were nonetheless expensive to produce, each requiring up to eighteen square metres of parchment for the entire oblong text of some 75,000 words – equivalent to the length of the New Testament. These manuscripts were encased in box bindings, although the advance of paper cheapened production from the tenth century in at least some parts of the Muslim world. Book artists flourished in medieval Persia, with deluxe productions commissioned from favoured scriptoria, and with particularly magnificent albums created for the Mughal rulers of northern India from the mid-sixteenth to the mid-nineteenth centuries. Even so, the great majority of books produced in Islamic lands were much simpler than the great courtly books and designed for daily worship. Manuscript Qu'rans in sub-Saharan regions of West Africa, for example, continued through the nineteenth century to be loose-leaf pages wrapped by a tooled leather wallet. It was again lithographed editions that cheapened production costs and began to supplant manuscript despite cultural resistance, but ultimately it was the transformation of mechanized letterpress in the twentieth century that provided a final revolution in the mass manufacture, circulation and increased translation of the Qu'ran. The holy book became, for example, a staple of production of the first printing press established in Bahrain in 1913, together, again typically, with associated interpretative pamphlets.

A further research horizon has developed with the pursuit of micro studies to map the place and space of book production and transmission. Questioning the neglected 'where' invites consideration of site in relation not only to physical geography but to its memory and tradition. Actor-network theory has been adapted effectively by William Warner and others to plot mediated interactions across greatly varying distances. A network is performed: the effect of a particular arrangement of actors and critics. Such history might involve many different societies and extends from study of shifts in media and oral-literacy to meticulous attention to the recovery of the history of commercial bookshops, booksellers and the book trade – and to the space of reading considered in chapter 5. In European and North American towns and communities, the place of selling and borrowing books and periodicals has been related to ideas of space and cultural topography, and to the role of the shop in the world of the polite and the public. Notable research is based on leases, insurance, probate and miscellaneous property records, and tax, customs, legal, court and local authority papers. In plotting book trading sites the notion of a 'bookscape' was also developed to combine place, space and memory in reinterpreting the character of commercial neighbourhoods.[6] Such research will continue to prompt thought about archives and records that can be exploited in new ways to profile book production and trading history.

Control: Copyright, Censorship and Circulation

An integral feature of the history of books since ancient times is how very different types of control exercised by different agents have affected book production and dissemination. Most originators of a book and its text were unable to supervise its effects or benefit from its success. The 'escape' of the text beyond the control of writers and those financing its publication challenges accepted ideas of authorship and demands fresh historical understanding of financial returns from a 'literary property' and the processes whereby the formation of canon of literature is related to the freer availability of certain books in all their various forms. The ultimate 'escape' of the text was also more fundamental: the different, individual interpretations of the text by readers and the effects of that reading upon them. It was the potency of the unfettered book that brought it into direct conflict with all those – state, church and even original patrons – who feared its consequences. Some of the most exceptional book historical studies in recent times have rigorously explored the role of the scribe, printer and publisher, methods of book circulation and the imposition of different controls in times of unrest, civil war or political and religious revolution.

Where no law or method of establishing rights over intellectual property existed, as in ancient Rome and indeed most of the premodern world, there was no authoritative way of establishing the original state of the text. In late Ming China, a relaxation of government censorship and the absence of copyright privileges of writers and publishers enabled anyone to reprint and circulate books. Yet the quest for intellectual and commercial rights, distilled into copyright issues, continues to be a fertile and far-reaching question in the history of the book. For copyright law or its absence is an integral part of the economic and political history of publishing, and one that resonates in today's world of digital piracy, internet authority and 'fake news'. Foundational Anglo-American treatments of copyright history by James Barnes, Mark Rose and John Feather were sensitive to changing author–publisher relations in the same way that Adrian Johns's exceptional study of piracy and 'intellectual property wars' responds to a vital and contemporary agenda.

The same responsiveness to current threats to freedom of expression has impelled many histories of the control exercised over publishing, book and press content and distribution by external authority, as well as the history of the evasion of censorship and the production and circulation of samizdat literature. The reactions to controlling attempts by political and religious authorities animate important studies in book history in all parts of the world, especially given the contrasting histories of censorship. The governments of China and Korea, for example, heavily shaped their respective book cultures by both sponsoring and censoring text production. By contrast, until modern times, Japanese governments seem to have been largely indifferent to the political uses and implications of print. Likewise, in early modern Europe, historical interpretations of the impact of new technologies in book production are critically inflected by an understanding of both direct interventions by church and state and more devolved forms of control and policing. In England, the relevant guild, the Stationers' Company, was endowed with powers to control its own industry. These powers inevitably came to conflict with the commercial interests of its own most powerful members. Elsewhere, as in France, the establishment of a privilege system of pre-publication licensing implicates censorship in state-sanctioned judgements of literary quality. These questions are developed, for example, not only by Elizabeth Armstrong for Renaissance France and Anne Goldgar in her study of Enlightenment 'impolite learning', but also by Robert Darnton in his review of censorship in British imperial India, where courts intervened in determining not just content but qualitative issues of publishing material.

Historians have searched for breaches and circumventions of censorship, examining, for example, evidence of resistance to the papal Index of forbidden, heretical publications. First established in the Catholic Netherlands in 1529, the more notorious papal Index Librorum Prohibitorum was established in Rome in 1559 and not abolished until 1966. Similar searches have been made of records of local licensing, such as that given to Moretus from the Council of Brabant to publish bibles and liturgical works. Licences and privileges were often printed at the front or back of the book, but more revealing legal challenges, deals and courtroom battles require assiduous archival digging such as that undertaken in Britain by Ronan Deazley and H. Tomás Gómez-Arostegui. By contrast, Hok-lam Chan's brief history of censorship in China describes more top-down efforts by the Song, Yuan and Ming rulers to ban the publication and transport of calendars and other sensitive texts, also demanding the vetting by local officials of all private manuscripts before publication. The extension of such histories will depend on careful interrogation of local sources, while the interpretation of broader state censorship such as that under the Qing and the even harsher literary inquisitions of the Kangxi, Yongzheng and Qianlong emperors from the late seventeenth century demand investigation of central archives and an understanding of the exact motivation behind decrees and government actions. Equally oppressive state and church control operated in Russia, but as Timothy Brook has suggested, the territorial vastness of China and the peripatetic and often elusive nature of woodblock printing ensured common evasion of authority. As other promising research reveals, in India an Act of 1835 allowed increased ownership of presses by Indians, so that lithography, again easier and cheaper than letterpress, was exploited by non-professionals, including many formerly engaged in the production of manuscripts. Such practice also evaded other laws and regulations, allowing communication and a diversity of opinion not sanctioned by any contemporary or later European governments.

In such ways, the history of the circulation of publications becomes integral to all histories of books worldwide, ancient and modern, crucially mediating between manufacture, attempts at control and reception, but also, as a continuing process, crossing time zones as well as geographical ones. Circulation ensures spatial distribution but also transport through the years and centuries, creating the temporal disorder of small shelves and large libraries alike, and the movement of books many years or centuries after their first publication. Such mediation takes many further forms, from private distribution and commercial bookselling to the lending of books by libraries and other institutions, but it also encounters variable and problematic survival rates, with much historical enquiry devoted to the reconstruction of the distribution and popularity of books. This research includes, notably, not simply the recovery of the first editions or appearances of publications, but the subsequent circulation of these and later editions as second-hand, frequently traded and also secreted books. Book travel was complex and mutable enough in Europe and the

Americas and in conveyance across the oceans, but elsewhere other institutional, cultural, political, economic, topographical and climatic complications are suggested, such as those brought to our attention by Nelly Hanna and Geoffrey Roper, among others, for the Middle East.

The turning-point in mass international and national trading in books came with the lessening of structural constraints on distribution from the late seventeenth century, fundamental transport changes and new financial organization interlinked with new social, urban, formations. By the second half of the eighteenth century almost every part of Europe was affected. Particularly as studied by Graham Pollard and Albert Ehrman, booksellers' catalogues, issued and used by both wholesalers and retailers, became primary vehicles for notification and promotion of booksellers' wares. A transnational and global history of the book is also not limited to international or centre-to-periphery relationships, but includes ways in which readers abroad influenced publishers and writers at home, as much as the other way round. It is also the case that any survey of commerce in print must recognize that sale was not the only means of distribution. At times when large collections represented a great proportion of the overall book market, books travelled as gifts, as the pawns of religious contest and as trophies of war. The *Reconquista*, the advance of the Ottomans, the Reformation and Counter-Reformation and looting during the Thirty Years War caused widespread upheaval in the book market. The revolutions of the late eighteenth and mid-nineteenth centuries rejuvenated the exchange of ancient books and manuscripts. *Säkularisation* under Joseph II and Napoleon forced monasteries to disgorge their holdings and sent crates of books across the mountains of western Europe and down the Danube and the Rhine – and there are scores of other major redistributive examples.

A further invaluable benefit of book circulation history is to break down the nationalism and falsely constructed boundaries and borders that have problematized the writing of book history, especially some of the series volumes of the History of the Book in Britain, in Scotland and the United States, among others.[7] Scientific expeditions, royal patronage, missionary publications, imported books and the gathering, channelling and delivery of news are all part of this history.

When considered from the perspective of an individual's reading of books, however, book circulation is most assuredly not restricted to publications that have only just been written or printed or that derive only from the reader's region or country. Studies such as those by Robert Darnton, Laurence Fontaine and Jeffrey Freedman have demonstrated the significance of the international, cross-border travel of books, extended by geographies of the book and emerging investigations of East–West contacts and comparisons. Darnton originally explored the extraordinary resources of the Swiss Société typographique de Neuchâtel (STN) and the travels of their 220 or so published works, 1769–94, the majority counterfeit and banned bestsellers in France. Fontaine traces the routes of pedlars as channels of news and communication, arguing that the peddling of new commodities from the sixteenth century such as books, watches and tobacco underpinned the European economy. The French Book Trade in Enlightenment Europe (FBTEE) digital project has now further transformed the potential of the STN and its mapping of the production, marketing, dissemination, policing and reception of books and ideas.

Records reconstructing the distribution networks, local, transnational and transoceanic, are varied and fragmentary. Shop inventories and stock sale records, for example, are a frustratingly haphazard or unfocused indication of the huge transactions in almanacs and chapbooks. The second-hand market, just visible from surviving sale catalogues and advertisements, spanned antiquarian and scholarly rarities, and remainders and cheap popular books. For wealthy bibliophiles, the hiring of book dealers and agents became indispensable. An increasingly active and organized second-hand market is evident by the end of the seventeenth century. Second-hand book and library auctions, which appear to have been uncommon before about 1650, rapidly increased in size and frequency. Few early auctioneers bought their stock of books; instead, most were selling on behalf of others, with relatively generous credit arrangements. Historical study of early modern enthusiasms for old volumes has further been overshadowed by renewed appreciation of the burgeoning market for incunables and rare first editions in the late eighteenth and early nineteenth centuries. The scale of the later revolution in the valuation and passion for early print and rare books dwarfs the bibliophilia of the seventeenth century, but this earlier period of collecting must also be measured in the context of relatively small but cumulative levels of book production, a limited economy and comparatively modest disposable incomes. And it made for some spectacular book hoarding (figure 5).

The distribution of new, old and imported titles was extended by private libraries, book clubs, subscription schemes, debating societies, religious societies and, by the early nineteenth century, mechanics' institutes. From at least the early eighteenth century, coffee houses in London and then Paris and other major European cities took multiple copies of newspapers for their customers. In the country towns, many debating societies formed their own book stock; this, like all these trends, was successfully transplanted to colonial towns and settlements in North America, the Caribbean, South America and India and the Far East. The transmission of books from Europe to its colonies and then between publishers in Europe and the Americas and all round the world developed with the increase in shipping routes and technologies, and the nineteenth-century development of the steamship, overseas credit arrangements and telegraphic communication. In the same way, internal distribution was transformed by the railways, banking and financial and commercial infrastructures. By contrast, the extensive networks for book distribution over many centuries in premodern China and India developed from production sites outside large urban centres, based on the simplicity and portability of the basic tools and technology of foundational woodblock printing.

Libraries

Histories of book collecting and of libraries have undergone notable revisions in recent years, testing evidence of use and perception and notably the design and occupancy of library space and the organization and taxonomy of holdings. Roger Chartier's *L'Ordre des livres* and contributions to journals such as *Library and Information History*, *Library Quarterly* and *Libraries and Culture* (significantly renamed *Information and Culture*), greatly expanded what has often been a limited

5 *A Bibliophile Caring for his Extensive Collection* by Carl Spitzweg, 1850

conceptual base. Pioneering historical analyses by Paul Kaufman in Britain and Bernhard Fabian and Paul Raabe in Germany have been extended by Alistair Black, Kenneth Carpenter and David McKitterick, among many others. As David Pearson has demonstrated, once-neglected provenance research crucially contributes to library history: without advances in determining past ownership, exchange and cataloguing of books we lose a vital dimension in the understanding of circulation and influence.[8] The meaning of the library – also the title of an essay collection edited by Alice Crawford – will continue to resonate as the materiality of the book is transformed and we redesign shared book reading and conservation spaces, an issue also developed in chapter 5.

Libraries, ancient and modern, often invest in conservation, guardianship, acquisition and access, but – to extend the point made at the close of chapter 1 – libraries can also contribute to the fracture of older assemblages and the reconfiguration of original records. Physical accumulations of ancient books, as collections or waste, presaged the origins of libraries, but most clusters comprised books specially guarded or removed from casual inspection or books collectively buried – instead of being destroyed – in veneration of inscribed sacred words. This guides our history of one such ancient treasury found buried in the palaces of Nineveh (modern Kuyunjik), comprising more than 30,000 cuneiform tablets and fragments of historical, epistolary, legal, divinatory, medical, literary and lexical inscriptions. Known as the library of Ashurbanipal, King of Assyria (*c*.668–630 BCE), and promoted as the oldest surviving royal library in the world, it is now at the centre of the most extensive investigation and public access since its rediscovery in 1850. In 2002, in cooperation with the University of Mosul in Iraq, and by use of digital technology, the British Library established the Ashurbanipal Library Project to introduce new readers to the contents of this ancient treasury of books. Such bureaucratic, religious and literary loot is firmly rooted in a militaristic state apparently anxious to control, if not censor, certain types of learning that ensured imperial success.

Libraries, book accumulation and the very notion of books recording things were resisted in many parts of the world. Scholars of early Indian and South Asian culture have long emphasized that belief in the spiritual efficacy of oral transmission, together with the sophisticated application of memorizing, explain why early teachers of the Vedas, the Sutras and Jaina scriptures rejected any idea of preserving texts in written form. The great Indian epic, the *Mahabharata*, despatches 'the writers of the Vedas', along with their sellers and mispronouncers, to hell. Nevertheless, by about the ninth century CE, Hindu, Buddhist and Jain elites all began to accept the utility of the graphic record. Disputes over the teachings of the Buddha and the devastation of a great famine weakening oral transmission have been given as two reasons for both Buddhists and the Jainas to create books of doctrine and to store them. And in the late twelfth century when the armies of the Muslim Muhammad Ghuri destroyed temples, monasteries and whole cities of northern India, followers of the Vedic cult also began written transcription of the Vedas to ensure preservation. In early India, manuscript collections accumulated at royal libraries, in addition to major royal publication projects and artisan scribal workshops like those at the monastic centres of Nalanda and Vikramasila (in modern Bengal). The libraries included the twenty-one established by Kumarapala (King of Gujarat, 1143–72) in the 'knowledge warehouses' of the Jainature and at other Buddhist monasteries.

Such writings were protected treasures, just as the ancient Ashurbanipal tablets were never meant to be borrowed or indeed publicly consulted. If the motives for the collection of these hoards have been correctly gauged, then they also suggest the active suppression and destruction of writings. Such devastation, caused by succession struggles and retribution as well as by rival regimes and enemies, again highlights the importance to historians of the book of appreciating loss. Similarly, and allied to destruction in terms of deliberate burial, the genizah, from the Hebrew הזינג for storage, developed as a separate area and then room of a Jewish synagogue or cemetery. The genizah usually served as a temporary storage location for discarded or worn-out Hebrew-language books and papers on religious topics prior to proper cemetery burial. Although there is great disagreement about this, the Dead Sea Scrolls, which are almost all Jewish religious texts and passages of Hebrew as well as translations into Greek and

Aramaic, might have been deposited over many generations as a genizah of cast-off holy texts too sacred to destroy. Similar deposits, such as those recovered from the Qubbah or mausoleum of the Great Mosque in Damascus, reveal linguistic roots in past cultures. The survival of materials meant to be occasional and often reused offers precious insight into the normal and the everyday, but differential rates of decay and damage between materials remain problematic. They remind us that the evidence offered by the book is often challenging and subtle.

Scholarship about Western libraries is particularly extensive, exploring many different aspects of private, commercial and public libraries as well as the ecclesiastical, institutional and university foundations that replaced medieval monastic libraries and that sometimes during the Reformation and the Enlightenment appropriated their books. The pioneering work of Sears Jayne in identifying catalogues, inventories, donations and household account books and booksellers' records has been extended by the ongoing Private Libraries in Renaissance England (PLRE) project. Different ways of hoarding or displaying test our use of the word 'private' for these activities. Different spaces used to contain and consult books make the word 'library' problematic. In this, as well as in later, more celebrated periods of book lust, the placing of the book collection or collections within houses, or moving between houses, forces us to think more widely about the relationship between books, their owners and their households. Truly public libraries were rare and always restricted in some way in Europe and its colonies before the mid-nineteenth century.

In China, before that time, no public libraries existed at all. Indeed, the sharing of knowledge through book collections was uncommon, offering an opportunity for book historians to ask comparative questions and explain why book collecting and sharing became so common among educated men and women in Europe between 1500 and 1850. Such investigation is further suggestive of the differing social support for scientific and humanist knowledge in Europe and China. A comparative global history of libraries furthers the understanding of knowledge creation and circulation but also forces a rethinking of the book in society – of acquisition, of the ideas of value and canon and of what a book culture might look like.

Cautions and Precepts

The recovery of the 'what' challenges a number of given precepts, supplementing ideas of a 'canon' and encouraging much greater discernment in our descriptive analysis of the impact of books, of which misuse of 'print culture' is a leading example. As noted, by a new understanding of what was published, circulated and critically well received at the time, we review what a literary canon might mean. Research has flourished on medieval manuscripts that are far removed from those of the 'canonical authors', breaching the boundaries of medieval English and French literary studies in particular. Such work contributes to the questioning of accepted canons, also unsettled by the identification of republication rates, edition sizes and movements within second-hand markets. Bibliographical listings of specific annual publications, including review references, also confirm the existence of books no longer surviving. A certain fissure separates those who believe that book history breaks down barriers between the products of genius and popular trash, and those who (for explicable reasons) resist such a muddying of critical standards and judgement. The failing comes when 'literature' is applied hastily or inconsistently to studies in the history of the book.

Histories of the European novel are particularly susceptible to this challenge, where some contributors have not been essentially concerned with literary form, and notably the 'formal realism' and 'narrative procedures' that Ian Watt advanced as the distinguishing feature of the novel. It is possible to construct a history that explores the management of the appeal of these publications and the entrepreneurship that advanced a product identified in its own time as a 'novel'. It becomes a moot question whether a cultural historian can refer to these 'novel' productions as 'literature'. The quest to understand how great writing came about sometimes rests uneasily with the interest of many cultural historians in the broader history of printing, publishing and print dissemination and reception. Brean Hammond, following Clifford Siskin, defines literature as 'professional imaginative writing', his starting point being the writer of talent and his or her lasting literary legacy.⁹ Many have little interest, for its own sake, in the broader commercial history of books and novels. As George Justice writes, 'I follow Siskin in using the capitalized form of "Literature" to describe a cultural realm solidified when the literary tradition and contemporary writers encounter, manipulate, and use print technology in the literary marketplace'.¹⁰ Yet commercial and technological advance brought not only a surge in the production of novels and their translations, but surprising developments in their valuation. In *The Function of Criticism*, Terry Eagleton writes of the early eighteenth century:

> Criticism here is not yet 'literary' but 'cultural': the examination of literary texts is one relatively marginal moment of a broader enterprise which explores attitudes to servants and the rules of gallantry, the status of women and familial affections, the purity of the English language, the character of conjugal love, the psychology of the sentiments and the laws of the toilet.¹¹

A quite different caution concerns the term 'print culture', an expression useful as a shorthand for connected propositions but often bandied about with little thought. The impact of the printing press is best seen as part of a broader history of human communication, in which the nature of 'printedness' spans many activities and in which printing amplified, enabled and even transformed existing practices and behaviours, not in isolation but in relation to other agencies and practices. Significantly, the exceptional Tokyo Printing Museum invites 'study of printing culture' rather than 'print culture'. And as Harold Love long ago pronounced, ' "Print culture", configured as a consciousness independent of individual acts of apprehension, is a kind of supernatural entity which, like other supernatural entities, we are driven to invoke in times of perplexity.'¹² Nicolas Barker is even blunter: 'When people talk of "print culture" I wish I had a revolver to reach for.'¹³

The first point to make is that 'print culture' is about more than books, more even than books, periodicals and newspapers. It is about all products of the press, of print considered in the widest remit, and indeed in relation to script and image, and notably maps, charts and varied engraved items. Above all, jobbing – or non-book – printing proved the financial mainstay of the vast majority of printers, and yet it remains relatively neglected by historians of 'print culture'. There are two broad hidden histories here: that of job printing in the printing house, and that of job printing in social and economic change. As Daniel Roche, Peter Stallybrass and others have shown, the creation of an expanding and highly inventive and flexible range of part-printed forms, documents, tickets, certificates and 'blanks' is a stimulating but far from straightforward study in understanding the making of the modern world. Historians of 'print culture' should pause over examples cited by Paul Needham and Clive Griffin of the non-survival of vast numbers of indulgences ordered from the great European printing houses. There is every reason to suppose, however, that there is an even greater archival loss, or rather burial, of records relating to jobbing work involved in commercial and financial transactions.

The second point to make is that small items of print further challenge boundaries between the printed and the written. The 'authority' so long held to be a singular characteristic of the printed text that replaced the scribal text has to be recast when one considers that it is the *written* mark or signature that actually confers authority on a pre-printed blank form, be it marriage certificate or insurance docket. Printers' jobbing work recast the production, material form and reception of everyday knowledge, reshaping intimate, private worlds and human relationships. Individuals and groups were bound, freed and defined by printed and by filled-in forms of understanding and obligation, but the relationship between the written and the printed also reshapes our idea of printedness.

Compounding this, Peter Beale and Harold Love wrote persuasively about the failure of historians of European printing to notice the continuing circulation of manuscripts in the early modern and modern age. More recently, Margaret Ezell, Alexandra Gillespie and Daniel Wakelin have urged further exploration of the development of printing *alongside* developments in manuscript production, just as manuscript culture remained very much alive in China even after the spread of woodblock printing. In this context, 'print culture' also disguises resistances and significance, most notably where some Chinese scholars such as Tsuen-hsuin Tsien argue that rather than there being a print revolution in China, the arrival of printing only reinforced an already bookish Chinese culture, strengthening government control by encouraging conformity to state orthodoxy.

Similarly, in Islamic lands the esteem given to manuscript books and the primacy of calligraphy in transcribing the Qu'ran and other holy texts delayed the acceptance of printed books, even though block printing of talismanic scrolls and amulets had advanced since medieval times. Jews and Christians resident in the Ottoman territories also printed after about 1500, and more soon came to accept the advantages of more rapid dissemination by print. The Hungarian convert Ibrahim Müteferrika was the first Muslim to establish a printing press, at Istanbul in 1727, but the continued respect for calligraphy ensured high values for manuscripts. In Asia generally, the collectors of books depended on copyists to supply important missing items, while poor scholars and students often copied works they could not afford to buy. Like scribes in other religious groups, Buddhist disciples notably copied sutras to express their faith. Village craftsmen, physicians and geomancers used manuscript to retain their secrets. Scriptures of popular religious organizations were usually manuscripts, as these organizations were interested in limiting circulation and keeping them secret.

The relative failure of print in colonial Asia before the mid-nineteenth century has long been a puzzle, given the introduction of the letterpress to the Indian subcontinent by Jesuits in 1556. Modern historians of India have suggested that print was rejected because of bazaar writer monopolies, religious ritual and local rulers' objections, and difficulties encountered by lithographers in rendering Persian and other scripts. Christopher Bayly, in his groundbreaking study of empire and information, adopted the idea, initially for northern India, of the 'ecumene' to describe unified communities of thought and communication. This was a world in which handwritten texts conveyed discussion of politics and religion, rights and duties, reinforcing traditional oral recitation. Discussants included the non-literate but also the 'literacy-aware' audiences of 'butchers, flower-sellers, bazaar merchants and artisans'. As Ajay Skaria, Mark Frost and others have shown, the cultural and political debate that predated print persisted in conjunction with printing technologies into the age of nationalism. In what is an important refinement of the 'print capitalism' developed by Benedict Anderson as part of his explication of imagined communities, the concept of the ecumene reveals a highly effective information order in which strategically placed written media reinforced a powerful culture of oral communication. The conclusion, which should make many book historians pause, is that printing by itself is largely redundant as a transformative force until very late in colonial rule.

5
Reading

We reach the most significant and challenging dimension of the history of books and the particular understanding of their reading. In the late 1980s, Jon Klancher claimed that 'audience' remained 'the most unexamined assumption in the armoury of cultural history and criticism'.[1] Increasingly, however, book history deepened audience and reception research by asking not just who read and what they read, but when people read, where they read and, above all, how and why they read.

Study of the reception of books and reading practices, the fourth and fifth of Lasswell's questions 'to whom?' and 'with what effect?', extends horizons in social and intellectual history. An investigation of reading contributes to our appreciation of how individuals in the past thought about and responded to the world around them – in effect, a *histoire des mentalités*. Bibliographical research remains indispensable to understanding the origination, distribution and transformative potential of the material text, but ultimately book history counts for historians when it concerns the history of the ways in which individuals read books, were affected by or acted upon their reading, or participated in practices and rituals involving books. By study of the reception of the various material forms of books and their texts, the history of the book is properly concerned with the recovery of past human memory, behaviour and experience.

The historical recovery of individual acts of reception draws upon both inter- and extra-textual research strategies. These are various. Studies of the intended reader as perceived by the author parallel reception theory based on an implicit idea of the reader in the text. Other studies relate aspects of the material text, including its morphology, orthography, typography and the presentation of illustrations and page and other design, to the written and often scribbled comments of readers (or 'marginalia') and other evidence of the use of the book. An often circumstantial but supporting understanding of reading competences, pedagogical methods and the phenomenology of cognitive procedures derives from investigation of many different types of historical sources. In addition, book historians continue to explore contemporary representations of reading practice and its consequences, written, drawn and, in modern times, filmed and recorded. Some of this testimony is deliberate, some incidental, some by observers, some by readers themselves.

There are many unknowns – and especially the earlier that any reading history is attempted. What we can tell about reading from cuneiform texts or even Roman wax tablets seems highly limited, although some of the strategies described, from occasional incidental reports about reading to images of reading from murals, paintings or illustrated texts, are applicable to premodern and medieval materials. But silences abound. Even the suggestion that text rubbings were taken of inscriptions on stelae and other carved monuments in Mesoamerica and South Asia, for example, begs the question of whether such rubbings were 'read' or put to more symbolic use such as to ward off evil or to celebrate a pilgrimage to the site. The reading of Central and South American khuipus as mnemonic aids drew on oral traditions, but parallels the memorizing of printed histories and the production of printed aids to ritualized recall in other parts of the world.

Literary scholars have debated the extent to which literary history and historicist approaches have been inattentive to the precise interaction between text and external context, and why this matters. Robert Hume has insisted that the meaning of texts 'is actuated only in readers or audiences' and he has warned, on the one hand, of disappointing interplay between cultural history and reader response theory and, on the other hand, of the limited consideration of audience and reception by many declared literary historians. David Simpson has counselled a return to the basics of historical research to advance historicist textual interpretation. Hume concludes that 'the historicist needs to be committed to the construction of a complex model from [historical] contextual (not purely literary) evidence'.[2]

All this is easier said than done, and especially so as histories of books pursue more challenging temporal and geographical horizons. In 1984 Janice Radway transformed the history of reading practices by her study of the response to popular romances in New England. Radway brought fresh conviction to the notion of 'popular', adapting oral history techniques to learn more about individual reading habits and responses to literary narratives. She argued that romance novels are 'the end products of a much-mediated, highly complex, material, and social process that involves writers, literary agents, publishing officials, and editors, as well as hundreds of other people who participate in the manufacture, distribution, and selling of books.' Radway further concluded that 'reading is not a self-conscious, productive process in which [readers] collaborate with the author, but an act of discovery during which they...accept without question the accuracy of all statements about a character's personality or the implications of an event'.[3] Such evidence is not available for most historians asking questions about long-dead recipients of texts, however many different, if partial and oblique, sources are available. The further result of Radway's study is to caution against making easy assumptions about the meaning of reception. Historians attempting to recover the diversity of past reading experiences must confront the identification and comparison of reading sites, reading competences and habits, and readers' own recognition of what and why they were reading.

The difficulties of evidence and interpretation aside, optimists outlined ambitious objectives. Michel de Certeau, one of the most creative advocates of cultural history, believed that many historians had appeared more concerned with calculating the correlations between objects read, social groups, and places frequented, than with analysing the very operation of reading, its modalities and its phenomenology. The crucial insistence of subsequent study was that texts cannot control response: rather, response derives from social circumstances which imbue every text with a certain instability rather than a predictable fixity. Following from this, histories of readers and reading were transformed by research aimed less at identifying numbers and types of readers, or at estimating literacy levels and the several types of text read, than at understanding reading practices, the nature of reading and the experience of the individual reader. The attention formerly given to the receivers and the received was transferred to the processes of reception and to an analysis of past reading strategies and competences.

Theoretically, past and present readerships could also be conceptualized not simply as aggregates of types of reader, but as the accumulation of many unique readings and therefore as the totality of different readings of the same text. Such an aggregation of past experiences is patently historically irrecoverable and cannot be applied in practical terms to book history and especially not to its global reach. Nonetheless, such an envisaging is helpful in encouraging us first to think carefully about the approach to understanding the experience of receiving a particular type of text and, second, to investigate the sorts of evidence upon which this new reception and reading history might draw. In many ways, case-by-case contextualization parallels revisions to the practice of textual criticism and bibliography already discussed. The pursuit of reading practice is embedded in the particular, in the microstudy and in the archivally and interpretationally challenging.

According to other, supportive criticism, different modalities of reception depended upon both the phenomenology of acts of reading and the culturally constructed means of receiving and understanding what was read. In particular, Paul Ricoeur considered how the figuration of a world was appropriated by readers and viewers of texts and pictures, while the construct of 'interpretive communities' (adopting the American 'interpretive' rather than 'interpretative') became a *sine qua non* of many late twentieth-century histories of textual reception. First proposed as a rhetorical, in-the-text presence by Stanley Fish, suggesting a collectivity of reading conventions, the notion of interpretive communities was given a more historical formulation by Roger Chartier, as groups of readers sharing the same style of reading and the same identifiable strategy of interpretation. Robert Hume's call to investigate 'historical reader-response groups' bears striking resemblance to this, and aimed, in his words, to be 'a kind of historicization of Stanley Fish'.[4] Such approaches paralleled the strategy proposed by Hans Robert Jauss and his group at Konstanz to understand the 'horizon of expectations' within which a work was created and received. The decoding of this reading experience, in which readers effectively create rather than receive texts, embraces study of diverse reading sites, different performative modes, including individual or communal reading aloud, and multiple effects upon auditors and participants. Texts foster unintentional meanings, which are, in effect, codes of perception ordered and enacted by individual readers.

Identifying Readers

Most historical studies of readers begin with the 'what', the identification of relevant materials, whether cuneiform tablets or printed newspapers and comic books. Bespoke books, those commissioned and created for a particular client, are most obviously mapped onto particular readers, but even here, as recent classical and medieval studies have demonstrated, it is all too easy to make false assumptions about who actually read custom-made texts. Where production was more commercial and market focused, a readership has been commonly defined by the type of literature read – or believed to have been read. Such a readership might be defined by literary content or more broadly by literary genre or form. It might be limited to a readership for a particular author or genre or defined according to the style of its publication and physical presentation. For reading history, the contrast between publishing in Asia and Europe also carries profound implications. The basic structural difference of book production, with most Asian books before modern times issued as private and bespoke copies, makes certain book-trade-based research strategies misleading and even redundant.

The further perspective is that of the construction by writers and editors of many specified or implied readerships within their texts, and associated references in advertisements, catalogues and the like. Many authors and compilers also tried to address multiple audiences, both explicitly and implicitly. Declarations to intended audiences are as old as books themselves, from cuneiform to papyrus, and their study is an important contribution to contextual study of medieval manuscripts. A short address in a colophon, title-page or preface, and more significantly, the advance of market-oriented productions rather than bespoke items with predetermined readers or audiences, spawned a plethora of addresses and pleas to projected readers. By the late seventeenth century, many designations from European printers and booksellers were highly specific. Some composed long lists of potential readers defined by gender, age, profession, interest, location, ability or skill. Perhaps because of this avalanche of material, relatively few studies address textually inscribed readerships of this kind, despite the advance in electronic cataloguing and retrieval possibilities. More commonly, research about such obviously projected readerships is embedded within larger histories of the social, economic or political groups to which these publications so explicitly appeal. Evidence ranges from title-page ascription to the subtlest of innuendo, requiring attention to the circumstances of writing and production, and sensitivity to irony, other rhetorical devices and knowledge taken for granted by the writer. Some authorial constructions of a readership claimed a group identity, by activity or by composition, while others were no more than assumed aggregates.

A much stronger historical tradition is the investigation of the production and distribution of print to provide general indicators of changing readerships. Numerous histories of the commercial chapbook, broadside, newspaper, part-issue, novel and magazine underpin assumptions about the numbers, gender, age and other types of reader. The increase in female readers, and calibrations within those readerships, has, for example, been inferred from the increased production of books and periodicals specifically designated for women. Examples include the *Ladies Mercury*, begun in London in 1693, the later *Ladies' Magazine* and its American equivalent similarly titled from 1792, and as celebrated in Germany, the magazine *Bibliothek der Frauenfrage* from 1888. Such understanding of reading from what was read requires some identification of the contemporary popularity of texts rather than studying those selected by modern canonical or heuristic criteria, and here the STCs and indexes of periodicals have provided invaluable indexes of title counts. It is also exactly by the use of these sources for readership evaluation, however, that we need to be reminded that the market for and the circulation of books require separate mapping from that of production figures for new titles and especially for new periodicals. In Europe, particularly, edition size varied, affecting the relative popularity of titles, while manuscript circulation thrived in the age of printing. The second-hand book market was diverse and expansive, and imports, particularly during the sixteenth and seventeenth centuries, were, for example, the mainstay of the scholarly English book market. Above all, access to reading involved far more than the buying of new productions.

Texts themselves influenced how people thought about how they read or ought to read, and what consequences would follow from their efforts. As Kathryn Sutherland has written, 'how we read (from paper or screen, from smartphone or iPad, in snippets or holistically) has consequences for what we make of what we read and for what we write. Changing publishing models affect us all.'[5] In the last hundred years of the dominance of the manual printing press, for example, the sensitivity of readers to categorization of readers and reading increased. The quickening production of texts included a multiplication of smaller formats across a range of literature. With the increased portability of texts, the sites for the reading of print – especially for shared and formalized reading occasions – increased and attracted much greater consideration and comment. In turn, this reinforced identifications of intentionalist reading groups, many confirming religious, occupational or single-sex profiles, where reading circles claimed particular books at hand and pursued particular reading practices. Many varieties of text were now aimed at these groups. In each of these an author, editor, scribe or compositor attempted, in effect, to impose control over the construal of a particular text, and the forms of reading within new sites and new types of reading groups were in varying degrees policed by new forms of textual emphasis and subtly embedded directions. Critical reviews offered reading protocols and attempted to regulate reading practices. Faster turnround of texts, notably of newspapers and magazines, also gave greater significance to the speed of reading about an event or notice and to the time of the day when the text was read.

Some centuries earlier, European readers and reading multiplied with the development of the carrying trade, provincial retailing, coffee houses, book clubs and circulating libraries. Books were acquired by gift and inheritance, direct purchase, as a result of subscription and by borrowing from a collection, private or commercial. Inventories or the sales catalogues of bookshops and, from the late seventeenth century, book auctions provide simple guides to reading tastes. The most useful list the quantities of particular titles either sold or remaining in stock. Study of individual early coffee houses and journals and books marked as belonging to them invite new reader histories such as those by Markman Ellis investigating copies of pamphlets from coffee houses. For the hundreds of later coffee houses, debating societies and even libraries where heads of households borrowed books and periodicals, however, there can be little agreement about the appropriate multiplier required to estimate readerships of newspapers and other shared texts. Subscription schemes, enabling the advance collection of financing for a book, were particularly popular in England and France from the late seventeenth century. Most books published by subscription carried printed subscriber lists with the sex, titles and, in many cases, the addresses and even the professions of supporters; but the lists must be treated with caution. There is no control to determine their accuracy, and many subscriptions were launched for specialist works or destitute authors. Like the few business records surviving, the subscription lists also tell us nothing about the motives for buying or borrowing and nothing about how exactly the books were read.

Much more generally, we are left to reflect that the number of books and pamphlets read – as well as those merely borrowed – was increased by private proprietary and subscription libraries, and a greater popular impact was achieved by the mid nineteenth-century advance of public libraries and the libraries of working men's clubs and similar institutions. In some places, public libraries succeeded more restrictive town library foundations. By then, commercial circulating libraries had also popularized reading, even though many such libraries and clubs were comparatively costly to join. Many people encountered new literature only as a result of borrowing from circulating libraries.

Given the invisibility of readers in most publishing, bookshop and even library records, a more reader-centred strategy is required. 'At-risk readerships'[6] might be constructed according to known characteristics of potential readers and their likelihood of acquiring books. This strategy becomes highly speculative for ancient societies, yet attainable, in different ways, for medieval Europe and Asia. Many studies of literacy attempt quantification based on evidence about writing skills. Yet even in early modern and modern Europe, the derivation of levels of sign literacy from occasional special censuses, wills, marriage registers or other official documents is highly problematic, either because of the extreme specificity of surviving sources or because the interdependency of the skills of reading and writing cannot be taken for granted. Reading – however characterized – is taken to have been a more common practice than writing. Many who could not write, or did not see why they should sign official papers, especially if their husbands marked, might certainly have had simple reading skills. Nevertheless, it is evidence of writing competence that has generally been the basis for the classification of literacy by profiles of age, gender, social status, wealth, occupation, religion, linguistic group or place of residence.

Different types of reading skill derive from pedagogical conditions, instructional methods and broader influences on textual access and acquisition. Some of the specific exertions of medieval and early modern tutors, as shown by Stephen Orgel, can be glimpsed from rare marginalia in schoolbooks, primers, bibles and prayer books. Motivations, religious and secular, have been the focus of much debate, and for some, commerce rather than religion acts as the prime motor to literacy. Certainly, pioneering work on the usage of numbers and the history of 'quantitative thought' is particularly suggestive and further questions simple polarities between literacy and non-literacy and also between literacy in different languages and dialects by the same reader. It is often better to acknowledge literacies rather than literacy. We have to rethink our appraisal of reading by considering not how many were reading texts, even a particular text, and not just the contingent circumstances of differences of gender and age, wealth, occupation, and religious and educational background, but how we categorize the different ways in which people were able or chose to read. The cultural and social resources of particular readers are not just grounded in economic circumstances but range across characteristics of aptitude, qualification, attitude and intention.

As an example of the interaction of the different variables, the case of the transformation of reading in Russia is illuminating. As Gary Marker has shown, in the kingdom of Muscovy the first printing press arrived in the late 1550s, only to fall rapidly under the control of the state-supported Russian Orthodox Church, so that by the end of the eighteenth century only one major publishing house had been set up in Moscow. Other presses were imported by modernizing Russian rulers, but their activity was frustrated by limited demand in a country with stubbornly low levels of literacy. Over the entire seventeenth century, Russian imprint production amounted to fewer than 500 titles, usually issued in runs of between 1,200 and 2,400 copies. The mass circulation of state-published alphabets and school primers by the twentieth century, however, has been the subject of contextualizing histories by Vadim Volkov and others. Their studies question the quality of literacy, especially in relation to numeracy and a range of other considerations which challenge any easy notion of what 'literacy' was. India offers an even greater challenge in relating its enduring low rate of print literacy not simply to the relative expense of book production and traditional practices of passing texts privately from teacher to pupil, generation after generation, but also to other literacies of text recognition. Foremost was the astonishing nineteenth-century advance of lithography and type-created publication in a dozen or more indigenous languages.

From the earliest times, the constraints of commissioning and acquiring and purchasing power were even greater than those of literacy, and even general calculations of the production costs of books suggest a powerful limitation upon the 'at risk' audience. In later and more commercial markets in the West, the price of books remained the major constraint. In early modern Europe but also in nineteenth- and early twentieth-century Europe and America many labourers and servants who might well have boasted modest reading skills were prevented from reading very much – certainly very much new literature – by the meagreness of their purse. The one qualification to this is the development of cheap print organizations, particularly religious charities, and most significantly of all, missionary societies and other organizations distributing books. Studies of such organizations in early nineteenth-century Britain, the antebellum United States, interwar Central Europe and modern South Africa, among others, also allow identification of further divisions in intended and 'at risk' reading groups by gender, ethnicity and age.

More significant for histories of reading by individuals are those records of sale or loans which detail specific clients. The records of bookshops, usually with more random custom than libraries, are also illuminating. The business ledgers of the Clay family, and in particular of John Clay, bookseller of Daventry, have featured in one debate between Jan Fergus and John Feather about the eighteenth-century provincial English book trade and its readers. Of individual sales records, further attention has been given to surviving ledgers of the late eighteenth-century London partnership of Hookham and Carpenter, but such business records are a rarity, and where they do survive, samples are often small. Surviving borrowing records range from those of the Vatican library from the fifteenth century to numerous cathedral libraries through the eighteenth and nineteenth centuries. Of other prominent subscription libraries, 77 ledgers survive from the Bristol Library Society, 1773–1857, where the earliest five volumes alone record 13,467 withdrawals of 900 titles between 1773 and 1784. Even so, such borrowing volumes are highly individual, as, for example, are the surviving circulation records from universities and colleges such as those of the Bodleian in Oxford from 1647 or from Tartu University library in Estonia, 1692–1707, Lyon public library in France 1899–1911, various North American society and subscription libraries from the late eighteenth century and during the nineteenth century, and small, fragmentary registers such as that of Witham parish library in Essex from about 1751. The What Middletown Read searchable database has been constructed from the circulation records of the Muncie Public Library in Indiana which document almost every book borrowed and its borrower 1891–1902. The Dissenting Academies Project includes an online searchable database of students' and tutors' loan records surviving between 1720 and 1860. The most notable feature of such records, however, is the serendipity of survival and the often narrow time span. Certain types of library may be comparable, but there is no representative type of library, with or without surviving usage records.

The further obvious but also problematic method of identifying readers is by direct evidence of individual book ownership, ranging from personal records to probate inventories gathered after the death of their owners. Inventories, post-mortem or taken during life, are often very general, however, often listing a number of books rather than specific titles, and it remains impossible to know whether such books were read and by whom without further corroboration. Such evidence might be found from reading references in diaries, letters and essays. Whether or not related to other sources, such references have been commonly used to speculate about the circulation of books and a general increase in those reading. The more difficult problem is that all memoirs of individual readers and of their contemporary observers beg particular questions about the subjectivity of the individual record. As will be discussed, we have to ask why the memoirs or observations were written and take heed of the special unreliability of anecdotal recall and self-justification. The most obvious control for this is the gathering of multiple case-studies of readers, and the use of the personal account – whether by reader or reader observer – in conjunction with other evidence and approaches. By such comparative work the history of reading is better aligned with the evidence of use left by actual readers. The further challenge is, then, to translate what we know of the circumstances in which a text was read to an understanding of the processes of reception.

Recovering Reading Practices

As a mental process, reading is a highly individualistic and culturally conditioned interpretation of written or printed signs – and also of much more. Skills are not independent. The ways of reading a picture, a building or even a landscape are transferable and cumulative. In different situations as well as in simple, direct comparison, variants in impressing or marking styles, in typefaces and in page layouts might invite radically different responses to the same sign and word. Responses vary between media, although much remains underexplored. In the centuries of print, for example, the relationship between the reading of printed and of handwritten letters was often problematic. Various suggestions have been made about both bifurcated and overlapping readerships according to the popularity of black-letter (also known as Gothic script, Gothic minuscule, or textura, used throughout Western Europe from the mid-twelfth century) and then roman and other type and script from the seventeenth and eighteenth centuries. There were also many further points of contact, from experiments in mock-script typography to the laborious copying of type forms in manuscript letters and simple book ownership labels.

Attempts to distinguish modes of reading have invited bold and fruitful assertions. Some have pointed to the replacement of communal, vocalized reading practices by silent internalized reading as both a reflection and an agent of change. In Paul Saenger's evaluation, the triumph of silent reading by the late fifteenth century resulted from the long-term historical development of writing with word separation and encouraged enhanced privacy and isolation. For printed books and periodicals circulating three centuries later, Rolf Engelsing identified a shift from intensive to extensive modes of reading. His influential argument was that less intensive and more partial and eclectic reading increased as a much broader range of printed materials became available.

In a parallel study, Anne McLaren has suggested that a new type of reactive, speedier and more selective reading and reading public developed in late Ming (sixteenth-century) China in response to new types of book. She argues that a new rhetoric of reading developed where the deep, 'intensive' reading of the Confucian Classics contrasted with a lighter vernacular reading. Like Engelsing's, this proposition is textually led, where expositions, encyclopaedias and the like are held to encourage *du* 讀, serious, 'deep' reading appropriate to Classics, histories and scholarship, at the expense of the *kan* 看, 'looking at' or 'viewing', suitable for vernacular works of fiction, drama and imaginative productions (appearing in print in large numbers only from the late sixteenth century). Those producing these texts introduced a new rhetoric of reading based on an 'extensive, discontinuous reading of an accessible, attractive text with a clear practical or didactic message'.⁷ Memorization, however, remained common and invites further parallels with changes in Europe, and what has been characterized as *lan* 覽, the 'surveying' of illustrations, opens up important new avenues for comparative research. Analysis of the history of different reading approaches in Asia is in its infancy.

'Study', as both McLaren and Daniel Gardner have emphasized, involved an intense and exhaustive process of memorization and recitation that allowed the student to make the text their own. Zhu Xi 朱熹, the late twelfth-century philosopher, described this recitative method as applied to the reading of the Confucian Classics and underpinning moral instruction. Zhu incorporated interlinear commentaries to reveal greater textual meaning, a guidance to reading practice that was replicated over successive generations, fixing a stylized form of 'interrupted' reading and learning. Such commentary allowed editors, authors and readers to shape and reshape the meaning of texts, while subtler deliberate changes in recopying over the centuries might be used to similar effect. This dialogic engagement with the text guided readers' interpretation in a manner akin to the reading and recitation of textual apparatus in medieval and early modern books in Europe. Just like classical and medieval European pedagogues, until the close of the Qing dynasty, Chinese schoolmasters taught their charges to recite the text of the Classics through memorization and before any meaning was construed.

Decoding of marginalia further reveals how texts, written and printed, precisely relate to readers' writing, glossing, correcting, reminding, emphasizing, arguing – cases in which reading constitutes an active and sometimes adversarial engagement with the book. Such research is much more advanced in Europe and the Americas than in Asia, although a study of anonymous marginalia defacing copies of the *Analects* of Confucius during the Cultural Revolution has gained some attention. Such evidence, partial and often serendipitous as survivals, reinforces the instability or perplexity in the reading process, encouraging misreadings and unexpected reactions. It also highlights motivations – a 'transactional reading' strategy brilliantly extended by the investigation by Anthony Grafton and Lisa Jardine of the marginalia of the writer Gabriel Harvey to reconstruct his programmatic reading of his 1555 copy of Livy between the early 1570s and the 1590s.[8] Successive studies by Grafton, William Sherman and others have exposed a rich reading recovery history, where singular reading experiences can also demonstrate similarities between readers and reading and annotating conventions and tropes. Marginalia are often difficult to decipher. Stephen Orgel, for example, using his own collection of late medieval and early modern annotated books, wrestles with small, only partly legible scrawls, baffling contractions of Latin and ancient vernacular and dialect musings.[9] He, like Grafton, does so to offer revealing insights into what individual readers learnt from books, how they reacted to particular passages and how they misread or eccentrically interpreted others. Orgel considers the mediation and quality of pedagogic practice, with an especially telling account of a teacher's interpolation of homoerotic passages in Virgil that contested contemporary humanist attempts to explain away the unacceptable.

Book usage, of course, need not correspond to what is generally regarded as reading. Exploration of historical reading practice is complicated by ritual attendant to an object whose reading is implied but not undertaken. Sometimes, individuals and institutions acquired books for reasons quite unrelated to reading. Books might be unread representations of faith, respectability or solidarity, critical to social and political display or religious ritual. As noted, Japanese men and women first encountered printing in a style known as 'hanga', woodblock printing intimately connected to belief, emotion and prayer and where the chanting accompanying its ritualized production and subsequent display as preventative shaman remained far more important than any reading of it. The kissing of the Bible in early modern and indeed modern Europe, to give a further example, offered a source of authority or talismanic protection. Clasped and cushioned or even carried on top of a pole, the adoration of the closed text contrasted with what David Cressy calls the English 'unsentimental, utilitarian attitude toward ordinary books'.[10]

Following from this, histories of 'publication', as the issuing of a text in whatever medium, must allow for a very broad interpretation of intended social functions, even before consideration of unintended functions. The spiralling output of printed books from the late eighteenth century through the twentieth century relates not only to an increase in the number of purchasers and, we infer, readers, but also from greater purchasing by those already buying books. Institutional and private library demand created greater potential for the stacking of unread books, a phenomenon often overlooked in studies relating readers to book production totals, but offering a different cultural history of book accumulation and symbolic authority. From the late seventeenth century, a more secular veneration of books transferred to new locales around the world, even though we might not at first recognize this. The establishment of private and public libraries, household collections and missionary donations presented with new potency the idea of books as the massed ranks of knowledge, status and conformity, outward or not. With this developed perceptions of 'reading' as an activity differentiated from simple reverence, even in physiological terms. Examples ranged from the medical effects of excessive or ill-reading, to the correct way to digest information and approach what was now commonly seen as the problematic deluge of print.

Accordingly, new assumptions were made about the permanence and authority of print, and many readers practised self-classification according to the activities and the aims of those engaged in reading. Correspondence, in particular, records how readers perceived themselves within groups seeking practical guidance, engaged in scholarship or religious devotion, as self-improving readerships, readerships interested only in entertainment, or ones, as many working-class autobiographies insist, interested primarily in 'discovery'. Timing and site also featured. An evening readership or a morning readership is perhaps most obviously associated with European newspapers, which first used this distinction in the eighteenth century, but it is also identifiable with particular works of devotion and particular bookish practices.

In such ways, differences between public or private reading are both more fundamental and more various than has been appreciated, and in turn, have a direct effect upon particular reading strategies. The difficulties of subjective reading records have already been noted, but many historians have attempted to identify shared perspectives from accumulated confessions of reading. Such studies include Margaret Spufford's pioneering analysis of 141 seventeenth-century spiritual autobiographies, David Vincent's examination of the autobiographies of 142 working-class readers in nineteenth-century Britain and Jonathan Rose's wide-ranging extrapolation of the intellectual life of those readers in the same period. Combinations of different types of record yield extended profiles of reading activity, such as Paul Benhamou's investigation of *cabinets des lectures*, or reading rooms, and Elizabeth McHenry's recovery of the reading history of African American library societies, as well as the magisterial studies of Richard Sher and Mark Towsey for Enlightenment Britain and North America.

As the innovative Reading Experience Database (RED) also establishes, certain parts of a book might be read, serial or intermittent reading might follow different routes through a text on different occasions, the number of participating readers and auditors might change according to venue or season, and there might be many variations to the manner in which a book was read aloud or in silence, in company or in solitude. RED currently hosts over 30,000 instances of written or printed 'recorded engagement with a written or printed text – beyond the mere fact of possession' by British subjects and visitors to the British Isles between 1450 and 1945. RED has also spawned similar database initiatives in Australia, Canada, the Netherlands and New Zealand. All suggest that as more books circulated, places of reading became more sensitive. A reader's permanent residential or professional location was contrasted with a readership when in the country, on military campaign, at the racecourse, in church, in the sedan chair, on the commode or in the barbershop. As a particularly striking example, Bill Bell's examination of reading on board ships offers a history in which site and purpose are critical to reading experience.

Reading practice might therefore be judged from evidence of changes in reading arrangements. The physical placement and reaction of the reader, or what has been called 'la posturologie de la lecture', can, when glimpsed from the historical record, offer further clues to the experience of reading. The exotic variety of reading furniture is displayed in the wonderful *Die Kunst des Lesens* by Eva-Maria Hanebutt-Benz. Much can be learned about reading space, whether grand chamber, lowly parlour or simple privy, from diary and contemporary commentary, household sale and other commercial records, and the representation of reading in drawings, paintings and prints. How a book was kept or arranged might suggest whether it was viewed as an object of veneration or derision, sedition or authority, for dispersal or retention, as decorative or informative. The book wheel (sometimes called a reading wheel, of medieval origin, and a vertically rotating book-holder allowing the reading of several heavy books in one location) was replaced by a vast assemblage of reading paraphernalia for use and display. Ideals in reading practice and purpose were suggested by the reading chairs, stands, desks, print-racks, ladders, rotating shelving, globes, busts and miscellanea, together with the actual design of library bays, windows, ceilings, wall shelving or space formerly enclosed by book presses (often freestanding cases to store books and read them on the cases' upper sloping tops). In recent years, the replacement of public libraries by 'idea centres' and the progress of makerspaces (sometimes called hackerspaces, hackspaces and fablabs) have transformed notions of physical locations where people meet to share resources and knowledge to learn, create and invent. Such sites challenge established concepts of libraries as literary browsing, reference or book-borrowing rooms, and of civic libraries especially as secluded, silent, privileged and significantly furnished – and funded – spaces.

The changing arrangements for reading have signalled particular, often political, messages about the use of books. Grand libraries, set up as temples to literary devotion, deepened the tension between reading as a strictly privileged and exclusive activity and reading as more public enlightenment. Ceiling murals, busts, imposing bookcases and fitments framed the library of an Enlightenment gentleman. For many, it was an archive of knowledge yet also an assertion of the perfectability of Man and a reassuring record of the advance of human achievement. In this Romantic vision of book collecting, the private library served as an enclosure for reflection, determinedly contrasting to the natural state of man, the primitive illiterate beyond the boundaries of the estate. Exactly the opposite is embodied in the agenda for public libraries in the late nineteenth and twentieth centuries and even more certainly in the digital age. The modern vision – democratic, inclusive, flexible, informal and responsive to new, if transitory, technologies – nevertheless remains one imposed upon readers (or 'customers'),

Readers' perceptions of readerships might be multiple and quite different from those envisaged by the text. Robert DeMaria's study of Samuel Johnson as reader offers an investigation of how one influential individual recognized the application of different modes of reading and his own conformity to different readerships. Johnson reported that he 'read like a Turk by tearing the heart out of a book', but also distinguished at least four different ways that he read: 'hard study' with note-taking, 'perusal', 'curious reading' and 'mere reading' or browsing.[11] The potential for broader enquiry is obvious. Contemporary commentaries on correct and incorrect ways of approaching books and print supplement and contradict the record left by the individual reader, with reports criticizing readers for reading in inappropriate places or for reading badly, quickly, insensitively or too much. Shared reading, reading groups and corporate reading, as in church or during rote learning, for example, all demand exploration.

Ultimately, such explorations remain in thrall to patchy evidential survival, but the challenge is to attempt a mediation between text and reader which involves the history of comparative reading competences, typographical recognition, changes in the physical form of the book and evidence of variations in the resources of the reader. The history of the construal of meaning by texts must consider how they were confronted and appropriated by the reader. Such attempts to understand the historical individual reader might, above all, check Whiggish accounts of the purpose and effects of reading. Even de Certeau, in writing of reading deterritorializing the reader, emphasized the primacy of the silent, modernized, internalized reader. Yet the history of reading is not self-evidently a history of improvement and enlightenment, of progress from ignorance and barbarism to democracy, humanitarianism and virtue. Reading is not necessarily liberating and can be an imprisoning experience. We must ask what reading inspired and what it constrained. This demands an open-minded absorption in the evidence. For many past observers, literacy was inappropriate for many social groups. Literacy was believed to lead to depravity or subversion, and social historians have been too ready to laugh and scorn. The ironic voice may intervene and handicap, both highlighting and belittling the failure of people's past accounts to describe their world. Similarly, serious attention must be given to the language of those describing the spiritual and material wealth derived from the learning of their letters and a love of books. Accounts of being 'ravished by the word', as one humble diarist put it, caution against the simple dismissal of the reader's self-perception. The practice of reading remained a prime agency for creating social and cultural variation against a history of common forms and patterns of exchange

Although the pursuit of historical interpretive communities enhanced and encouraged the study of reading experience drawn from individual testimonies, the extension of the 'how' posed new questions about the authority of such case studies. Early modern and European studies led the way. A dozen or more editions or interpretations of the testimony of early modern literate artisans recreated a mental universe based to varying degrees on the testimony of textual reading (or misreading) experiences. Distinguished studies explored exactly how reading interpreted texts and made printing and the acquisition of books both dangerous and revelatory. Particularly influential was the pioneering micro-history by Carlo Ginzburg of the trial and reported reading of Domenico Scandella, miller of late sixteenth-century Friuli).[12] Out of the Inquisition archives of Udine, Scandella, known as 'Menocchio', resurfaced as the twentieth-century hero of Ginzburg's classic courtroom drama. An inspiration for dozens of analogous studies, Ginzburg invites us to understand the mediation of print between randomly acquired and often imperfect texts and a semi- or, more accurately, strangely literate and learned early modern artisan. Nevertheless, such memoirs and recorded encounters, so effective in recovering past mental states in all their vividness and idiosyncrasy, often outshine broader consequences of 'printedness' in society, politics and the economy.

Micro-histories based on reading experiences offer rich material, but their distinctiveness appears to highlight issues of representativeness. How could we, in the words of Roger Chartier, 'organize this indistinguishable plurality of individual acts according to shared regularities'?[13] An answer implicit in recent studies is to downplay the importance of broad uniformities and to focus instead upon the qualitative differences of experience. Exploration of the range of variability of individual experience revises emphasis upon the typicality of those individuals whose record is written and has survived by often singular circumstance and luck. New histories of reading, grounded in the notion that the text does not exist until given signification by readers, reject sharp divides between the literate and the non-literate, acknowledging instead different literacies and different ways of revisiting the same text. At issue are different ways of performing reading and of readers believing in their empowerment by reading performance, whether by an individual alone with the text, or by communal activity, and ritual.

6
Consequences

There have been various French neologisms in this volume – *livres sans frontières*, *livres sans auteurs* and *livres sans lecteurs* – which might leave us wondering what books *do* have: free to be everywhere and yet also not to have writers and readers. It is of course true that once produced by human agency, books might be left abandoned or stored unread. A certain intervention does ensure even basic preservation, but if that were all then we have *livres* and *histoires* but not history of the book.

Books in all their forms carry texts whose reading conveys intellectual and ideological significance. Books transmit knowledge by physical form, or the message by the medium, and share some of the characteristics of other material goods. Tactility, design and ornamentation convey meaning even before a book is read. The connections supplied by sign, script and print fall short of the interactive exchanges possible between people not parted by distance. In many ways, however, books offer the same connectedness provided by letters and other received communication. Portable, legible and durable manuscript, printed and other forms of books, notably including periodicals and newspapers, extended and widened the reach of exchange. Such exchange altered according to the mutations of religious allegiance, war, invasion, colonialism, migration, exile, commerce, nationalism, revolution and political independence.

In Europe by about the mid-eighteenth century, and in Asia by about the end of the nineteenth century, most men and women directly or indirectly encountered printed products, whether or not they were read. Print, however, is not restricted to what is usually thought of as 'books' and 'publications', while even by the end of the eighteenth century only a minority of Europe's population confidently read pamphlets, newspapers and books, even including bibles, prayer books and hymn books. Study of the processes by which they were read greatly contributes to the historian's conceptualization of the changing social contingencies of past belief. For reading, no more than the construction of particular ideas, is no universal or timeless experience: it is conditioned by historical circumstance in which reading becomes part of the recovery of the historical identity of a text. It is at the very core of the history of the book. By recovering and offering an interpretation of a range of texts available, we help rescue the history of popular thought and discursive practice from the canon of great texts studied in isolation, review the differences between authorial meaning and intention, magnify the absences and illuminate the unexpected. Book history continues to break down perceived polarities between popular and elite, explores mental constructions and undermines falsely oppositional categories such as 'literate' and 'illiterate'.

As illustrated, there are many examples of where 'book historical' methodologies have revised influential historical arguments and in so doing developed fresh and provocative research agendas. In the 1980s, Martin J. Wiener's *English Culture and the Decline of the Industrial Spirit, 1850–1980* gained great influence not only among historians but in business schools worldwide. Sir Keith Joseph gave a copy of the book to every member of Margaret Thatcher's Cabinet. Wiener argued that literature and culture promulgated an anti-business ethos and contributed to long-term economic malaise during the very years of late Victorian economic success. Objections were numerous: anti-business values were not new and Britain's economic rivals similarly produced a strong dose of anti-business culture. The most obvious questions, however, concerned Wiener's use of literary examples without attention to the popularity of the texts, their reception and historically verified interpretation. Not only could an alternative history be constructed by analysis of greatly reprinted publications – in the late nineteenth century but also in the decades before – but the debate about 'frames of mind' demanded thoroughgoing revision to the historian's determination of the popularity and readership of a diverse range of literature (of the type developed by Janice Radway and many others discussed in this volume).

What reading meant offers new research challenges but ones which build upon past forays into book-based *histoires des mentalités* and the function of books in the transmission of knowledge. To revisit another example, the attempt to understand 'collective psychologies' by Robert Mandrou in 1964 paralleled similar investigations by Philippe Ariès, Jean-Louis Flandrin and Michel Vovelle. Mandrou defined a popular culture of shared sensibilities from inference from the titles of *La Bibliothèque bleue de Troyes*. He also followed Daniel Mornet's 1933 pursuit of the pre-Revolutionary reading of the masses, discussed earlier.[1] Both accounts are vulnerable to criticism about the partiality and particularity of the sources, but in the wake of such studies Carla Hesse and Jeremy Popkin, among others, have drawn on bibliographical approaches to offer fresh and challenging interpretations of the causes of the Revolution. Robert Darnton has similarly revivified study of small and popular books, their reading, distribution and policing in eighteenth-century France, in work which continues in new and stimulating directions.

Histories of readers and reading contribute to larger claims about long-term political and cultural change, even though many of the studies are highly confined by time and place. Anyone examining print reception in Europe and its colonies, for example, works in the shadow of a number of general assertions, many based on varieties of collective consciousness and emotion. Emphasis upon growing audiences – more books, more readers – tempts generalizations about the emergence of various modernities, where histories of reading, subsumed within larger narratives, contribute to a teleological chronicle of progress, of the march of literacy, enlightenment, individualism, participative debate, empowerment and democracy. All are situated as progressive forces in which so-called 'print culture' is part nursemaid and part chronicler. As David Cressy has warned of allied research, low literacy rates in the early modern period are not necessarily 'indicators of retardation or deprivation, awaiting rectification by progress'.[2] The past, often romantic history of reading in the eighteenth and nineteenth centuries, however, includes accounts of democratization from the vantage point of later success. For Richard Altick, for example 'the history of the mass reading audience is, in fact, the history of English democracy'.[3]

The more nuanced analyses of current social and cultural historians adept at broad bibliographical and book-historical research and understanding have continued to refine the social history of ideas and knowledge. These histories include scrutiny of the impact of different communication technologies, including print and printedness, upon language and social and political representations. Such enquiry also helps avoid the dangers of grand hypothesizing. The effects of print, for example, feature prominently in debates about an overarching development of civil society and distinctions between public and private. With an influence as great as Anderson and his exposition of imagined communities, Habermas proposed the evolution of a 'public sphere' where practical reason was institutionalized in a discourse of reasoned arguments which overrode status and tradition. Such a public sphere is presented as the prerequisite of a democratic polity, and as founded on refined discourse and greater participation. Propelling this were print, books, journals, literary criticism and a bourgeois world of letters. Resulting summaries of both Anderson and Habermas, however, tend to chart a linear development of an increasingly active 'press', enlarging public debate and creating an authentic public opinion, all apparently as new phenomena with little or no similarity to pre-print 'publicness'.

To highlight another consequence, the gender of writers, producers and audiences has become of increasing significance in book history, although comparative research in different societies is limited and requires extension. Gender remains relatively unimplicated, however, in concepts like print capitalism and the public sphere. Peter Kornicki has contrasted the reading materials and practices of women readers in Europe and East Asia, while, as McDermott has cautioned, the approaches to reading identified for early modern China are problematically gendered. *Du* 讀 was applied only to male readers studying the ancients, and *kan* 看 to women and some men reading material considered more trivial. The distinction echoes comparisons between readers of fiction and readers of scientific works and the classics in Europe since the eighteenth century and yet such a characterization, common in contemporary accounts, fails to match the more complicated reality of mixed audiences, by gender as well as age, profession and social status, for books, periodical and newspapers.

In pursuit of past reading practices, the history of the book continues to draw on new disciplinary expertise and insights. Fresh questioning of the translatable and untranslatable, for example, has extended understanding of the book in colonial encounters and the effect of particular types of imported books, texts and linguistic and typographical signs upon peoples who commanded a particular, if then unrecognized, type of literacy and book culture. Scott Manning Stevens, historian of the Mohawk peoples, has written about 'linguistic fantasy' in which apparent readers and users of the 'other' language assumed belief in their own expertise.[4] They claimed a confidence in their command of another language, culture and interpretation of meaning that they simply did not have. Conversely, the orthographic and, later, the typographical translation of the oral resulted not only in the denial of a proper language until it was cast in metal and read in print, but in the assumed denial to other peoples of an acceptable means of communication other than that which was imposed upon them, be it under the Song in the tenth to twelfth centuries, in Central and South America in the sixteenth and seventeenth centuries, in India and North America in the eighteenth century, or in many Muslim territories, South Africa, New Zealand and other occupied lands in the nineteenth and twentieth centuries.

The history of the book is unavoidably political – both in its concerns and its effects, and the writing of book history has inevitably brought political criticism. The relations between media and society are patently and essentially political, where control of the press and the means of public communication from ancient times to the present threatens fundamental freedoms. The modern newspaper press, in particular, establishes its claim to freedom by its conveyance of opinions and political and financial information. The alternative and the radical are integral to the history of communications. Of equal sensitivity – and drama – is the history of invasion and colonialism. A pivotal feature of most conquests is missionary and proselytizing activity, where 'the book' is the holy book – the Bible or the Qu'ran and other scriptures. Among several critics, however, Trish Loughran has decried 'mainstream book history' as a reification of nationalism which 'rehearses a passion play about modernization' and 'a justification for the world as we know it that absorbs local differences within a totalizing picture of the Gutenberg book's global spread'.[5] Caroline Davis and David Johnson have eloquently called for greater understanding of the precolonial book in Africa and castigated the perpetuation by Henry Louis Gates, as one who should have known better, of the false division between a literate world and premodern Africa.[6] An obvious parallel is with the debate between Gananath Obeyesekere and Marshall Sahlins over the Western-inspired notion that Captain Cook seemed a god to savages and the Western condescension meted out to 'natives' and their misunderstood and misdescribed culture.[7] The eloquent plea by Davis and Johnson, however, appears in a preface to a collection of book history essays where attention to pre-1800 Africa is still more desired than explored.

The development of bibliographical studies, tied to the nation-state because of pragmatic as well as the more obvious linguistic and literary association, has already been described, and the residual conservatism of some bibliographers, preferring empirical and technical evaluation to suggestive theoretical intervention, has not always been misplaced. Nonetheless, the challenge to decolonize and remove unhelpful political and national boundaries in book history remains, as does the redefining of concepts such as print capitalism which occlude many of the intellectual goals suggested in this volume. The multiplicity of book histories is also energizing and enriching. By themselves, analytical bibliography, critical theory, reading history, library history and bibliographical history, widely conceived, all answer different types of question and are motivated by different impulses and epistemological concerns, but they are deepened and given greater critical acuity by their collision – painless or not.

If we conclude that there cannot and should not be one type of history of the book, but many types, there cannot therefore be a rigidly defined 'book history' or '*the* history of the book' as projected by its more ardent modern advocates.

Collaboration between disciplines has been beneficial, but this does not mean that collaboration results in one monolithic idea of what book history might be. For some, including this contributor, the history of the book is still too little concerned with comparative social histories of ideas. Ideographic, pictographic, alphabetic and other writing systems recording verbal sounds, and graphic signs, script, print and other technologies determined the manner in which thought was materially produced and consumed. In similar ways, in the digital age, the internet provides the opportunity but also the boundaries for new forms of social networking and textual formation and reception. The words and ideas conveyed by published texts are the *meaningful* result of the production, circulation and reading of the material text. The history of the book has been dominated by discussion of the impact and characteristics of print and also of particular modern forms such as periodicals and newspapers. Just as important however, are early books in all their unfamiliar and challenging forms, books in non-literate societies or societies with differential literacies, and the continuing and changing significance of manuscripts and written correspondence.

Examination of the actual artefact will never be circumvented in scholarly analysis of the material book, but, as exemplified by this volume, the ways in which we think of the book and its history and of what a book has been are revolutionized by what a book might now be. Many commentators associate contemporary 'books' less with their material *form* than with their *function* as a means of communication. The revival and adaptation of such words and concepts as 'icon', 'font', 'tablet', 'scrolling' and 'the virtual' are cyphers for a reconceptualization of what a book is. Hyperlinked texts, digital editions and the ebook, screen adaptations, audiobooks and podcasts change the ways in which texts are acquired, transmitted, circulated, read, interrogated, searched and stored. Authorship identities and rights are made more complex, and automated cross-lingual translation accentuates issues of untranslatability. And in such transformative times, more books are published than ever before, whether through conventional means, print-on-demand, or by the World Wide Web. Facsimile editions of ancient Chinese classics or Mesoamerican codices, or almost anything mentioned in this book, can be read on smartphones or included in blogs and email attachments; David Mitchell and Philip Pullman (among others) have published short fiction using Twitter, 140 characters at a time; and self-publishing opens to everyone the possibility of publication, uncontrolled dissemination and unknown readerships.

Books of the digital age enable the encoding of and a new interactivity with information and knowledge, and extend metafiction and narrative techniques. Digital books offer revisions and tests to our consideration of sign and character design and recognition, the composition and comprehension of the page, of what a 'page' is and where it ends, of the complexity of 'paratexts', and of the variety of our reading practices and motivations. In the world of digitized texts and of Google Books, we are challenged not only by questions of the archiving and retrieval of knowledge through 'books', but of what copyright is and of the implications of Open Access, licensing agreements and inequitable information supply. Authors, publishers and readers confront new forms of global piracy, of how censorship operates and of how new technologies change and are changed by commercial, political, religious and national interests. The digital revolutionizes the commercial structure and business models of modern publishing and international conglomerates. Many physical books were and are, of course, never read at all and the majority of the copies of certain misconceived editions are pulped and destroyed, but what is now the digital equivalent of the unread and the destroyed? Loss, deletion and redundancy take on different and challenging meanings. Publishers, meanwhile, are digitizing backlists and keeping books 'in print' to an unprecedented extent. And there are many other questions. What is the future of the public and institutional library in the age of makerspaces, hackerspaces and a 'shared knowledge economy'? How might we now measure reading and reader response, where we find new and different evidence – much perhaps overwhelming in quantity and ephemerality – from feedback reviews and information such as Goodreads, digital reading group records, Amazon order histories, and easily accessible and monitorable school and university reading lists?

Self-evidently, the history of the book is relatable to and draws conceptual inspiration from our fast-changing media world. Contemporary parallels have informed continuing research about communications shifts, what counts as 'knowledge', the manner in which it was created and the consequences of how it was stored and used. Some histories of the relationship between an advancing, and often glibly asserted, 'print culture' and its enabling of social behaviour and perception might well be seen as exercises in the recovery of past 'social media'. Other sophisticated systems of conveying meaning now challenge books as vehicles for communicating knowledge and cultural and political expression. Questions of replication, standardization, authority and authenticity are all under scrutiny. In concluding an anniversary piece for the Bibliographical Society in 1992, Don McKenzie predicted that ' "the book" and its history will become something more than the history of books'.[8] Since then, the history of the book has unavoidably and rightly been implicated in debates about digitization and the future of the book, contributed to comparative social histories of knowledge, and, somewhat belatedly, informed the writing of intellectual history. New technologies challenge our assumptions about what books are and were in many ways, coupled with the transformative research potential of digital humanities.

Most conspicuously, the 'global turn' in book history advances histories of knowledge that took their inspiration from the challenges of early modern and Enlightenment Europe – of changes in the organization of knowledge, the circulation and impact of ideas, the intellectual and social history of libraries and the global transmission of European cultures. The ways in which the accumulation of knowledge is offset by loss parallel the balance between advances and constraints examined by histories of the book. In an increasing number of case histories from different parts of the world, the focus of study is of displaced, subsumed and corrupted oral cultures and previously written ones, but also of creatively composite cultures in which imposed and invented languages and traditions have their own positive contribution. Ultimately, it is an agenda that speaks to our current digital, globalized and yet intellectually and ideologically fragmented and often mutually uncomprehending world.

Notes

1 The Scope of Book History

1 Robert Darnton, 'What is the History of Books?', *Daedalus*, 111 (Summer, 1982): 65–83, at 65.
2 Margaret Cohen, *The Sentimental Education of the Novel* (Princeton, 1999), p. 23.
3 David S. Shields, *Civil Tongues and Polite Letters in British America* (Williamsburg, VA, 1997), pp. xxx–xxxi.
4 Movable type processes are various and include East Asian carved ceramic, wood and metal tablets of individual characters from the eleventh century CE. The European method from the fifteenth century, replicating the alphabetic writing system of recording verbal sounds, involves casting letters and symbols in metal in a mould of adjustable width (the 'printing type'). This provides identical forms for each letter and other symbols of the same body and design which are assembled (or 'set' or 'composed') to create words. The surface of the printing types, coated with ink and impressed on paper, provides the printed words or characters on a page. One or more pages are printed on each side of a sheet of paper, according to the 'format' of the book. When sufficient sheets are printed, the individual printing types are taken out and redistributed back into cases compartmentalized to store the different sorts of type.
5 Elizabeth Eisenstein, *Divine Art, Infernal Machine: The Reception of Printing in the West from First Impressions to the Sense of an Ending* (Philadelphia, 2011), p. xi.

6 Gérard Genette, *Paratexts: Thresholds of Interpretation*, trans. Jane. E. Lewin (Cambridge and New York, 1997), p. 13.
7 Roger Chartier, *The Author's Hand and the Printer's Mind*, trans. Lydia G. Cochrane (Cambridge, 2014), p. 135.
8 An outstanding guide is Joseph P. McDermott, *A Social History of the Chinese Book: Books and Literati Culture in Late Imperial China* (Hong Kong, 2006); see in particular his 'Bibliographical Notes', pp. 263–78.
9 More simply, *shu* for book (书, the simplified form used in mainland China, or 書, the traditional form used in the past and today in Taiwan and Hong Kong).
10 Genette, *Paratexts*, p. 2, citing Philippe Lejeune, *Le Pacte autobiographique* (Paris, 1975), p. 45.
11 D. F. McKenzie, *Bibliography and the Sociology of Texts* (London, 1985).
12 'A fount of type was a set of letters and other symbols in which each sort was supplied in approximate proportion to its frequency of use, all being of one body- [or point-] size and design'; Philip Gaskell, *A New Introduction to Bibliography* (Oxford, 1972), p. 33. In US English, 'font' has also been used to mean a set of types of the same design cast on the same body at the same time. In modern, more general – and seemingly universal – usage, 'font' means digital simulations of a set of types of the same design.
13 Eleanor Robson, 'The Ancient World', in James Raven (ed.), *The Oxford Illustrated History of the Book* (Oxford, 2018).
14 Notably Harold Innis, *The Bias of Communication* (Toronto, 1951); Harold Innis, *The Strategy of Culture* (Toronto, 1952); and Harold Innis, *Changing Concepts of Time* (Toronto, 1952).
15 Joseph Needham and Tsuen-hsuin Tsien, *Science and Civilization in China*: vol. 5: *Chemistry and Chemical Technology, Part 1: Paper and Printing* (Cambridge, 1985), p. 40.
16 Galen's letter *De indolentia* (Περὶ ἀλυπησίας) or 'On the Avoidance of Distress', discovered in the Vlatadon monastery in Thessaloniki, probably originating in Constantinople; this English translation is quoted from Clare K. Rothschild and Trevor W. Thompson (eds), *Galen's 'De indolentia': Essays on a Newly Discovered Letter*, Studien und Texte zu Antiken und Christentum 88 (Tübingen, 2014), pp. 21–36 (quotation is 19 at p. 25).
17 Germaine Warkentin, 'In Search of "The Word of the Other": Aboriginal Sign Systems and the History of the Book in Canada', *Book History*, 2 (1999): 1–27.

2 The Early History of Book History

1. Pliny the Elder, *The Natural History*, Book XIII, 70.
2. Cassiodorus, *Variae*, trans. S. J. Barnish (Liverpool, 1992), p. 160.
3. Colin H. Roberts and T. C. Skeat, *The Birth of the Codex* (London, 1987), p. 25.
4. Cassiodorus, *Variae*, XI, pp. 383–6.
5. Rothschild and Thompson, *Galen's 'De indolentia'*, 7 at p. 22; further context is offered on pp. 65–78 by Matthew C. Nicholls, 'A Library at Antium?'.
6. Cf. Peter Kornicki, 'Books for Women and Women Readers', in Joseph P. McDermott and Peter Burke (eds), *The Book Worlds of East Asia and Europe, 1450–1850: Connections and Comparisons* (Hong Kong, 2015), pp. 283–325.
7. McDermott, *A Social History of the Chinese Book*, pp. 11ff.
8. *Laboryouse journey and Serche of Johan Leylande for Englandes Antiquities*, sig. Cv r–v, cited in Jennifer Summit, *Memory's Library: Medieval Books in Early Modern England* (Chicago, 2008), p. 141.
9. Karl Immanuel Gerhardt (ed.), *Die philosophischen Schriften von Gottfried Wilhelm Leibniz*, 7 vols (Berlin, 1875–90), vol. 7, p. 160.
10. Peter Burke, *A Social History of Knowledge: From Gutenberg to Diderot* (Cambridge, 2000), pp. 81–2, 93–4, 174–6, 194–6; and Peter Burke, 'The Proliferation of Reference Books, 1450–1850', in McDermott and Burke, *Book Worlds of East Asia and Europe*, pp. 237–81, at pp. 267–70.
11. Yu Xiangdou 余象斗 (also known as Yu Wentai 余文台 and Yu Santai 余三台), *Xinke tianxia simin bianlan Santai wanyong zhengzong* 新刻天下四民便覽三台萬用正宗 [Santai's infinitely useful (guide to) how to do everything correctly for the convenient consultation of all the four classes under heaven, newly cut] (Shulin, in what is now Jianyang, 1599), p. 1a; I am grateful to Cynthia Brokaw for this reference and its translation.
12. Henry Woudhuysen, 'Before Moxon: The Public Face of the English Book Trade, 1475–1680', Presidential lecture, Bibliographical Society, 2016.
13. Joseph Moxon, *Mechanick Exercises on the Whole Art of Printing (1683–4)*, ed. Herbert Davis and Harry Carter, 2nd edn (London, 1962), p. vii.
14. Jacqueline Glomski, 'Incunabula-Typographiae: Seventeenth-Century Views on Early Printing', *The Library*, 2: 4 (2001): 336–48.

Notes to Pages 42–50

15 Thomas Cogan, *The Rhine: Or, A Journey From Utrecht to Francfort; Chiefly by the Borders of the Rhine, and the Passage down the River, from Mentz to Bonn*, 2 vols (London, 1794), vol. 2, p. 183; see also vol. 2, pp. 190–8, 208–9.
16 Isaac D'Israeli in Marvin Spevack (ed.), *Isaac D'Israeli on Books: Pre-Victorian Essays on the History of Literature* (London, 2004), p. 46.
17 Woudhuysen, 'Before Moxon', citing Percy Simpson, *Proof-Reading in the Sixteenth, Seventeenth and Eighteenth Centuries* (Oxford, 1955), p. 176.
18 David Pankow, *The Printer's Manual: An Illustrated History: Classic and Unusual Texts on Printing from the Seventeenth, Eighteenth and Nineteenth Centuries* (Rochester, NY, 2005), p. 14.
19 Joseph Ames, *Typographical Antiquities: Being an Historical Account of Printing in England* (London, 1749), preface, p. [v].
20 Obituary of William Caslon, 17 August 1778, newspaper cutting in Cambridge University Library's copy of Ames, *Typographical Antiquities*.
21 Kristian Jensen, *Revolution and the Antiquarian Book: Reshaping the Past, 1780–1815* (Cambridge, 2011).
22 David McKitterick, *Old Books, New Technologies: The Representation, Conservation and Transformation of Books since 1700* (Cambridge, 2013), p. 170.
23 William Blades, *The Life and Typography of William Caxton*, 2 vols (London, 1861–3).

3 Description, Enumeration and Modelling

1 W. W. Greg, 'Bibliography – An Apologia', *The Library*, 4th ser., 13: 2 (Sept. 1932): 113–43.
2 G. Thomas Tanselle, *Bibliographical Analysis: A Historical Introduction* (New York, 2009).
3 Neil Harris, 'Definitions of bibliography, and in particular of the variety called Analytical', in 'Panorama des enjeux et méthodes de la bibliographie matérielle', Institut d'histoire du livre, ENSSIB online.
4 David D. Hall, 'Erudition and Learned Culture', in Scott E. Casper et al., *A History of the Book in America: The Industrial Book, 1840–1880* (Chapel Hill, NC, 2007), pp. 347–59.
5 E. Gordon Duff, *Early Printed Books* (London, 1893), the title to chapter 13.

6 The material form is critical here: 'juan' 卷, usually translated as 'scroll' or 'fascicle' for pre-Song dynasty texts, is best translated as a 'chapter' and is the measuring unit of preference for Chinese book collectors. The alternative 'ce' is best reserved for 'volume'. The number of *juan* in a *ce* varied enormously.
7 Ye Dehui, 'A Critique of *Youxian jinyu*', in Su Yu (ed.), *Collected Essays on Defending Confucianism*, 6 vols (Taipei, 1971 [1898]), vol. 4, pp. 173–218; translation from Wm. Theodore de Bary and Richard Lufrano (eds), *Sources of Chinese Tradition*, vol. 2: *From 1600 through the Twentieth Century*, 2nd edn (New York, 2000), p. 280. I am grateful to Leon Rocha for this reference.
8 McDermott, *A Social History of the Chinese Book*, p. 263.
9 D. F. McKenzie, 'History of the Book,' in Peter Davison (ed.), *The Book Encompassed: Studies in Twentieth-Century Bibliography* (New Castle, DE, and Winchester, 1998), pp. 290–301, at p. 290.
10 Carla Giunchedi and Elisa Grignani, *La Società bibliografica italiana (1896–1915)* (Florence, 1994).
11 Martin Boghardt, *Analytische Druckforschung:Ein methodischer Beitrag zu Buchkunde und Textkritik* (Hamburg, 1977), p. 16.
12 Bettina Wagner, 'Introduction', in Bettina Wagner and Marcia Reed (eds), *Early Printed Books as Material Objects* (Berlin and New York, 2010), p. 1.
13 A. W. Pollard and G. R. Redgrave, comps, *A Short-Title Catalogue of Books Printed in England, Scotland and Ireland and English Books Printed Abroad 1473–1640* (STC); 2nd edn, rev. and enlarged by W. A. Jackson, F. S. Ferguson and Katharine F. Pantzer (London, 1976–86).
14 Marcus A. McCorison, 'The Annals of American Bibliography, or Book History, Plain and Fancy,' *Libraries & Culture*, 26: 1 (Winter, 1991): 14–23, at 15.
15 K. I. D. Maslen and John Lancaster, *The Bowyer Ledgers: The Printing Accounts of William Bowyer, Father and Son: With a Checklist of Bowyer Printing, 1699–1777, a Commentary, Indexes, and Appendixes* (London, 1991).
16 David McKitterick, 'Bibliography, Population, and Statistics: A View from the West', in McDermott and Burke, *Book Worlds of East Asia and Europe*, pp. 65–104, at pp. 98–100.
17 Sarah Zhang, 'The Pitfalls of Using Google Ngram to Study Language', *Science*, 350: 6260 (12 Oct. 2015); see also Jean-Baptiste Michel et al., 'Quantitative Analysis of Culture Using Millions of Digitized Books', *Science*, 331: 6014 (14 Jan. 2011): 176–82.

18 The *bibliothèques bleues* were a publishing scheme introduced in Troyes in 1602, but more generally it is a term used for certain ephemera and popular literature published in France between then and about 1830, and similar to English chapbooks and German *Volksbuch*.
19 Robert Darnton, *Édition et sédition. L'Univers de la littérature clandestine au XVIIIe siècle* (Paris, 1991), pp. i–ii (my translation).
20 Factotum printing involved a block or plate with an empty space in the centre into which was fitted type, another block or an engraved plate.
21 Notable single- or dual-author national histories also continued, including, for example, Harald L. Tveterås, *Den norske bokhandels historie* [to 1900], 3 vols (Oslo, 1988), and vol. 4, Harald L. Tveterås and Egil Tveterås, *Den norske bokhandels historie* [since 1900] (Oslo, 1996).
22 An early account is given in C. Berkvens-Stevelinck, H. Bots, P. G. Hoftijzer and O. S. Lankhorst (eds), *Le Magasin de l'Univers: The Dutch Republic as the Centre of the European Book Trade* (Leiden, 1992).
23 Walter Ong, *Orality and Literacy: The Technologizing of the Word*, 2nd edn (New York, 2002).
24 Darnton, 'What is the History of Books?', pp. 66–7.
25 Thomas R. Adams and Nicolas Barker, 'A New Model for the Study of the Book', in Nicolas Barker (ed.), *A Potencie of Life: Books in Society: The Clark Lectures, 1986–1987* (London, 1993), pp. 5–43, at p. 7.
26 Peter D. McDonald, *British Literary Culture and Publishing Practice 1880–1914* (Cambridge, 1997).

4 Who, What and How?

1 Among many examples are Jack Stillinger, *Multiple Authorship and the Myth of Solitary Genius* (Oxford, 1991); Zachary Leader, *Revision and Romantic Authorship* (Oxford, 1996); Grantland S. Rice, *The Transformation of Authorship in America* (Chicago, 1997); and Helen Smith, *Grossly Material Things: Women and Book Production in Early Modern England* (Oxford, 2012); among more internal literary, yet historicized approaches, see Stephanie A. V. G. Kamath, *Authorship and First-Person Allegory in Late Medieval France and England* (Cambridge, 2012).
2 McDermott, *A Social History of the Chinese Book*; Christopher A. Reed, *Gutenberg in Shanghai: Chinese Print Capitalism, 1876–1937* (Vancouver, 2004).

3 Cynthia Brokaw and Kai-wing Chow (eds), *Printing and Book Culture in Late Imperial China* (Berkeley, 2005).
4 These also revise the standard S. H. Steinberg, *Five Hundred Years of Printing* (London, 1955), even as revised and edited by John Trevitt (London, 1996).
5 Lotte Hellinga, 'Printing', in Lotte Hellinga and J. B. Trapp (eds), *The Cambridge History of the Book in Britain*, vol. 3: *1400–1557* (Cambridge, 1999), p. 72.
6 James Raven, *Bookscape: Geographies of Printing and Publishing in London before 1800* (Chicago and London, 2014).
7 Listed in the final section of the Bibliography.
8 David Pearson, *Provenance Research in Book History: A Handbook* (London, 1995).
9 Brean S. Hammond, *Professional Imaginative Writing in England, 1670–1740: Hackney for Bread* (Oxford, 1997).
10 George Justice, *The Manufacturers of Literature: Writing and the Literary Marketplace in Eighteenth-Century England* (Cranbury, NJ, 2002), p. 24.
11 Terry Eagleton, *The Function of Criticism* (London, 1984), p. 18.
12 Harold Love, 'Early Modern Print Culture: Assessing the Models', *Parergon: Journal of the Australian and New Zealand Association for Medieval and Early Modern Studies*, 20: 1 (2003): 45–64, at 56.
13 Nicolas Barker, *Form and Meaning in the History of the Book* (London, 2003), p. 27.

5 Reading

1 J. P. Klancher, *The Making of English Reading Audiences, 1790–1832* (Madison, 1987), p. 8.
2 R. D. Hume, 'Texts within Contexts: Notes toward a Historical Method', *Philological Quarterly*, 71 (1992): 69–100, at 81; David Simpson, 'Literary Criticism and the Return to "History"', *Critical Inquiry*, 14 (1988): 721–47.
3 Janice A. Radway, *Reading the Romance: Women, Patriarchy, and Popular Literature* (Chapel Hill, NC, and London, 1984), pp. 12, 190.
4 Hume, 'Texts within Contexts', pp. 80, 84. The US English 'interpretive communities' has always been preferred to the English 'interpretative'.
5 Kathryn Sutherland, post on 'The Academic Book of the Future' project, 2016, https://academicbookfuture.org/advisory-board/kathryn-sutherland/.

6   I borrow 'at risk' from historical demographers meaning the proportion of a given population of sufficient age, physical abilities, skills and propensities to be liable to act (in this case to read books).
7   Anne E. McLaren, 'Constructing New Reading Publics in Late Ming China,' in Brokaw and Chow, *Printing and Book Culture in Late Imperial China*, pp. 152–83, at p. 173; Anne E. McLaren, *Chinese Popular Culture and Ming Chantefables* (Leiden, 1998), pp. 73–6.
8   Anthony Grafton and Lisa Jardine, ' "Studied for Action": How Gabriel Harvey Read his Livy', *Past and Present*, 129: 1 (1990): 30–78.
9   Stephen Orgel, *The Reader in the Book: A Study of Spaces and Traces* (Oxford, 2015).
10 David Cressy, 'Books as Totems in Seventeenth-Century England and New England', *Journal of Library History*, 21 (1986): 92–106, at 93.
11 Robert DeMaria, *Samuel Johnson and the Life of Reading* (Baltimore, 1997), pp. 10ff.
12 Carlo Ginzburg, *Il formaggio e i vermi: Il cosmo di un mugnaio del '500* (Turin, 1976), trans. John and Anne Tedeschi as *The Cheese and the Worms: The Cosmos of a Sixteenth-Century Miller* (London, 1980).
13 Roger Chartier, 'Texts, Printings, Readings', in Lynn Hunt (ed.), *The New Cultural History* (Berkeley, 1989), pp. 154–75, at p. 156.

6   Consequences

1   Robert Mandrou, *De la culture populaire aux XVIIe et XVIIIe siècles. La Bibliothèque bleue de Troyes*, 2nd edn (Paris, 1975); Daniel Mornet, *Les Origines intellectuelles de la Révolution française, 1715–1787* (Paris: 1933), based on Daniel Mornet, 'Les Enseignements des bibliothèques privées 1750–1780', *Revue d'histoire littéraire de la France* (1910): 449–96.
2   David Cressy, 'Literacy in Context: Meaning and Measurement in Early Modern England' , in John Brewer and Roy Porter (eds), *Consumption and the World of Goods* (London and New York, 1993), pp. 305–19.
3   R. D. Altick, *The English Common Reader: A History of the Mass Reading Public 1800–1900* (Chicago and London, 1957), p. 3.
4   Manning Stevens, 'Mother Tongues and Native Voices: Linguistic Fantasies in the Age of the Encounter', in E. Hoffman-Nelson

and M. Nelson (eds), *Telling the Stories: Studies in Native American Literature* (New York: Peter, 2001), pp. 3–18.
5   Trish Loughran, 'Books in the Nation', in Leslie Howsam (ed.), *The Cambridge Companion to the History of the Book* (Cambridge, 2015), pp. 36–52, at p. 49.
6   Caroline Davis and David Johnson, 'Introduction', in Caroline Davis and David Johnson (eds), *The Book in Africa: Critical Debates* (Basingstoke and New York, 2015), pp. 1–17.
7   The debate is examined in Robert Borofsky, 'Cook, Lono, Obeyesekere, and Sahlins', *Current Anthropology*, 38: 2 (1997): 255–82.
8   McKenzie, 'History of the Book', p. 301.

Bibliography

1 The Scope of Book History

Barker, Nicolas, *Form and Meaning in the History of the Book* (London, 2003).
Baron, Sabrina Alcorn, Eric N. Lindquist and Eleanor F. Shevlin (eds), *Agent of Change: Print Culture Studies after Elizabeth L. Eisenstein* (Boston, 2007).
Barthes, Roland, *Image, Music, Texts*, trans. Stephen Heath (London, 1977).
Burke, Peter, *A Social History of Knowledge*, vol. 1: *From Gutenberg to Diderot* (Cambridge, 2000).
Burke, Peter, *A Social History of Knowledge*, vol. 2: *From the Encyclopédie to Wikipedia* (Cambridge, 2012).
Carter, Thomas Francis, *The Invention of Printing in China and its Spread Westwards* (New York, 1925).
Cavallo, Guglielmo, and Roger Chartier, *A History of Reading in the West: Studies in Print Culture and the History of the Book* (Amherst, 1999).
Chartier, Roger, *Inscription and Erasure: Literature and Written Culture from the Eleventh to the Eighteenth Century*, trans. Arthur Goldhammer (Philadelphia, 2007).
Darnton, Robert, 'What is the History of Books?', *Daedalus*, 111 (Summer 1982), 65–83
Darnton, Robert, '"What is the History of Books?" Revisited', *Modern Intellectual History*, 4: 3 (2007): 495–508.
Davis, Caroline, and David Johnson (eds), *The Book in Africa: Critical Debates* (Basingstoke and New York, 2015).

Eliot, Simon, and Jonathan Rose (eds), *A Companion to the History of the Book* (Chichester, 2009).

Febvre, Lucien, and Henri-Jean Martin, *L'Apparition du livre* (Paris, 1957); trans. by David Gerard as *The Coming of the Book: The Impact of Printing, 1450–1800* (London and New York, 1976).

Frasca-Spada, Marina, and Nick Jardine (eds), *Books and the Sciences in History* (Cambridge, 2000).

Hall, David D., 'The History of the Book: New Questions? New Answers?', *Journal of Library History*, 21: 1 (1986): 27–38.

Hofmeyr, Isabel, *The Portable Bunyan: A Transnational History of "The Pilgrim's Progress"* (Princeton, 2004).

Howsam, Leslie, *Old Books and New Histories: An Orientation to Studies in Book and Print Culture* (Toronto, 2006).

Howsam, Leslie (ed.), *The Cambridge Companion to the History of the Book* (Cambridge, 2015).

McDermott, Joseph P., and Peter Burke (eds), *The Book Worlds of East Asia and Europe, 1450–1850: Connections and Comparisons* (Hong Kong, 2015).

McElligott, Jason, and Eve Patten (eds), *The Perils of Print Culture: Book, Print and Publishing History in Theory and Practice* (Basingstoke, 2015).

McKenzie, D. F., *Bibliography and the Sociology of Texts* (London, 1985).

McKitterick, David, *Print, Manuscript and the Search for Order 1450–1830* (Cambridge, 2003).

Raven, James (ed.), *The Oxford Illustrated History of the Book* (Oxford, 2018).

Shields, David S., *Civil Tongues and Polite Letters in British America* (Williamsburg, VA, 1997).

Suarez, Michael F., and H. R. Woudhuysen (eds), *The Oxford Companion to the Book*, 2 vols (Oxford, 2010).

Warner, Michael, *The Letters of the Republic: Publication and the Public Sphere in Eighteenth-Century America* (Cambridge, MA, 1990).

Xiumin, Zhang, *The History of Chinese Printing*, trans. Chen Jiehua et al. (Paramus, NJ, 2009).

Ancient communities

Bagnall, Roger S. (ed.), *The Oxford Handbook of Papyrology* (Oxford, 2009).

Balke, Thomas E., and Christina Tsouparopoulou (eds), *Materiality of Writing in Early Mesopotamia* (Berlin, 2016).

Black, Jeremy A., Graham Cunningham, Eleanor Robson and Gábor G. Zólyomi, *The Literature of Ancient Sumer* (Oxford, 2004).
Boone, Elizabeth H., and Walter D. Mignolo (eds), *Writing without Words: Alternative Literacies in Mesoamerica and the Andes* (Durham, NC, 1994).
Boone, Elizabeth H., and Gary Urton (eds), *Their Way of Writing: Scripts, Signs and Pictographies in Pre-Columbian America* (Washington, DC, 2011).
Brown, Michelle (ed.), *In the Beginning: Bibles to the Year 1000* (Washington, DC, 2006).
Cohen, Matthew, and Jeffrey Glover (eds), *Colonial Mediascapes: Sensory Worlds of the Early Americas* (Lincoln, NE, 2014).
Engelhardt, Joshua (ed.), *Agency in Ancient Writing* (Boulder, CO, 2012).
Gamble, Harry Y., *Books and Readers in the Early Church: A History of Early Christian Texts* (New Haven, 1995).
Hilgert, Marcus (ed.), *Understanding Material Text Cultures: A Multidisciplinary View* (Berlin, 2016).
Jansen, Maarten, and Gabina Aurora Pérez Jiménez, *The Mixtec Pictorial Manuscripts: Time, Agency and Memory in Ancient Mexico* (Leiden, 2010).
Lewis, Mark Edward, *Writing and Authority in Ancient China* (Albany, NY, 1999).
Li, Feng and David Prager Branner (eds), *Writing and Literacy in Early China* (Seattle and London, 2011).
Piquette, Kathryn E., and Ruth D. Whitehouse (eds), *Writing as Material Practice: Substance, Surface and Medium* (London, 2013).
Postgate, Nicholas, *Bronze Age Bureaucracy: Writing and the Practice of Government in Assyria* (Cambridge, 2013).
Quilter, Jeffrey, and Gary Urton (eds), *Narrative Threads: Accounting and Recounting in Andean Khipu* (Austin, 2002).
Roberts, Colin H., and T.C. Skeat, *The Birth of the Codex* (Oxford, 1983).
Rollston, Christopher, *Writing and Literacy in the World of Ancient Israel: Epigraphic Evidence from the Iron Age* (Atlanta, 2010).
Shaughnessy, Edward L., *Rewriting Early Chinese Texts* (Albany, NY, 2006).
Tsien, Tsuen-hsuin, *Written on Bamboo and Silk: The Beginnings of Chinese Books and Inscriptions*, 2nd edn (Chicago, 2004).
Wang, Haicheng, *Writing and the Ancient State: China in Comparative Perspective* (Cambridge, 2014).
Winsbury, Rex, *The Roman Book: Books, Publishing and Performance in Classical Rome* (London, 2009).

Woods, Christopher (ed.), *Visible Language: Inventions of Writing in the Ancient Middle East and Beyond* (Chicago, 2010).

2 The Early History of Book History

Barrett, Timothy H., *The Woman Who Discovered Printing* (London, 2008).
Blair, Ann, *Too Much to Know: Managing Scholarly Information before the Modern Age* (New Haven, 2010).
Brokaw, Cynthia J., and Kai-wing Chow (eds), *Printing and Book Culture in Late Imperial China* (Berkeley and London, 2005).
Brokaw, Cynthia, and Christopher Reed, *From Woodblocks to the Internet: Chinese Publishing and Print Culture in Transition, 1800 to 2008* (Leiden, 2010).
Davison, Peter (ed.), *The Book Encompassed: Studies in Twentieth-Century Bibliography* (New Castle, DE, and Winchester, 1998).
Ezell, Margaret J. M., *Social Authorship and the Advent of Print* (Baltimore and London, 1999).
Kornicki, Peter, *The Book in Japan, A Cultural History from the Beginnings to the Nineteenth Century* (Leiden, 1998).
McDermott, Joseph P., *A Social History of the Chinese Book: Books and Literati Culture in Late Imperial China* (Hong Kong, 2006).
McKitterick, David, *Old Books, New Technologies: The Representation, Conservation and Transformation of Books since 1700* (Cambridge, 2013).
McMullen, David, *State and Scholars in Tang China* (Cambridge, 1988).
Raven, James, *Bookscape: Geographies of Printing and Publishing in London before 1800* (Chicago and London, 2014).

3 Description, Enumeration and Modelling

Benson, Charles, *A Dictionary of Members of the Dublin Book Trade, 1801–1850* (London, forthcoming).
Besterman, Theodore, *The Beginnings of Systematic Bibliography* (London, 1935).
Bibliographical Society, *The Bibliographical Society, 1892–1942: Studies in Retrospect* (London, 1949).
Black, Fiona, Bertrum H. MacDonald, J. Malcolm and W. Black, 'Geographic Information Systems: A New Research Method for Book History', *Book History* 1 (1998): 11–31.

158 Bibliography

Blayney, Peter, *The Bookshops in Paul's Cross Churchyard*. Occasional Papers of the Bibliographical Society, 5 (London, 1990).

Braddock, Richard, 'An Extension of the "Lasswell Formula"', *Journal of Communication*, 8 (1958): 88–93.

De Bolla, Peter, *The Architecture of Concepts: The Historical Formation of Human Rights* (New York, 2013).

Eisenstein, Elizabeth, *The Printing Press as an Agent of Change: Communications and Cultural Transformations in Early-Modern Europe*, 2 vols (Cambridge, 1979), recast as *The Printing Revolution in Early Modern Europe*, 2nd edn (Cambridge, 2005).

Gaskell, Philip, *A New Introduction to Bibliography* (Oxford, 1972).

Goldschmidt, E. P., *Gothic and Renaissance Bookbindings* (London, 1928).

Hobson, G. D., *Studies in the History of Bookbinding: Selected Studies* (London, 1985).

Kornicki, Peter, *The Book in Japan: A Cultural History from the Beginnings to the Nineteenth Century* (Leiden, 1998).

Lasswell, Harold, 'The Structure and Function of Communication in Society', in Lyman Bryson (ed.), *The Communication of Ideas: A Series of Addresses* (New York, 1948), pp. 37–51.

Le Roux, Elizabeth, *A Social History of the University Presses in Apartheid South Africa: Between Complicity and Resistance* (Leiden, 2016).

McCorison, Marcus A., 'The Annals of American Bibliography, or Book History, Plain and Fancy', *Libraries & Culture*, 26: 1 (Winter, 1991): 14–23.

McKerrow, R. B., *An Introduction to Bibliography for Literary Students* (Oxford, 1927); repr. 1994 with intro. by David McKitterick.

McMurtrie, Douglas C., *Modern Typography and Layout* (Chicago, 1929).

McMurtrie, Douglas C., et al., *A History of Printing in the United States: The Story of the Introduction of the Press and of its History and Influence during the Pioneer Period in Each State of the Union* (New York, 1936).

McQuail, Denis, *McQuail's Mass Communication Theory*, 6th edn (Los Angeles, 2010).

Moretti, Franco, *Atlas of the European Novel, 1800–1900* (Chicago, 1998),

Morison, Stanley, *The Typographic Book, 1450–1935: A Study of Fine Typography through Five Centuries* (London, 1963).

Nagatomo, Chiyoji, *Edō jidai no tosho ryūtsu* [The Book Trade in the Edo Period] (Tokyo, 2002).

Pickwoad, Nicholas, 'Onward and Downward: How Binders Coped with the Printing Press before 1800', in Michael Harris and Robin

Myers (eds), *A Millennium of the Book: Production, Design and Illustration in Manuscript and Print 900–1900* (Winchester, 1994), pp. 61–106.

Pollard, Graham, and Albert Ehrman, *The Distribution of Books by Catalogue from the Invention of Printing to A.D. 1800, Based on Material in the Broxbourne Library* (London, 1965).

Pollard, Mary, *A Dictionary of Members of the Dublin Book Trade, 1550–1800, Based on the Records of the Guild of St Luke the Evangelist, Dublin* (London, 2000).

Simpson, Percy, *Proof-Reading in the Sixteenth, Seventeenth and Eighteenth Centuries* (Oxford, 1955).

Siskin, Clifford, and William Warner (eds), *This is Enlightenment* (Chicago, 2010).

St Clair, William, *The Reading Nation in the Romantic Period* (Cambridge, 2004).

Stoddard, Roger, *Marks in Books, Illustrated and Explained* (Cambridge, MA, 2005).

Stokes, Roy, *The Function of Bibliography* (London, 1969).

Suzuki, Toshiyuki, *Edō no dokusho netsu: Jigaku suru dokusha to shoseki ryutsu* [The Reading Fever in Edo: The Self-Taught Readers and the Circulation of Books] (Tokyo, 2007).

Tabor, Stephen. 'ESTC and the Bibliographical Community', *The Library*, 7th ser., 8 (2007): 367–86

Twyman. Michael, *Printing 1770–1970: An Illustrated History of its Development and Uses in England* (London, 1970).

Wallerstein, Immanuel, *World-Systems Analysis: An Introduction* (Durham, NC, 2004).

Werner, Michael, and Bénédicte Zimmermann, 'Beyond Comparison: *Histoire Croisée* and the Challenge of Reflexivity,' *History and Theory*, 45: 1 (2006): 30–50.

4 Who, What and How?

Amory, Hugh, *Bibliography and the Book Trades: Studies in the Print Culture of Early New England*, ed. David D. Hall (Philadelphia, 2004).

Anderson, Benedict, *Imagined Communities: Reflections on the Origin and Spread of Nationalism*, rev. edn (London and New York, 1991).

Armstrong. Elizabeth, *Before Copyright: The French Book-Privilege System 1498–1526* (Cambridge, 1990).

Atiyeh, George N., *The Book in the Islamic World: The Written Word and Communication in the Middle East* (Syracuse, NY, 1995).

160 Bibliography

Augst, Thomas, and Kenneth E. Carpenter (eds), *Institutions of Reading: The Social Life of Libraries in the United States* (Boston, 2007).
Bagnall, Roger S. (ed.), *The Oxford Handbook of Papyrology* (Oxford, 2009).
Bayly, C. A., *Empire and Information: Intelligence Gathering and Social Communication in India, 1780–1870* (Cambridge, 1996).
Beetham, Margaret, *Domesticity and Desire in the Woman's Magazine, 1800–1914* (London, 1996).
Black, Alistair, *The Public Library in Britain, 1914–2000* (London, 2000).
Blagden, Cyprina, *The Stationers' Company: A History, 1403–1959* (London, 1960).
Blair, Ann, *Too Much to Know: Managing Scholarly Information before the Modern Age* (New Haven, 2010).
Blair, Sheila S., and Jonathan M. Bloom, 'The Islamic World', in James Raven (ed.), *The Oxford Illustrated History of the Book* (Oxford, forthcoming).
Blayney, Peter, *The Stationers' Company and the Printers of London, 1501–1557*, 2 vols (Cambridge, 2013).
Boone, Elizabeth H., and Walter D. Mignolo (eds), *Writing without Words: Alternative Literacies in Mesoamerica and the Andes* (Durham, NC, 1994).
Boone, Elizabeth H., and Gary Urton (eds), *Their Way of Writing: Scripts, Signs and Pictographies in Pre-Columbian America* (Washington, DC, 2011).
Brook, Timothy, *The Confusions of Pleasure: Commerce and Culture in Ming China* (Berkeley, 1998).
Brokaw, Cynthia, *Commerce and Culture: The Sibao Book Trade in the Qing and Republican Periods* (Cambridge, MA, 2007).
Carruthers, Mary, *The Book of Memory*, 2nd edn (Cambridge, 2008).
Chan, Hok-lam, *Control of Publishing in China: Past and Present* (Canberra, 1983).
Chartier, Roger, *The Cultural Uses of Print in Early Modern France* (Princeton, 1987).
Chia, Lucille, *Printing for Profit: The Commercial Publishers of Jianyang, Fujian (11th–17th Centuries)* (Cambridge MA, 2003).
Chia, Lucille, and Hilde de Weerdt (eds), *Knowledge and Text Production in an Age of Print: China, 900–1400* (Leiden, 2011).
Chow Kai-wing, *Publishing, Culture, and Power in Early Modern China* (Stanford, 2004).
Crawford, Alice (ed.), *The Meaning of the Library: A Cultural History* (Oxford and Princeton, 2015).

Darnton, Robert, *The Business of Enlightenment: A Publishing History of the Encyclopédie, 1775–1800* (Cambridge, MA, 1979).

Darnton, Robert, *Censors at Work: How States Shaped Literature* (London and New York, 2014).

Deazley, Ronan, Martin Kretschmer and Lionel Bently (eds), *Privilege and Property: Essays on the History of Copyright* (Cambridge, 2010).

De Hamel, Christopher, *A History of Illuminated Manuscripts*, 2nd edn (London, 1994).

Eyre, Chris, *The Use of Documents in Pharaonic Egypt* (Oxford, 2013).

Ezell, Margaret J. M., *Social Authorship and the Advent of Print* (Baltimore, 2003).

Fabian, Bernhard, *Buch, Bibliothek und geisteswissenschaftliche Forschung: Zu Problemen der Literaturversorgung und der Literaturproduktion in der Bundesrepublik Deutschland* (Göttingen, 1983).

Fontaine, Laurence, *Histoire du colportage en Europe* (Paris, 1993); trans. as *History of Pedlars in Europe* (Cambridge, 1996).

Foot, Mirjam M., *The History of Bookbinding as a Mirror of Society* (London, 1998).

Fraser, Robert, and Mary Hammond (eds), *Books without Borders*, 2 vols (London, 2008).

Freedman, Jeffrey, *Books without Borders in Enlightenment Europe: French Cosmopolitanism and German Literary Markets* (Philadelphia, 2011).

Frost, Mark, 'Pandora's Post Box: Empire and Information in India, 1854–1914', *English Historical Review*, 131 (Oct. 2016): 1043–73.

Fyfe, Aileen, *Steam-Powered Knowledge: William Chambers and the Business of Publishing, 1820–1860* (Chicago, 2012).

Gaskell, Philip, *A New Introduction to Bibliography* (Oxford, 1972; rev. edn, New Castle, DE, and Winchester, 1995).

Giesecke, Michael, *Der Buchdruck in der frühen Neuzeit* (1991; rev. edn., Frankfurt, 1998).

Gillespie, Alexandra, *Print Culture and the Medieval Author: Chaucer, Lydgate, and their Books, 1473–1557* (Oxford, 2006).

Gillespie, Alexandra, and Daniel Wakelin (eds), *The Production of Books in England 1350–1500* (Cambridge, 2011).

Gitelman, Lisa, *Always Already New: Media, History and the Data of Culture* (Cambridge, MA, 2006).

Goldgar, Anne, *Impolite Learning: Conduct and Community in the Republic of Letters, 1680–1750* (New Haven, 1995).

Golvers, Noël, *Building Humanistic Libraries in Late Imperial China* (Rome, 2011).
Gómez-Arostegui, Tomás, 'The Untold Story of the First Copyright Suit under the Statute of Anne in 1710', *Berkeley Technology Law Journal*, 25: 3 (2010).
Goody, Jack, and Ian Watt, 'The Consequences of Literacy,' *Comparative Studies in Society and History*, 5: 3 (April 1963): 304–45
Grafton, Anthony, *The Culture of Correction in Renaissance Europe* (New Haven, 2011).
Griffin, Clive, *Journeymen-Printers, Heresy, and the Inquisition in Sixteenth-Century Spain* (Oxford, 2005).
Hall, David D., *Ways of Writing: The Practice and Politics of Text-Making in Seventeenth-Century New England* (Philadelphia, 2008),
Hanebutt-Benz, Eva, Dagmar Glass and Geoffrey Roper (eds), *Middle Eastern Languages and the Print Revolution: A Cross-Cultural Encounter* (Westhofen, 2002).
Hanna, Nelly, *In Praise of Books: A Cultural History of Cairo's Middle Class, Sixteenth to the Eighteenth Century* (Syracuse, NY, 2003).
Hemmungs Wirtén, Eva, 'The Patent and the Paper: A Few Thoughts on Late Modern Science and Intellectual Property', *Culture Unbound*, 7: 4 (2015): 600–9.
Hesse, Carla, *Publishing and Cultural Politics in Revolutionary Paris, 1789–1810* (Berkeley, 1991).
Houston, George W., *Inside Roman Libraries: Book Collections and their Management in Antiquity* (Chapel Hill, NC, 2014).
Howsam, Leslie, *Cheap Bibles: Nineteenth-Century Publishing and the British and Foreign Bible Society* (Cambridge, 1991).
Howsam, Leslie, and James Raven (eds), *Books between Europe and the Americas: Connections and Communities, 1620–1860* (London and New York, 2011).
Jackson, H. J., *Marginalia: Readers Writing in Books* (Toronto, 2001).
Jensen, Kristian (ed.), *Incunabula and their Readers: Printing, Selling and Using Books in the Fifteenth Century* (London, 2003).
Jensen, Kristian, *Revolution and the Antiquarian Book: Reshaping the Past, 1780–1815* (Cambridge, 2011).
Johns, Adrian, *The Nature of the Book: Print and Knowledge in the Making* (Chicago and London, 1998).
Johns, Adrian, *Piracy: The Intellectual Property Wars from Gutenberg to Gates* (Chicago, 2009).
Kaufman, Paul, *Libraries and their Users: Collected Papers in Library History* (London, 1969).
Knight, Jeffrey Todd, *Bound to Read: Compilations, Collections, and the Making of Renaissance Literature* (Philadelphia, 2013).

König, Jason, Katerina Oikonomopoulou and Greg Woolf (eds), *Ancient Libraries* (Cambridge, 2013).
Kornicki, Peter, *The Book in Japan: A Cultural History from the Beginnings to the Nineteenth Century* (Leiden, 1998).
Kwakkel, Erik, Rosamond McKitterick and Rodney Thomson, *Turning over a New Leaf: Change and Development in the Medieval Manuscript* (Leiden, 2012).
Lewis, Mark Edward, *Writing and Authority in Ancient China* (Albany, NY, 1999).
Li, Feng and David Prager Branner (eds), *Writing and Literacy in Early China* (Seattle and London, 2011).
Lyons, Martyn, *A History of Reading and Writing in the Western World* (Basingstoke, 2010).
Maclean, Ian W. F., *Learning and the Market Place: Essays in the History of the Early Modern Book* (Boston, 2009).
Marker, Gary, *Publishing, Printing, and the Origins of Intellectual Life in Russia, 1700–1800* (Princeton, 1985).
Martin, Henri-Jean, *The History and Power of Writing* (Chicago, 1994).
McCleery, Alistair, 'The Book in the Long Twentieth Century', in Howsam, Leslie (ed.), *The Cambridge Companion to the History of the Book* (Cambridge, 2015), pp. 162–80.
McDowell, Paula, *The Women of Grub Street: Press, Politics and Gender in the London Literary Marketplace, 1678–1730* (Oxford, 1998).
McGann, J. J., *A Critique of Modern Textual Criticism* (Chicago, 1983).
McGann, J. J., *The Beauty of Inflections: Literary Investigations in Historical Method and Theory* (Oxford, 1985),
McGill, Meredith, *American Literature and the Culture of Reprinting, 1837–1853* (Philadelphia, 2003).
McKitterick, Rosamond, *The Carolingians and the Written Word* (Cambridge, 1989).
Mollier, Jean-Yves, *Louis Hachette (1800–1864). Le fondateur d'un empire* (Paris, 1999).
Patten, Robert L., *Charles Dickens and 'Boz': The Birth of the Industrial-Age Author* (Cambridge, 2013).
Needham, Paul, *The Printer and the Pardoner* (Washington, DC, 1986).
Pedersen, Johannes, *The Arabic Book*, trans. Geoffrey French, ed. Robert Hillenbrand (Princeton, 1984).
Pettegree, Andrew, *The Book in the Renaissance* (London and New Haven, 2011).
Popkin, Jeremy, *Revolutionary News: The Press in France, 1789–1799* (Durham, NC, 1990).

Price, Leah, *How to Do Things with Books in Victorian Britain* (Princeton, 2012).
Quilter, Jeffrey and Gary Urton (eds), *Narrative Threads: Accounting and Recounting in Andean Khipu* (Austin, 2002).
Raabe, Paul, *Bücherlust und Lesefreuden: Beiträge zur Geschichte des Buchwesens im 18. und frühen 19. Jahrhundert* (Stuttgart, 1984).
Raven, James (ed.), *Lost Libraries: The Destruction of Great Book Collections since Antiquity* (Basingstoke, 2004).
Raven, James, *The Business of Books: Booksellers and the English Book Trade 1450–1850* (London and New Haven, 2007).
Raymond, Joad, *Pamphlets and Pamphleteering in Early Modern Britain* (Cambridge, 2003).
Reed, Christopher A., *Gutenberg in Shanghai: Chinese Print Capitalism, 1876–1937* (Vancouver, 2004).
Rhodes, Dennis E., *The Spread of Printing: Eastern Hemisphere: India, Pakistan, Ceylon, Burma, and Thailand* (Amsterdam, 1969).
Roberts, Colin H., and T. C. Skeat, *The Birth of the Codex* (Oxford, 1983).
Rollston, Christopher A., *Writing and Literacy in the World of Ancient Israel: Epigraphic Evidence from the Iron Age* (Atlanta, 2010).
Roper, Geoffrey (ed.), *World Survey of Islamic Manuscripts* (London, 2002).
Roper, Geoffrey, 'The Printing Press and Change in the Arab World,' in Sabrina Alcorn Baron, Eric N. Lindquist and Eleanor F. Shevlin (eds), *Agent of Change: Print Cultural Studies after Elizabeth L. Eisenstein* (Boston, 2007), pp. 250–67.
Rose, Jonathan, *The Intellectual Life of the British Working Classes* (New Haven, 2001).
Rose, Mark, *Authors and Owners: The Invention of Copyright*, rev. edn (Cambridge, MA, 1995).
Rouse, Mary A., and Richard H. Rouse, *Authentic Witnesses: Approaches to Medieval Texts and Manuscripts* (South Bend, IN, 1991).
Saenger, Paul, *Space between Words: The Origins of Silent Reading* (Stanford, 1997).
Shaw, Graham, *Printing in Calcutta to 1800* (London, 1981).
Skaria, Ajay, 'Writing, Orality and Power in the Dangs, Western India, 1800s–1920s,' in Dipesh Chakrabarty and Shahid Amin (eds), *Subaltern Studies*, 9 (1996), pp. 13–58.
Spufford, Margaret, *Small Books and Pleasant Histories: Popular Fiction and its Readership in Seventeenth-Century England* (London, 1981).
St Clair, William, *The Reading Nation in the Romantic Period* (Cambridge, 2004).

Twyman, Michael, *The British Library Guide to Printing, History and Techniques* (London, 1998).
Vincent, David, *Literacy and Popular Culture: England 1750–1914* (Cambridge, 1989).
Wakelin, Daniel, *Scribal Correction and Literary Craft: English Manuscripts 1375–1510* (Cambridge, 2014).
Wang, Haicheng, *Writing and the Ancient State: China in Comparative Perspective* (Cambridge, 2014).
Watt, Ian, *The Rise of the Novel: Studies in Defoe, Richardson and Fielding* (London, 1956).
Watt, Tessa, *Cheap Print and Popular Piety, 1550–1640* (Cambridge, 1991).
Weedon, Alexis, *Victorian Publishing: The Economics of Book Production for a Mass Market 1836–1916* (Basingstoke, 2003).

5 Reading

Bayly, C. A., *Empire and Information: Intelligence Gathering and Social Communication in India, 1780–1870* (Cambridge, 1996).
Chartier, Roger, *The Order of Books: Readers, Authors, and Libraries in Europe between the Fourteenth and Eighteenth Centuries* (Cambridge and Stanford, 1994).
Clanchy, Michael, *From Memory to Written Record: England, 1066–1307*, 3rd edn (Oxford, 2013).
Darnton, Robert, 'First Steps towards a History of Reading', *Australian Journal of French Studies*, 23 (1986): 5–32; repr. in Peter Burke (ed.), *New Perspectives on Historical Writing* (Cambridge, 1991), pp. 1–75.
Ginzburg, Carlo, *The Cheese and the Worms: The Cosmos of a Sixteenth-Century Miller*, trans. John and Anne Tedeschi (London, 1980).
Goody, Jack (ed.), *Literacy in Traditional Societies* (Cambridge, 1968).
Grafton, Anthony, and Lisa Jardine, ' "Studied for Action": How Gabriel Harvey Read his Livy', *Past and Present*, 129: 1 (1990): 30–78.
Hannebutt-Benz, Eva-Maria, *Die Kunst des Lesens: Lesemöbel und Leseverhalten vom Mittelalter bis zur Gegenwart* (Frankfurt, 1985).
Houston, R. A., *Literacy in Early Modern Europe: Culture and Education 1500–1800* (London, 1988).
Hume, R. D., 'Texts within Contexts: Notes toward a Historical Method', *Philological Quarterly*, 71 (1992): 69–100.

Johnson, William A., *Readers and Reading Culture in the High Roman Empire: A Study of Elite Communities* (Oxford, 2010).
Klancher, Jon P, *The Making of English Reading Audiences, 1790–1832* (Madison, 1987).
McHenry, Elizabeth, *Forgotten Readers: Recovering the Lost History of African American Literary Societies* (Durham, NC, 2002).
Orgel, Stephen, *The Reader in the Book: A Study of Spaces and Traces* (Oxford, 2015).
Radway, Janice A., *Reading the Romance: Women, Patriarchy, and Popular Literature* (Chapel Hill, NC, and London, 1984).
Raven, James, Helen Small and Naomi Tadmor (eds), *The Practice and Representation of Reading in England* (Cambridge, 1996).
Ricoeur, Paul, *From Text to Action: Essays in Hermeneutics, II*, trans. Kathleen Blamey and John B. Thompson (London, 1991).
Sher, Richard B., *The Enlightenment and the Book: Scottish Authors and their Publishers in Eighteenth-Century Britain, Ireland, and America* (Chicago, 2006).
Thompson, John B., *Books in the Digital Age* (Cambridge, 2005).
Thompson, John B., *Merchants of Culture: The Publishing Business in the Twenty-First Century*, 2nd edn (Cambridge, 2012).
Towsey, Mark, *Reading the Scottish Enlightenment: Books and their Readers in Provincial Scotland 1750–1820* (Leiden and Boston, 2010).
Volkov, Vadim, 'Limits to Propaganda: Soviet Power and the Peasant Reader in the 1920s', in James Raven (ed.), *Free Print and Non-Commercial Publishing since 1700* (Aldershot and Burlington, VT, 2000), pp. 177–93.
Wakelin, Daniel, *Humanism, Reading and English Literature 1430–1530* (Oxford, 2007).

Multi-contributor national histories of the book

Bell, Bill (gen. ed.), *The Edinburgh History of the Book in Scotland*, 4 vols (Edinburgh, 2007–).
Curtain, John (founding ed.), *History of the Book in Australia*, 4 vols (Brisbane, 2001–).
Fleming, Patricia Lockhart, and Yvan Lamonde (gen. eds), *The History of the Book in Canada / Histoire du livre et de l'imprimé au Canada*, 6 vols [3 in each language] (Toronto and Montréal, 2004–7).
Hall, David D. (gen. ed.), *A History of the Book in America*, 5 vols (Chapel Hill, NC, 2000–10).

Hoare, Peter (gen. ed.), *The Cambridge History of Libraries in Britain and Ireland*, 3 vols (Cambridge, 2006).

Martin, Henri-Jean, and Roger Chartier (eds), *Histoire de l'édition française*, 4 vols (Paris, 1983–6).

McKenzie, D. F., David McKitterick and I. R. Willison (gen. eds), *The Cambridge History of the Book in Britain*, 7 vols (Cambridge, 1999–).

Welch, Robert, and Brian Walker (gen. eds), *The Oxford History of the Irish Book*, 5 vols (Oxford, 2006–).

Index

Abydos 19
account books 23, 65, 109;
    ancient 18, 20
actor-network theory (ANT)
    79, 99
Adams, Thomas 77
advertisements 14, 58, 61, 90,
    104, 119
Afghanistan 22, 26
Africa 2, 10, 13, 17, 19, 67,
    74, 141; West 98; see also
    South Africa
Aguateca, Guatemala 27
albums 41, 46, 98
almanacs 25, 104; see also
    calendars
Alnander, Johan Olaf 43
alphabets (letters), alphabetic
    systems 14, 17, 19, 29, 35,
    77, 93, 97, 98, 124, 126,
    142; see also graphemes
Altick, Richard D. 85, 139
Amazon (company) 143
American Antiquarian Society
    (AAS) 66, 71, 73, 75
American Bibliographer 46, 59
American Historical
    Association 73
American Library Association
    59
*American Library Book
    Catalogues* 61
American Printing History
    Association 71
American Society for
    Eighteenth-Century Studies
    73
Americas 4, 26, 29, 91, 103,
    105, 128; see also Central
    America, North America,
    South America
Ames, Joseph 43–4, 46
Amory, Hugh 84
Amsterdam 76, 91
Analects of Confucius 128
Anderson, Benedict 114, 139
Annales school 68
Annenberg School for
    Communication and
    Journalism 80
anonymity 89, 128
annotation *see* marginalia
antiquarian booksellers 38, 45,
    53, 104–5
Antwerp 72, 91, 96–7
Anyang, China 20

apograph (transcript) 88
apprenticeship records 50, 79, 90
Arabic 96, 98; use of papyrus 23–4
Arabiske bog (*The Arabic Book*) 55
Aramaic 19, 23, 34, 109
Arber, Edward 50, 52
archaeology 16, 19–20, 22, 26–7, 30, 54, 67
archives 5, 11, 24, 50, 58, 59, 65, 67, 72, 73, 77, 79, 84, 86, 89–92, 99, 100–02, 134; lost 112; of knowledge 132, 143; *see also* history of the book sources
Ariès, Philippe 138
Aristotle 71
Armstrong, Elizabeth 101
Ashurbanipal, King, and tablets 107–8
Asia 5, 34, 64, 67, 87, 97–8, 113, 119, 128, 137; Central 2, 18, 19, 67; South 3, 4, 9–10, 17, 22, 31, 107–8, 116; *see also* China; East Asia
Association internationale de bibliophilie 54
Association paléographique internationale: culture, écriture, société (APICES) 56
Associazione italiana biblioteche 54
Assyria 22, 107
Atkyns, Richard 40
atlases 61; *see also* maps
audiobooks 142
Australia 72, 75, 131; Australasia 74, 87; Australasian Rare Books School 74

authors 13, 37, 63, 45, 48, 53, 84, 86–7, 95–6, 110, 116, 119, 121–2, 128; anticipating readers 116–7, 120; canonical 110, 137; identities and rights 142; intent 83; and challenges 143
authorship 4, 7, 11, 13, 38, 42, 75, 77, 79, 83, 85, 89–90, 100; attributions 58, 61, 63; and gender 94–5
autobiographies 130–1
Aztec pictographs 14, 26, 28

Badius, Jodocus 41
Bahrain 99
Bailyn, Bernard 86
Bale, John 37
ballads 62, 67, 86
Baltic 76, 97
bamboo 17, 34; and wooden strip books 20, 21
banben 9, 51
banned books 38, 52–3, 101–2, 104; *see also* censorship; Index
bark 10, 21, 22, 25–6, 27, 31, 33, as liber 32–3; fig tree 29
Barker, Nicolas 77, 111
Barnes, James 100
Barrett, Timothy H. 37
Barthes, Roland 14–15
Baseler Papiermühle, Switzerland 72
Bayerische Staatsbibliothek Inkunabelkatalog 61
Bayly, Christopher 86, 113
Beale, Peter 112
Beijing 72, 96
Beinecke Library, Yale 74
Belanger, Terry 74
Bell, Bill 131

Bellingradt, Daniel 89
Benhamou, Paul 131
Bennett, H.S. 86
Benson, Charles 50
Berkeley, California 56
Bertelsmann 92
Besterman, Theodore 54
bestsellers 85, 89, 104; *see also* popular literature
bibles 24, 25, 30, 32, 36, 65, 85, 101, 123, 129–30, 137, 141; translated 70, 97
bibliographical lecture series 74–5
bibliographical societies 53–4, 71; Bibliographical Society 53, 55, 59, 144; of America 53; of Australia and New Zealand 53; of Canada 53
bibliography 7, 10, 36, 49, 56; analytical 7, 15, 47–8, 49, 53, 56, 69, 141; definitions 47–9; descriptive 15, 48–51, 53; enumerative (or systematic) 7, 47–8, 49, 52, 57, 61, 64, 66, 68; historical 15, 48, 49, 61, 58, 76; national 58, 69; precursors to 40–6; textual 48, 49, 69; 'new' 47, 50
bibliologie 68
bibliomania (bibliomanie) 38–9, 44–5
bibliometrics 58, 68–9, 76, 92
bibliophiles 41–2, 43–5, 52–3, 55, 104–5, 106; associations of 54; bibliophilia 74, 105
Biblioteca Nacional de España 63
Bibliotheca universalis 38
Bibliothek der Frauenfrage 120

Bibliothèque nationale de France 62, 63
bibliothèques bleues 68; *Bibliothèque bleue de Troyes* 138
Bidwell, John 86
binding (of books) 14, 16, 20, 26, 40, 48, 49, 57, 65, 87, 98; inventory 57; research and history 54–5, 86–7, 88
Black, Alistair 107
Black, Fiona 79
Blades, William 46, 52
Blagden, Cyprian 86
Blair, Ann 38, 39
Blair, Sheila 98
blanks 10, 23; as forms 112–13
Blayney, Peter 85–6
Bloch, Marc 68
block prints 3, 5, 14, 22, 37; *see also* woodblock printing
Bloom, Jonathan 98
Bodleian Library, Oxford 125
Bodoni, Giambattista 44
Boghardt, Martin 55
Bogtrykmuseet, Denmark 72
bones 16–17, 19
book(s): ancient 16–32; arrangements 132; artists 98; as objects 129; auctions 68–9, 90, 122; bespoke 119–20; 'biographies' 13; business and financing 92, 90, 99, 100, 122, 124–5; circulation 76, 92, 99–105; clubs 45, 105, 122; cupboard 36; dealers and agents 104–5; definition of 9–11, 20, 32; design 136; digital 142–4; distribution 40, 76, 84, 94, 103–5,

117; donations 122, 130; folded 20, 23; fragility 24–5, 31; function 10, 11, 29; illustration 86; images 36; imported 121, 140; 'in print' 143; interrupted appreciation 27; lost 17, 31, 34, 58, 89, 108, 110, 143; market 38–9, 45, 84, 99, 103, 104, 119–20, 124, 130; materiality 16, 107; ownership 48, 88; patronage 84, 92; phonographic 29; portability 19, 121, 136; provenance 48, 58; 'pyro-osteomantic' 17; records 90, 104, 123, 126; rediscovery 31; scholarly 121; second-hand 65, 102, 104, 121; superfluity 38–9; survival 17, 27, 29, 62, 64; symbolic use 14, 35, 116, 129, 135; tactility 136; unintended functions 129–30; unread 14; and language 34; and national interests 143; and religion 136; and revolution 96, 100, 103, 14; and war 103, 136; *see also* binding, editions, reading, history of the book
Book Collector, The 55
Book of Zhuangzi 20
book studies 8, 74; ancient 35; medieval 123; *see also* history of the book
book trade 65, 50, 99, 125; international agreements 92; studies of 54; *see also* publishing
book wheel (or reading wheel) 132

Book History 55
book history, see history of the book
bookplates 43, 61
booksellers 45, 46, 50, 65, 78–9, 84, 99, 102, 120, 125; antiquarian 53; catalogues 103; records 109; trade sales 62
bookshops 99, 122, 123; records 125
Boorstin, Daniel 71
borrowing (of books) 99, 108, 122–3, 132; registers 125–6; *see also* libraries
Boswell, Eleanor 50
Bourdieu, Pierre 78
Bowers, Fredson 53
Bowyer, William 45, 62; firm 59
Boxhorn, Marcus Zuerius 42
Braddock, Richard 81
Bradshaw, Henry 46, 47
Brazil 72, 87, 96
Briggs, Asa 86
Bristol Library Society 125
Britain 3, 44, 50, 53, 54, 56, 58, 61, 65, 68, 75, 88–9, 101, 103, 107, 125, 131, 138; Roman 22–23; and territories 61
British Book Trades Index 50
British Library 46, 59, 61, 79, 107
British Museum 46, 49
broadsides 40, 50, 120
Brokaw, Cynthia 34, 95
Brook, Timothy 102
Buddhism 108, 113; sutras 14, 22
Bulletin du bibliophile 54
Bunyan, John 13
Buringh, Eltjo 64
Burke, Peter 39, 86–7

Bury, Richard de 38
Byblos, Phoemicia 32
Byzantine 88

Cai Lun 21
Cairo 23, 98
calendars 14, 19, 27, 29, 30, 102; see also almanacs
calf skin (vellum) 10; see also skins
calligraphy 93, 113
Cambridge 73, 75;
    Bibliographical Society 53
Cambridge History of the Book in Britain 65
Cambridge Project for the Book Trust 73
Cambridge University 73;
    Library 17, 47
Canada 61, 75, 131
canonicity 4, 38, 95, 100, 110–11, 120, 137
capsa (book box) 33
Cardanus, Hieronymus 42
Carpenter, Kenneth 107
Carter, Harry 41
Carter, Thomas F. 9, 37
Casa da xilogravura, Brazil 72
Cascajal Block 26
Caslon: William 44
Cassiodorus 32, 33, 36
Catalogue Collectif de France (CCFr) 62
Catalogue of English Literary Manuscripts 63
Catalogue of English Printers 43
catalogues 37, 40, 43, 44, 52–3, 56–8, 67, 68, 69, 89, 90, 103, 104, 109, 119, 122; manuscripts 63–4; publishers' 58; retrospective 58–66; and cataloguers 48

Catalogues of Dated and Datable Manuscripts 56
cataloguing 38, 40, 49, 51–2, 56, 83, 88, 107; Asian 66; electronic, on-line 92, 120; rules 74, 83; systems 36, 60–2; and readerships 120
Catullus 33
Caxton, William 41, 46, 97
censorship 2, 7–8, 48, 69, 83–5, 99–105, 107, 143
Center for the Book, Washington DC 71, 73
Center for the Study of Books and Media, Princeton 73
Central America 10, 14, 26, 67, 140
Centre for Manuscript and Print Studies, London 73
Centre for Material Texts, University of Cambridge 73
Centre for the Book, Pretoria 74
Centre for the History of the Book, University of Edinburgh 73
Centre for the History of the Media at University College Dublin 63
Centre for the Study of the Book, Oxford 73
Centre national de la recherche scientifique (CNRS) 88
Century of the English Book Trade 50
certificates 112–13
Chan, Hok-lam 101–2
Chang'an (Xi'an) 21
Changsha rolls, China 20
chapbooks 62, 86, 104, 120
Chartier, Roger 4, 7, 13, 87, 105, 118, 134

cheap books and print 84, 85, 92, 93, 102, 104, 125
Cheongju Early Printing Museum, South Korea 72
children's books 86
China 9, 16, 17, 26, 34, 39–40, 51, 64, 72, 87, 89–95, 100, 105, 109, 128, 139; and censorship 100–1; manuscripts 112–3; origins of printing 42; reading 127
Chinese: characters 93; classics 34, 142; language 17; listing of book titles 51; printing 35–6, 37 (and European awareness of 37); script 22; women authors 95–6; as a *lingua franca* 34
Christianity 24, 95, 113
Clark Library, University of California at Los Angeles 75
clay tablets 10, 11, 17–20; endurance of 22
Clay, John and family 125
cloth 16, 25, 26
Cockerell, Sydney 56
Codex Amiatinus 36
Codex Argenteus 24–5
Codex Cospi 27, 28
Codex Sinaiticus 30–31
codices 2, 15, 27, 33–4, 88; ancient 30–31; Mayan 27; Mesoamerican 142; and parchment 24
codicology 6–7, 87–8; *see also* handwriting; palaeography
coffee houses 105, 122
Cogan, Thomas 42
Cohen, Margaret 4
Cole, John Y. 71

collation 36, 48, 53, 56–7, 74; Collators 56–7
collecting and collections (of books) 15, 37, 46, 49, 58, 86, 103, 105, 130, 132; and guides 52
collectors (of books) 15, 37, 39, 45, 48, 53, 93–5; Asian 113
colonialism 2, 5, 6, 30, 105, 114, 136, 140–1
colophon 7, 120
Columbia University, New York 74
Comet Portable Optical Collator 57
comic books 119
Comité international de paléographie latine (CIPL) 56
communications 1, 3, 11, 16, 19, 86–7, 102, 104–5, 113–14, 136, 139–44; 'circuit' 77; graphic forms 27–9; history 31, 32–3, 51–2, 55, 111; models 77–82; 'shift' 70–1; studies 76–7
compositors 43, 47, 84, 121
computers 33, 64, 66
Confucianism 51, 53, 127
Confucius 128
Congreve, William 83
conservation (of books) 1, 2, 11, 17, 53, 60, 86–87, 107, 141
Constantinople 96; *see also* Istanbul
Copernicus 71
copyright 48, 83, 85, 89, 99–105, 143
copy-texts 47–8, 53, 83
Corpus of British Medieval Library Catalogues 56

correctors (of the press) 40
correspondence 76, 142
Corsellis, Frederick 41
Coster, Laurens 41
cotton 14, 25–6, 30; *see also* cloth
Counter-Reformation 103
Crandall Historical Printing Museum, Utah 72
Crawford, Alice 107
Cressy, David 129, 138–9
Crete 20
critical theory 6, 7, 141
criticism and critics 13, 53, 84, 85, 89, 99, 110–11
Crombergers (Seville) 91
Cultural Revolution 128
cuneiform 18–19, 30, 34, 107, 116, 119
Cuthenbergus 42; *see also* Gutenberg
Cyprus 19

D'Israeli, Isaac 42
Dai Kan-Wa jiten 51
Damascus 109
Danmarks Grafiske Museum 72
Danube 103
danyinben 53; *see also* editions
Darnton, Robert 3, 4, 7, 69, 77–8, 101, 104, 138
Daventry 125
Davies, Myles 39
Davis, Caroline 141
Davis, Herbert 41
de Bolla, Peter 66
de Certeau, Michel 117
De Jing 20
De ortu et progressu artis typographicae 42
de Worde, Wynkyn 41, 97
Dead Sea Scrolls 25, 108–9
Deazley, Ronan 101

debating societies 105, 122
deerskin 15, 29; Mayan 27; *see also* skins
DeMaria, Robert 133
Denucé, Jan 92
Depositio cornuti typographici 43
Descriptive Checklist of Book Catalogues 61
Deutsches Schreibmaschinenmuseum, Germany 72
Dewey, Melvil 59
diaries 12, 126, 131, 134
Dibdin, Thomas Frognall 44, 46
dictionaries 10, 19, 41, 45–6, 50, 51, 59
Dictionary of Printers and Printing 45–6
Die wol eingerichtete Buchdruckerei 43
Digita Vaticana Onlus 88
digital 88; facsimiles 61; humanities 66–7; images 57, 64; library collaborations 67; projects 57; reproduction 94; scanning 66–7; technology 107; *see also* editions
Digital Scriptorium 56
diplomatic 88
Dissenting Academies Project 125
divination 16–17, 20, 27, 107
documents 17, 20, 23, 25, 32, 42, 47, 55, 88, 112, 123
Dublin 50, 72
Duff, E. Gordon 49, 50, 52

Eagleton, Terry 111
Early English Books Online (EEBO) 66

Early modern manuscripts
  online (EMMO) 56
East Asia 9, 34, 37, 45,
  52, 55, 92–3, 96,
  97, 139; authorship
  89–90; bibliographical
  development 50–51; *see
  also* Asia
*East Asian Publishing and
  Society* 55
ebooks 142
École Nationale Supérieure des
  Sciences de l'Information
  et des Bibliothèques, Lyon
  73
economics in book history 2,
  5, 7, 49, 60, 69, 78–80,
  81, 83–6, 90–6, 100, 103,
  112, 120, 124, 137; labour
  costs 90
ecumene 113, 114
Edinburgh 73; Bibliographical
  Society 53; Rare Books
  School 74
EDIT 16 (Censimento
  nazionale delle edizioni
  italiane del XVI secolo) 63
editing 1, 13–14, 39, 40, 45;
  annotation 83; decisions
  47–8; processes 84, 93;
  studies 6, 15; and female
  authors 95–6
editions 9, 13, 21, 36, 38, 51,
  53, 55, 61–2, 70, 71, 76,
  98, 99, 102, 132, 134,
  143; digital 31, 56, 142;
  'ideal' 83; rare 104; sizes
  57, 62, 68, 110, 121;
  title counts 64–5; *see also*
  collation; STCs
editors 55, 59, 117, 119, 121,
  128; of newspapers 7
Eesti Trükimuuseum, Estonia
  72

Egypt 17, 19, 20, 22, 23, 30
Egyptian language 19, 23
Ehrman, Albert 103
Eighteenth Century Collections
  Online (ECCO) 66
Eighteenth Century Short Title
  Catalogue (ESTC) 60–2,
  65, 66
Einbanddatenbank (German
  Database of Book
  Bindings) 57
Eisenstein, Elizabeth 6, 69–70,
  71, 97
Electronic Enlightenment,
  Oxford 76
electronic media 30, 41, 66,
  76, 77, 85, 120; *see also*
  digital
Eliot, Simon 92
Ellis. Markman 122
*Encyclopaedia of Literary and
  Typographical Anecdote.*
  46
encyclopaedias 39, 43, 46,
  127
Encyclopédie 43
Enemies of Books 46
Engelsing, Rolf 127
English Short Title
  Catalogue (ESTC) 60–1,
  62, 65
engraving 4, 5, 40, 42, 43, 46,
  57, 61, 86, 111; *see also*
  intaglio
Enlightenment 69, 85, 109,
  131, 132, 144
ephemera 61, 62, 84, 143
epigraphy 1, 17
epitext 12
Ernesti, Johann Heinrich
  Gottfried 43
Estienne, Robert and Henri
  41
Estonia 72, 125

Europe 3–4, 18, 38, 44, 49, 50, 54, 57, 67, 69, 75, 87, 99, 102, 119, 122, 128, 137, 139, 140, 144; central 87, 125; medieval 85, 87–88, 123; printing in 5, 9, 14, 34, 36–7, 41, 42, 44, 61, 64; in comparative perspective 34, 39; Western 127
European Library 63
Evans, Charles 52, 59; *American Bibliography* 66
Evelyn, John 40
Ezell, Margaret 112

Fabian, Bernhard 107
fablabs 132
factotums 74
Fang, Achilles 52
Fanshu ouji (*Casual Notes of a Book Monger*) 52–3
Feather, John 100, 125
Febvre, Lucien 7, 9, 68, 69, 96
Fell, John 42
Fergus, Jan 125
Fertek, Martin-Dominique 43
fibre 10, 11, 16, 21, 56, 57; *see also* hemp
Fish, Stanley 118–9
Flanders 62
Flandrin, Jean-Louis 138
Folger Library, Washington DC 56
font (fount) 41, 142; definition 12, 146 n. 12
Fontaine, Laurence 104
Foot, Mirjam 86
Fournier, Pierre Simon 43–4
Foxon, David 59
France 3, 8, 16–17, 40, 54, 61–2, 63, 67, 68, 72, 75, 76, 85, 101, 104, 122, 125, 138

Freedman, Jeffrey 104
French Book Trade in Enlightenment Europe (FBTEE) 104
French Revolution 68, 69, 138
French Vernacular Books 63
Froben, Johan 41
Frost, Mark 113
Fyfe, Aileen 91

Gabriel (Gateway and Bridge to Europe's National Libraries) 63
Gaelic 61
Galen 24, 34, 71
Gallica 63, 88
Gandhara 26; Buddhist canon 31
Gardner, Daniel 128
Gates, Henry Louis 141
Genadendal Museum and Printing Works, South Africa 72
gender 2, 34, 81–2, 90, 123–4, 139, 140; and literacy 123; studies 4; and readers 120–1, 125; *see also* women authors
Genette, Gérard 7, 11
genizah 108–9
Geographic Information Systems (GIS) 79
Gerbner, George 80, 81
German 61, 62
Germany 55, 56, 57, 72, 76, 85, 107, 120
Gesamtkatalog der Wiegendrucke 61
Geschichte des Buchwesens 8; *see also* history of the book
Gesner, Conrad 38
Ghuri, Muhammad 108
Gillespie, Alexandra 89, 112

Gilmont, Jean-François 97
Ginzburg, Carlo 134
Giunti, Lucantonio and Bernardo 41
Glasgow Bibliographical Society 53
Glomski, Jacqueline 42
glossing 128
glyphs 27; Mesoamerican 30
Goldgar, Anne 101
Goldschmidt, E.P. 54
Gómez-Arostegui, H. Tomás 101
Goodreads 143
Google Books 67, 143
Gothic language 25; script 127
Grafton, Anthony 40, 84, 128–9
graphemes 17, 98
Greek 20, 88, 98, 108; books 24, 96
Greg, W. W. 47, 50, 52, 53
Griffin, Clive 112
Grolier Club 45
Grotte de Thaïs, France 16–17
Guatemala 26
guilds 101; control 40, supervision 84
Guileville, Guillaume de 36
Gujarat 108
Gutenberg, Johannes 36, 37, 141; dispute over 41–2; prize 55
Gutenberg's Galaxy 76
Gutenberg-Jahrbuch 55
Gutenberg-Museum, Mainz 72

Haarlem 41
Habermas, Jürgen 92, 139
hackerspace 132, 143
Hague, The 76
Hailey, Carter 57
Hall, David D. 49, 84
Hamburg 98

Hammond, Brean 110–11
Han period, China 20, 21
Hand Press Book Database 63
Handlist of the Latin Writers 89
Handschriftenkunde 88
handwriting 7, 48, 57, 88, 89, 113, 127; *see also* codicology, writing
Hanebutt-Benz, Eva-Maria 131
hanga see moku-hanga
Hangzhou 96
Hanna, Nelly 103
Hansard, Thomas Curson 44
Hansol Paper Museum, South Korea 72
Harris, Neil 49
Harry Ransom Center, University of Texas at Austin 73
Harvard University 52, 74
Harvey, Gabriel 128–9
HathiTrust Digital Library 67
Hawaii 97
Hebrew 23, 96, 108
Heidenreich,Tobias 40
Hellinga, Lotte 97
Hemmungs Wirtén, Eva 92
hemp 10, 22
Herbert, William 44
Herculaneum 30
Heritage of the Printed Book Database 63
Hesse, Carla 138
hieroglyphs 19, 20, 26; script 23; Cretan Hieroglyphic 20
ḥijāzī script 98
Hindu scriptures 22
Hinduism 108
Hinman Collator 56–7
Hinman, Charlton 57
histoire du livre 3, 8, 68; *see also* history of the book

Index

Histoire et civilisation du livre 55
Historia artis typographicae in Svecia 43
Historical Manuscripts Commission 59
History of Printing in America 44
history of the book: branding 3; Centres 63, 71, 73–4, 88; Chinese 9, 35–6, 37, 39–40, 51–2, 64–5, 94–5; controversy about 6; degree courses 74; early 32–40; French 7, 8, 68–9, 87, 104; geographical extent 2–4, 5; global 5, 13–14, 34, 73–4, 76, 80, 92, 94, 95–6, 103–4, 109, 118, 141, 143–4; Japanese 35, 36, 55, 86, 87; Korean 35; lecture series 74–5; models, circuits and diagrams 77–82; multiple 141–2; national 2–3, 5, 7, 44–6, 58–61, 69, 141; national biases 42–4, 45, 75; national volumes 75–6, 86, 103, 166–7; programmes 74; scope 1–16; seminars 74, 86–7; sources 2–3, 27, 48, 56, 60–8, 70–84, 87, 88, 90, 99, 102, 116, 121, 123, 126, 138; terminology 8–9; and the 'global turn' 144; and nationalism 46, 51, 53, 103–4, 114, 136, 141; and politics 2, 74, 134, 140–1
Hittite 19
Hobbes, Thomas 36–7
Hobson, G.D. 54
Hoe, Robert 45
Hofmeyr, Isabel 13
holy books 99, 109, 113, 141; *see also* bibles; Qu'ran
Hornschuch, Hieronymus 40
'hoso-e' (woodblock prints) 14
Hume, Robert 116–7, 118
Hurrian 19
hymn books 137
hyperlinked texts 142
hyperspectral imaging 57

Iberian Book Project 63
İbrahim Müteferrika Kağıt Müzesi, Turkey 72
ideograms / ideographic systems 11, 16–7, 142
illustrations (in books) 10, 11, 36, 43, 48, 86, 87, 116, 128
imagined communities 114, 139
impression techniques 3–4, 17–18, 35, 57; *see also* engraving; printing; woodblock printing
imprints 62–6, 76, 124; false 61, 76
Incas 10, 29–30
incunables (incunabula) 50, 55, 85, 89, 97; catalogues 61–2; and early printed books 56–7; and recording of 57; market for 104–5
Incunabula Short Title Catalogue (ISTC) 61
Index Librorum Prohibitorum 101
Index of English Literary Manuscripts 63
Index of Printers and Publishers 59
indexes 53, 87

Index   179

India 22, 25, 26, 31, 45, 61, 87, 95, 98, 101, 105, 107–8, 113, 140; literacy 124; scribes 26; scripts 98
indulgences 112
Information and Culture 105
information management 85; networks 86; overload 38
ink 6, 10, 20, 26, 33, 42, 57, 145 n. 4; gold and silver 24; smudged 66; inkpots 27
Innes, Harold 19, 76
Inquisition 134
inscriptions 11, 17, 19, 26, 107, 116
Institución y origen del arte de la imprenta 43
Institut d'Histoire du Livre, Lyon 73
insurance 90, 99; docket 112
intaglio 57, 86; *see also* engraving
intellectual history 4–5, 31, 39, 68–9, 85, 115, 136, 144
Intellectual Origins of the French Revolution 68
International Dunhuang Project (IDP) 67
International Society for Eighteenth-Century Studies 73
Internationale Gutenberg-Gesellschaft 55
interpretive communities 118
Introduction to Bibliography for Literary Students 47
inventories 57, 92, 104, 109, 122, 126
iPad 121
Ireland 72, 75, 89
Islam 98, 108; printing 113; territories 98, 140
Istanbul 96, 113; *see also* Constantinople
Italian 63
Italy 8, 54, 63, 72
ivory 19, 33

Jackson Lectures, Toronto 75
Jackson, William A. 50
Jaina scriptures 108
James, M.R. 56
Japan 14, 22, 34–6, 51, 52, 63–4, 67, 72, 86, 87, 91, 92–3, 101, 129; bibliographical studies 55; printing 34–5
Jardine, Lisa 128–9
Jauss, Hans Robert 119
Jayne, Sears 109
Jensen. Kristian 45
Jenson, Nicolas 41
Jeonju Hanji Museum, South Korea 72
Jesuits 113
Jewish books 108–9, 113
Jiake 89
jinhuishu 53; *see also* banned books
jobbing printing 10–11, 75, 112
John Rylands Library, Manchester 49
Johns, Adrian 100
Johnson, David 141
Johnson, Samuel 65, 133
journalism 5, 45, 80, 84–5
Justice, George 111

Kangxi 102
Karmiole Lectures 75
Kaufman, Paul 107
Ker, Neil 56, 89
khipus (quipus) 10, 29–30, 116
Kikuya, Nagasawa 52
Klancher, Jon 115

Knossos 20
knowledge 142–4; formation 95; history of 144; social history of 87.
Konstanz 119
Korea 9, 22, 34–5, 72, 92–3; censorship 101; printing 34–5, 37
Kornicki, Peter 34, 55, 86, 139
Kumarapala, King 108

L'Apparition du livre (The Coming of the Book) 69, 71
L'Ordre des livres 105
La Bibliofilia 54
La Science pratique de l'imprimérie 43
La Società bibliografica italiana 54
labels 61, 127
Lakota people 29
Lancaster, John 59
Langley, Thomas 42
language(s) 2, 4, 6, 8, 14, 17–19, 26, 29, 42, 43, 51, 61, 66, 111, 123, 134, 139, 144; Asian 34–5; barriers 94; carried by papyrus 23; formed in print 97–8, 124, 140; semitic 19; vernacular 19, 58–9, 70, 97; and STCs 60–4; *see also* translation
Lankhorst, Otto 76
Laozi 20
Lasswell, Harold Dwight 80–1, 155
Late Medieval English Scribes (catalogue) 88
Latin 4, 13, 18–19, 32, 33, 36, 40, 50, 56, 62, 88–9; annotations 129; as lingua franca 19
Lazarsfeld, Paul 81

Le Roux, Elizabeth 78
leaves (as a book) 10, 22–3, 24, 26; in bibliography 48
Lebanon 96
Leibniz, Gottfried 38
Leiden Centre for the Book 73
Leipzig 30, 40, 55
Lejeune, Philippe 11
Leland, John 37
Leo S. Olschki Editore 54
letter writing 78, 90, 91, 126–7, 136
letterpress 41, 56, 60–1, 66, 70, 93, 95, 102, 113; letter-founding 44; mechanized 99; *see also* printing
letters see alphabets
Liberia 97
Librarian of Congress 71
librarians 33, 39, 53, 84, 86; librarianship 40
libraries 3, 40, 42, 45, 46, 49, 56, 58, 60, 61, 63, 95, 102, 105–10, 121–22, 130–1, 143; African American 131; auctions 104; catalogues 56, 68–9, 83, 89, 90, and codes 49–50; cathedral 125; circulating 122; design 132; digital 64, 67; history 8, 55, 68, 86, 105, 107, 141; monastic 37, 64, 108, 109; national 59, 63, 71, 74; North American 125; private 68–9, 95, 105, 109, 122, 130, 132; public 71, 95, 109–10, 122, 125, 132–3, 143; records 64, 123, 126; subscription 122, 125; university 67, 125
Library and Information History 105

Libraries and Culture 105
Library, The 47, 54
Library Quarterly 105
licensing 84; agreements 143;
   pre-publication 101
Linear A and B scripts 20
Linotype 92
literacy 16, 20, 26, 76, 99,
   118, 123–4, 133–4, 140;
   differentials 15, 142;
   initiatives 71; rates 138–9;
   categories 137; gender
   divisions 34; reflections
   35–6, 113; working-
   class 85; and premodern
   division 141
literary history 4–5, 17, 47,
   56, 67, 68, 116–17, 137;
   property 84, 100; research
   3, 58, 83; significance 15;
   studies 7, 9, 14, 78, 84,
   110
literature 4, 15, 19, 33, 51,
   60, 67, 76, 85, 120, 124;
   Chinese 34–5, 52–3;
   definition 84–5, 89–91,
   101, 110–11, 137–8;
   European medieval 36, 37;
   samizdat 101
lithography 45, 57, 95–98,
   99, 102, 113; and reading
   124; in India 95; photo-
   lithography 46
Liu Xin 36
Livy 129
logograms 16, 29
London 23, 30, 43, 46, 71,
   72, 73, 74, 75, 92, 105,
   120; Rare Books School
   74; records 50, 59, 79, 91,
   125
Longmans 91
lost books 17, 31, 58, 89, 108,
   110, 143; lost records 112
Loughran, Trish 141

Love, Harold 111, 112
Luchtmans 91
Luiten van Zanden, Jan 64
Lyell Lectures, Oxford 75
Lyon 72, 73, 96; public library
   125; rare books school 74

MacDonald, Bertrum 79
Maclean, Ian 85, 94
Maclise, Daniel 46
Macmillans 91
Madan, Falconer 56
magazines 7, 43, 65, 120, 121;
   see also periodicals
Mahabharata 108
Mainz 41, 42, 72, 96
Mainz Psalter 45
makerspaces 132, 143
Mallinckrodt, Bernhard von
   42, 50
Manchester 45, 49
Mandragore, base des
   manuscrits enluminés 64
Mandrou, Robert 68, 138
Mann, Susan 95–6
Manning Stevens, Scott 140
Manuale tipografico 44
Manuel typographique 43
manuscripts 6, 10, 12, 24, 25,
   26, 27, 28, 31, 36, 48,
   52, 95, 73, 83, 84, 88, 98,
   112–13, 126–7, 136, 142;
   catalogues 58–9, 64, 67;
   Chinese 53, 64, 90, 95;
   circulation 3, 35, 85, 112,
   121; collections 40–1, 108;
   decipherment 57; medieval
   85, 88–9, 110, 120;
   monastic 41; preservation
   37, 85; publication 5,
   90, 98, 102; sale and
   exchange 55, 103; sources
   63; studies 53, 55–6, 63,
   110; Western 56; *see also*
   codicology

Manutius, Aldus 41
maps 10, 61, 86, 111
Mare, Albinia de la 56
marginalia 12, 116, 123, 128–9
Marker, Gary 124
market (books) 7, 38–9, 40, 45, 78–9, 84, 94, 103, 111, 119, 124, English 121; expansion 92; provincial 122; second-hand 104, 110, 121
Martial 33
Martin, Henri-Jean 7, 9, 69, 96
Maslen, Keith 59
Mass Communication Theory 80
mass production 19, 38, 92, 95, 98, 99, 103, 124; mass communications studies 80–1
Mayans 14, 26–7; recording systems 10
Mazarin, Cardinal 40
McCleery, Alistair 92
McCorison, Marcus 60
McDermott, Joseph 34, 39, 52, 94, 95, 139
McDonald, Peter 78
McGann, Jerome J. 83
McHenry, Elizabeth 131
McKenzie Lectures, Oxford 75
McKenzie, D. F (Don) 4, 7, 10, 13, 49, 50, 53, 77, 83, 84, 144
McKerrow, R.B. 47, 52
McKillop, Beth 93
McKitterick, David 46, 64, 107
McKitterick, Rosamond 89
McLaren, Anne 127–8
McLuhan, Marshall 76, 77

McMullen, David 39
McMurtrie, Douglas 57
McQuail, Denis 80
Mechanick Exercises 41
media 1, 19, 20, 99, 114, 127; electronic 85, 143–4; studies 4, 19, 63, 73, 76, 80; theory 77; and society 140–1; *see also* communications
Mediemuseet, Denmark 72
Mediterranean 19, 24, 26
Melbourne Museum of Printing 72
Merchants of Culture 92
Mesoamerica 14, 17, 26, 27, 30, 116, 142
Mesopotamia 17
Mexico 63, 87, 96
Middle East 17, 26, 96, 103
Ming 39, 100, 101–2, 127
mise-en-page 74, 87
missionaries 4, 95, 103, 125, 130
Mitchell, David 143
Mixtec manuscript 27; pictographs 26
Modern Language Association 73
Mohawk 140
moku-hanga 35, 129
Mollier, Jean-Yves 86, 91
Mollins, Nikolajs 97
monasteries 30, 31, 37–8, 40, 41, 103, 108, 109
Mongol printing 37
Mongolia 14
Monotype 92
Moretti, Franco 66
Moretus 101
Morison, Stanley 54
Mornet, Daniel 64, 68–9, 138
Morocco 96

Morrison, Paul G 59
Moscow 96, 124
Mossul University 107
Moulin à Papier de Brousses, France 72
movable type 5, 34–5, 36–7, 98; anniversaries 42; earthenware 35; inefficiencies 93; wooden 35
Moxon, Joseph 41, 43–4, 46
Mughals 22, 98
multispectral imaging 57
Münchener DigitalisierungsZentrum (MDZ) 64
Muncie Public Library 125
Murray, John I 91
Musée de l'Imprimerie, Lyon 72
Musée des arts et métiers du livre, Montolieu, France 72
Museo Bodoniano Museum, Parma 72
Museo de artes gráficas, Colombia 72
Museo della Carta, Amalfi, Italy 72
Museo della Carta, Fabriano, Italy 72
Museu do Papel Terras de Santa Maria, Portugal 72
Museum of Historic Typewriters, Germany 72
Museum of Printing, Haverhill, MA 72
Museum of Typography, Souda, Greece 72
Museum Plantin-Moretus, Antwerp 72
music 4, 10, 14, 61, 86
Müteferrika, Ibraham 113
Mycenea 20

Nagatomo, Chiyoji 55
Nalanda 108
namazu-e (catfish-motif prints) 14
Napier University 73
National Gallery. London 59
National Library of South Africa 74
National Portrait Gallery, London 59
National Print Museum, Dublin 72
National Typefounding Collection (on-line) 72
nationalism 103, 114, 136, 141
Naudé, Gabriel 40, 49
Needham, Paul 112
Nelson, Carolyn 59
Netherlands 61, 76, 97, 131
New England 84, 117
New Testament 97, 98
New York 45
New Zealand 96, 131, 140; Australasian Rare Books School 74
news 85, 103, 104; fake 100
newspapers 10, 38, 61, 62, 84, 85, 86, 92, 105, 111, 119, 120–2, 130, 136, 140, 142
Ngram 67
Nichols, John 45
Nineteenth-Century Short Title Catalogue (NSTC) 61
Nineveh (Kuyunjik) 107
North America 17, 29, 60–1, 63, 86, 97, 99, 105, 120, 124, 125, 128, 131, 140
North American Imprints Project 60
notes 7, 11, 12, 14, 48, 51, 52, 53, 61, 87; *see also* marginalia

novels 53, 58, 66, 86, 110–11, 117–20, 143

Obeyesekere, Gananath 141
Olmec 26; recording systems 10
omens 17, 19
Ong, Walter 76
Online Computer Library Center (OCLC) 63
Open Access 143
Oporinus, Johannes 41
optical character recognition (OCR) 64, 66
oracle texts 17
orality 16, 19, 76, 99, 108, 140; oral communication 114; cultures 17, 144; traditions 116; transmission 31, 70, 108
Oregon 97
Orgel, Stephen 123, 129
Orthodox Church, Russian 124
Orthotypographia 40
Osterreichisches Papiermachermuseum, Austria 72
ostraka (broken pottery) 20, 30
Ottomans 103; empire 96; territories 113
Oxford 41, 42, 75, 76, 125; University 73
Oxford Bibliographical Society 53
Oxford English Dictionary. 41

pages 24, 116, 143; construction 14, 27, 98; imaging 31, 57, 63; layouts (*mise-en-page*) 57, 74, 87, 88, 120; limitation 58, 60, 62; and reading 120, 126–7
Pakistan 22, 26
palaeography 6–7, 56, 85, 87, 88; palaeographers 1, 3, 56
palimpsests 57
palm-leaf books 9, 10, 22, 26, 31
palmyra 26
pamphlets 10, 50, 59, 61, 63, 84, 99, 137; from coffee houses 122
Panizzi Lectures 75
Panizzi, Anthony 49
Pankow, David 43
Pantzer, Katharine 59
paper 2, 6, 10, 15, 23, 25, 48, 91, 93, 98, 121; availability 89; Chinese 21–2; derivation 32; fibres 57; history 86; Indian scrolls 25; making 23, 43, 45, 55; mills 72; money 37; sheets 16; supposed invention 21
Papers of the Bibliographical Society of America 54
Papers of the Bibliographical Society of Canada 54
papyrus 10, 16, 23, 24, 32, 91, 120; fragments 23, Greek 23; robustness 33
paratexts 7, 11–12, 14, 87, 143
parchment 10, 24, 33, 91; codices 16; resilience 25 *see also* vellum
Paredes, Alonso Víctor de 43
Paris 40, 56, 74, 79, 88, 96, 105
Parker Library on the Web 64

Parker, Matthew 41
Parma 44, 72
part-issues 120
paste-ins 88
patronage 7, 54, 84, 91, 92, 94, 100, 103
Pearson, David 107
pedagogy 74, 116, 123–4, 128, 129
Pedersen, Johannes 55
pedlars 85, 104
Pelliot, Paul 9
Penguin (Ltd) 92
Pennsylvania 75
Pepys, Samuel 43
periodicals 45, 58, 84, 85, 92, 10, 111, 136, 142; indexes 46, 120–21
peritext 11
Persia 22, 98
Peru 63, 96
Philides the grammarian 34
phonograms 16
photography 57; photogravure 86; phototypesetting 52
Pickwoad, Nicholas 86
pictograms 19, 142; pictographs 26
piety 85
Pilgrim's Progress 13
pilgrimage 26, 36, 116
Pinakes database 88
piracy 84, 100; digital 100; global 143
Piyujing Sutra 21–22
plant fibres 10, 16
Plantin, Christophe 41; Plantin-Moretus 91; and ledgers 91–2
playbills 61
playing cards 61
plays 10, 42, 53, 127
Pliny the Elder 32, 71

Plomer, H.R. 50, 52
podcasts 142
Pollard, Alfred W. 52, 59
Pollard, Graham 54, 103
Pollard, Mary 50
Pompeii 22
Poole, William F. 46
Popkin, Jeremy 138
popular literature 23, 39, 58, 62, 68–9, 71, 76, 85, 89, 92, 102, 104, 110, 117, 120, 122, 137–8; *see also* bestsellers
Portuguese 61, 63
postcolonialism 2, 5, 6, 30
prayer 19, 35; prayer books 65, 123, 137
prefaces 11, 65, 120
press freedom 44–5, 69–70, 92, 139; control 78, 102, 124, 140
primers 123, 124
Princeton University 73, 74
Principles of Bibliographical Description. 53
print, deluge of 130; democratization of 97; 'fixity' 71, 117–8; and script 127; and nationalism 114; and the written 112–3
print capitalism 113, 139, 141
'print culture' 70, 110, 111–2, 144
print runs 58, 62, 65, 90; and readership 124
printedness 134, 139
printers 7, 15, 40, 84, 97, 120; images 41–2, 43; manuals 43, 40, 44, 45, 90; working practices 84, 93

printing 3–4, 5, 6, 8–11, 13, 14, 16–18, 22, 36–7, 93, 101, 112–14, 129, 141–3; accounts of 46, 93, 134; archives 91–2; 'art and 'mystery' 41; bad effects 38, 44; concurrent 84; expansion 91, 92; history 85–6, 96, 110, 112; houses 91; images 41–2, 43, 46; jobbing 112; origins 34–7; overproduction 39; paper money 37; play about 43; presses 93, 96, 97, 99, 124; printing museums 71, 72; prints 86, 132; revolution 69–70; sacks 14; technical terms 41; 'technologically determinist' 69–70; technologies 34–5, 45; undercapacity 91; *see also* letterpress, lithography, print culture, printers
Printing Historical Society 71
Printing Museum, Beijing 72
Printing Museum, Bunkyo-ku, Tokyo 72
Private Libraries in Renaissance England (PLRE) 109
Program in the History of the Book in American Culture 73
proof correction and reading 47, 54
provenance (books) 48, 58; research 107
publishers 11, 13, 53, 54–5, 60, 89, 93, 95, 100, 105, 143; advertisements 90; catalogues 58; international conglomerates 80, 85, 92, 143; multinationals 80, 92; records 59, 90–1

publishing 13–14, 64–8, 77, 85, 101, 117, 119, 121, 142–4; business records 58, 91; by women 85, 95–6; capital outlay and overheads 93; economics 85, 100, 105; expansion 35; history 42–4, 45, 73, 85–6, 90–91, 110, 124; in the United States 86; labour 87–8; models 77–82, 121; nature of 10; non-commercial and private 91, 92, 94; records 79, 123; scholarly 94; *see also* book trade
Publishing History 55
Pullman, Philip 143
punch-cutting, automation of 92
punctuation marks 17
Pylos 20

Qianlong 102
Qing dynasty 51, 52, 102, 128
Qu'ran 98, 99, 113, 141
Quærendo 55
Quaritch, Bernard 45
Qubbah 109
Quechua 29
quill pens 27
quipus *see* khipus

Raabe, Paul 107
Radway, Janice 117, 138
railways 105
Random House 92
Raphelengius, Franciscus 41
rare book(s) schools 74
rare books 1, 9, 45, 66, 93, 104–5; Chinese 51, 52
reader response 68, 116–7
readers 7, 8, 11, 12–14, 22, 24, 39, 68, 70, 81, 99–100, 103–4, 107,

119–26, 141–4; age 123–4; anticipated 78, 120; histories 118, 138–9; intended 116; implied 119–20; mass audience 139; self-classification and perception 130, 133–4; unknown 143; women 117, 120, 138, 139–40; *see also* reading, readerships
readerships 74, 118, 119, 122, 127, 130–3, 138; anticipated 120; 'at-risk' 123–4; unknown 143
Readex Microprint-AAS Early American Imprints 66
reading 7, 8, 11, 35–6, 71, 76, 81–2, 85–6, 99, 103, 107, 115–35, 137, 140; aloud 131; as 'viewing' 127; censuses 123; 'distant' 66; 'deep' 127; evidence 118–35; furniture 131–2; gendered 139–40; habits 88; history 8, 12, 141; incorrectly 130; intensive and extensive 127; intermittent 131; meaning of 29, 138–9; memoirs of 126, 130–1, 133; micro-histories 134–5; on ships 131; practices 126–35, 143; place of 131–2; silent 127, 131; speed and time 121; testimonies 134; and modernities 138; and democracy 138–9
reading groups 121, 133, 143
reading rooms 131, 132
Reading Experience Database (RED) 131
reception 12, 13, 32, 35, 76–7, 80, 84–5, 94, 102, 105, 115, 126, 142; history 86, 118; theory 116–17; *see also* reading
Reconquista 103
recopying 22, 128
Record of Known Banned Books 52
Red Sea 23
Redgrave, G. R. 59
Reed International 92
Reed, Christopher 95
Reformation 96, 103, 109
Regystre of the Names of Englysh Wryters 37
religion 14, 71, 84–5, 113, 123; religious publication 86; societies 105; *see also* Buddhism; Christianity
Renaissance 31, 35, 101, 109
Renaissance Society of America 73
retrospective bibliography 7, 58–68, 75; Asian and Chinese 64; British 69; *see also* bibliography, STCs
reviews 46, 54, 58, 110, 121, 143; by women 85
revolution (political) 2, 3, 5, 36, 68–70, 96, 100, 103, 136, 138
Revue d'histoire ecclésiastique 88
Revue française d'histoire du livre 55
Rhine 103
Ricoeur, Paul 118
Riga 97
Rist, Johann 43, 46
rituals 6, 14, 19, 31, 113, 115, 116, 129, 135
Robert Smail's Printing Works, Scotland 72
Robson, Eleanor 17
Roche, Daniel 87, 112
Roman 22–3, 30, 96, 98, 101, 116

Rome 24, 34, 96, 100, 101
Roper, Geoffrey 103
Rose, Jonathan 131
Rose, Mark 100
Rosenbach Lectures 75
Rousseau, Jean-Jacques 69
Roxburghe Club 45
royalties 89–90
rubrication 87, 88
Russia 14, 76, 87, 102, 124

Saenger, Paul 127
Sahlins, Marshall 141
säkularisation 103
sale catalogues 104, 122;
    records 104, 125
Sammelbände 89
samplers 11
Sandars Lectures, Cambridge 75
Sanskrit 4, 34, 95
Scandella, Domenico (Menocchio) 134
Schoepflin, Jean-Daniel 42
scholarship 1, 4, 6, 7, 9, 36–8, 51, 53, 69, 70, 94, 104, 114, 127, 130; history of 56, 85
schoolbooks 123, 124
science 36, 45, 51, 69, 71, 76, 86, 103, 109, 140
Scotland 61, 72, 75, 103
Scottish Centre for the Book, Edinburgh 73
scribal culture 69; production 89; workshops 27, 108
scribes 7, 15, 22–3, 24, 26–7, 70, 84, 88, 100, 113, 121
script 10, 16, 19–20, 21–4, 88, 98, 111, 113, 142; and language 97; and print 76, 87, 127; *see also* manuscript
Script and Print 54

scriptoria 55, 70, 98
scrolling 33, 142
scrolls 9–10, 14, 20, 24–6, 31, 33, 34, 108; birch-bark 26; and amulets 113
Seccombe, M. 59
Secord, James 13, 86
self-publishing 89, 90, 143
semasiograph 29
Senefelder, Alois 95
Seville 91, 96
Shang dynasty 17
Shannon, Claude 80
Sharpe, Richard 89
Shaw, Graham 95
Shaw-Shoemaker 66
shells 16–17, 27, 29
shelves 33, 92, 102, 132
Sher, Richard 131
Sherman, William 129
Shields, David 4–5
shipping 105, 131; registers 80, 90
Short Title Catalogue Netherlands (STCN) 62
Short Title Catalogus Vlaanderen (STCV) 62
short-title catalogues (STCs) 58–68, 75, 120–1; cautions about 58–68
shuji 9
Shulin qinghua (*Plain Talk on the Forest of Books*) 52
signs 2, 12, 15, 16–18, 20, 70, 126–7, 136, 140, 142–3
Siku quanshu zongmu 52
silk 10, 14, 20, 21, 34
Silk Road 37, 67
Simpson, David 116–7
Simpson, Percy 54
Singerman, Robert 61
Sippar 18
Siskin, Clifford 110
Skaria, Ajay 113

skins (of animals) 10–1, 16, 25; calf (vellum) 10; *see also* deerskin
smartphones 121, 142
Société bibliographique de France 54
Société des bibliophiles 54
Société typographique de Neuchâtel (STN) 79, 104
Society for the History of Authorship, Reading and Publishing (SHARP) 73–4
Song dynasty 9, 52, 93, 101–2, 140
South Africa 72, 74, 78, 87, 125, 140
South America 10, 29–30, 67, 74, 105, 140
Sozialgeschichte der deutschen Literatur 85
Spanish 62, 63
Springer Verlag 92
Spufford, Margaret 130–1
Sri Lanka 3, 14, 26
St Catherine's Monastery, Sinai 30
St Clair, William 78–9, 91
St Petersburg 30, 76
Stallybrass, Peter 112
Stanford University 74
Stationers' Company 50, 54, 79, 86, 101
Steinberg, S.H. 96
stereotyping 3, 92, 97
Stevens, Henry 46
Stoddard, Roger 57
Strahan, William 91
Strasbourg 42
Studies in Bibliography 53
stylus 22, 26
Suarez, Michael 64
subscription 67, 122; libraries 122, 125; lists 62; schemes 89, 105, 122

Suho Memorial Paper Museum, Taiwan 72
Sumeria 17–18, 19
Sumerian 19
Sun Dianqi 52–3
Sutherland, Kathryn 121
sutras 14, 21–22, 108
Suzhou 39
Suzuki, Toshiyuki 55
Switzerland 72, 104
Syriac 96, 97

tablets 10, 16, 17–18, 19–22, 33, 107, 108, 116, 119; digital 10, 142
Taejong of Joseon, King 35
talipot palm 26
Tang dynasty 39, 52
Tang Shunzhi 39
Tanselle, Thomas 47
Tartu University library 125
Tetsujirō, Morohashi 51
texere 13
texts 10, 13, 14–15; access and acquisition 123; definition 11, 12, 84; made by reading 135; material 142; Mesoamerican 26; popularity 120–1; trawling 66–7
textual criticism 36, 56, 118
textura 127
thangkha scrolls 14
Thebes 20
Thomas, Isaiah 44
Thomason Collection of Civil War Tracts 59
Thompson, John 86, 92
Thym, Moses 40
Tibet 14
tickets 10, 14, 112
tillet blocks 14
Timperley, Charles Henry 45, 97

titles 11, 33, 92–3; recording 48, 51, 53, 61–5, 69; title counts 121–2, 138; title-pages 46, 120; see also STCs
Tokyo 72; Printing Museum 111
Toronto 75
tortoise shells, inscribed 16–17
Toulouse 69
Towsey, Mark 131
translation 70, 75, 97, 108–9, 111; and translator 89; see also language
Traube, Ludwig 56
Trevitt, John 96
Trinity College, Cambridge 64
Ts'ang-shu Shih-yüeh, The Bookman's Decalogue 52
Tsuen-hsuin Tsien 112–3
Turkey 14, 72
Twitter 143
Twyman, Michael 57, 86
type 4, 5, 17, 42, 51, 92, 96, 98, 124, 127; design 57, 87; founding 41, 44, 46, 94, 97; mechanical setting 92; specimens 40, 42, 43, 46; see also movable types
Type Museum, London 72
typeface conventions 97; and reading 126–7
Typographical Antiquities 44
typography 3, 12, 41, 72, 75, 83, 116; mock-script 127; see also type

Überlieferungsgeschichte. 56
Udine 134
Ugaritic 19
Ulpian 33
ultraviolet radiation (UV) 57
Understanding Media 76–7

United States of America 3, 49, 53, 59, 61, 72, 73–4, 75, 86, 88, 103, 125
Universal Magazine 43
Universal Short-Title Catalogue (USTC) 63
University of California at Los Angeles (UCLA) 73, 75; Rare Book School 74
University of Pennsylvania 74, 80
University of Reading 91
University of St Andrews 63
University of Virginia 74
Upcott, William 47, 49
Uppsala 24, 55
Uruk, Sumeria 17–18

Vatican Library 88, 125
Vedas 108
Vedic cult 108
vellum 10
Venice 96, 98
Vergil, Polydore 42
Verzeichnis der im deutschen Sprachraum erschienenen Drucke (VD16, VD17, VD18) 62–3
Vietnam 22
Vikramasila 108
Vincent, David 131
Vindiciae typographicae 42
Vindolanda 22
Virgil 129
Virginia, USA, Rare Book School 74
Vivarium 36
Volkov, Vadim 124
Vovelle, Michel 138

Wadi Daliyeh 23
Wadi el-Jarf 23
Wagner, Bettina 57
Wakelin, Daniel 112

Walde, Otto 55
Wallerstein, Immanuel 80
wampum beads 29
Warkentin, Germaine 29
Warner, Michael 4
Warner, William 79, 99
Washington, DC 56, 73, 74
watermarks 57
Watt, Ian 86, 110
waxed boards 22–3, 91, 116
Weaver, Warren 80
Weedon, Alexis 92
Wellek, René 37
Wen xian (*Documents*) 55
Werner, Michael 79
Westminster 41, 46, 96
What Middletown Read database 125
Widmer, Ellen 96
Wiener, Martin J. 137
Wiggins Lectures 75
Wilkinson, Alexander 63
William Andrews Clark Memorial Library 73
Winan, Robert B. 60
Windahl, Sven 80
Wing, Donald 59
winter counts 29
Witham parish library 125
Wolfe, Heather 89
women authors 85, 95–6; readers 139–40
woodblock printing (xylography) 5, 35, 93, 95, 98, 102, 112, 129; *see also* block prints

woodcuts 67; positioning 57
wooden tablets 22; writing boards 22
working men's clubs 122
World Digital Library (of UNESCO) 67
World Wide Web 142
Woudhuysen, Henry 41
Wren Digital Library 64
writers 21, 22, 38, 46, 85, 89, 95–6, 100, 103, 108, 111, 117, 119–20, 136, 139
writing 20–1, 22–4, 29, 33, 56, 57, 74, 77, 85, 120, 127–8; skills 19, 34, 123; systems 16–17, 26, 142; *see also* handwriting, letter-writing,

Xi, Zhu 128
Xiumin, Zhang 9
Xuanzang 26
xylography 35, 93; *see* woodblock printing

Yangzi delta 39
Ye Dehui 51–2
Yellow River valley 16
Yongzheng 102
Yuan 101–2
Yuanming, Zhu 39
Yun Zhu 96

Zapotec 26
Zimmermann, Bénédicte 79